BEYOND TRADITIONAL JOB DEVELOPMENT

THE ART OF CREATING OPPORTUNITY

DENISE BISSONNETTE

A Milt Wright & Associates, Inc. Publication

Recognizing the importance of preserving what has been written, it is a policy of Milt Wright & Associates, Inc. to have books of enduring value published in the United States printed on acid-free paper, and we exert our best efforts to that end.

Library of Congress Cataloging-in-Publication Data

Bissonnette, Denise.
Beyond traditional job development: the art of creating opportunity / Denise Bissonnette.
    p. cm.
    Includes bibliographical references.
    ISBN 0-942071-29-8 (alk. paper) : $29.95
    1. Job creation--United States
    2. Job vacancies--United States.
I. Title.
HD5724.B534 1994
650.14--dc20   94-21858
                                                      CIP

Printed in the United States of America

CONTENTS

ACKNOWLEDGMENTS

This book is the result of ideas, opportunities and support offered me by many people whom I am very privileged and pleased to acknowledge.

To the hundreds of job developers I meet week to week in various parts of North America, I offer unending praise and humble thanks for your stories of success (and distress), your enthusiasm, and the relentless spirit you bring to the important task of assisting people to find dignity and value in their communities. This book was inspired by you.

In awe of his ability to conceive and articulate what most of us can only dream of, I am forever indebted to Richard Pimentel, my partner and co-author of *The Performance Based Placement Manual: Job Development Techniques That Work*. The seeds sown by Rich in our earlier work continue to blossom throughout this book.

I thank my lucky stars for having had the good fortune of meeting up with my partner, Milt Wright, ten years ago. He is a brother and a friend who continually encourages me to try new wings.

Kudos are enthusiastically extended in admiration and appreciation of Barbara Wexler, editor extraordinaire, for her quick and insightful treatment of this book. This writing benefits not only from the mastery of her craft, but from the zeal and enthusiam she brought to the task. Thank you, Barbara!

Hats off (and thrown high in the sky) to Tony De Savia for his talent and artistry reflected in the layout, formatting and cover of this book!

Every writer needs an Anita Lee Wright and I am one of the fortunate few to have benefitted from the one and only! I hereby deliver a bouquet of bright red roses to Anita for innumerable hours of editing and proofing and for the ultimate completion and production of this book.

For their generous gifts of time and energy in reading the first draft, I offer my wholehearted thanks to the following people whose invaluable insights and suggestions are reflected throughout this book: Ken Glover, Rob McInnes, Mark Donovan, Curt Hansen, Carolyn Thompson, George Tilson, Suzanne Bergeron, Milt and Anita Wright, Louise Baker and Mark Griffiths. Take a bow, respected friends!

There are two additional readers who deserve special thanks: my father and his wife, Maynard and Diane Bissonnette, whom I love and respect beyond measure. Congratulations for balancing the roles of critic and cheerleader with true aplomb!

To Lynda Jean Groh I offer applause (in fact, a standing ovation) for the unrelenting effort, passion and humor she pours daily into the wellspring of Milt Wright & Associates!

I am truly grateful to the remarkable team of the Canadian Council on Rehabilitation and Work in Winnipeg — Karen, Rose Marie, Rob, Rosanna, Gary, Peter, Louise and Faye — for making my work in Canada possible and giving me a second home.

I owe a tremendous intellectual debt to Tom Jackson, the person who has most influenced my thinking in the field of employment. It was his book, *Guerilla Tactics in the Job Market,* that dramatically expanded my view of what I could aspire to as a job developer. I hope to thank him in person some day.

The number of other people who have influenced my thinking and writing is too numerous to list. I have quoted them throughout the book and included a bibliography of their work. I have learned so much from so many that I am certain there are few truly original thoughts put forth in this book. Since it is impossible to trace the origins of every idea and thank my many teachers, I will instead thank you, the reader, for continuing the circle and further cultivating these ideas for your own purposes.

Similar to the way tides move at the invitation of the moon, my thoughts become words only with the prompting of music. These acknowledgments would not be complete without mentioning Tracy Chapman, Tony Bird, Joe Cocker, Chris deBurgh, Neil Young, Kashtin, Enya, Ottmar Liebert, Loreena McKennit, 10,000 Maniacs and the many other musical artists who nudge me daily out of what would otherwise be a permanent writer's block and who, instead, inspire an eager voice.

More personally, for their ongoing support and encouragement throughout the writing of this book, I lovingly acknowledge my sisters, Maria and Michelle, and my dear friends Renee, Maureen, and Roxanne.

If I were to share a by-line on this book with anyone it would be with my extraordinary mate, Robert John, who has walked every step of this journey with me. I stand in renewed and constant awe of his gifts to me — too many and too wondrous for words. I will simply thank you, Rob, for putting a dance in my step, a song in my heart, and a strong, gentle wind in the sails of my soul.

And finally, in loving memory of Joe Cooney and Esther Stone, who served as mentors early in my career and whose confidence in me far surpassed my own.

This book is dedicated to
my precious Jessica Rose
and her beloved grandmothers,
Felicia Lamendella and Charlotte Bissonnette.

PREFACE

As a job developer you are in a unique position to affect real change in the lives of those you serve and in the economic life of your local business community. If it is true that for everything there is a season, I believe this is ours.

For those who are travelling an inspired path, may this book provide a bit of well-deserved reinforcement as you continue your pilgrimage. For those of you whose job development journey seems lacking in purpose and direction, it is my fond hope that this book will provide a fresh vision of new possibilities.

It is only fair to warn you from the beginning that this book is intended to present more than a compilation of random strategies and techniques to increase your effectiveness as a job developer. This is, rather, an impassioned plea and a call to arms to job developers to look again, not only at *how* we do what we do, but the *what* and the *why* behind our actions. The vision, direction and expectations of job developers must be as flexible as the strategies we use to bring them about. This recurring theme is examined throughout the book. I am writing not only as a comrade to a cause, but as a cohort in an important movement to create more and better employment opportunities for the people we serve, and to radically change the way(s) in which we do business. This book is about changing the very context of the job development endeavor, not just bettering our immediate situation.

Today the challenges and opportunities of the job developer are greater than ever, and the need for our services is felt more acutely than ever by those we serve. Never has there been a greater need for job developers to take an intelligent, business-minded, proactive and revolutionary approach to creating employment opportunities in our local communities.

No two job developers approach their work in exactly the same way because job development requires a personal approach. Please use the ideas presented in this book as grist for your own mill. It is not my intention to simply replace one approach to job development with another. Rather, I invite you to consider your present approach in light of some new ideas. My hope is that you will use the ideas presented as an artist might use paint, or clay, or musical notes. Take what you like, add your own perspective, and continue shaping the work you do as time and experience unfolds.

For those of you looking for straightforward methods and techniques, you will find them in these pages. Hopefully you will abide the musings and philosophies as well. If this work smacks of idealism, that is as it is intended. Ralph Waldo Emerson once said, "If your dream is somewhere in the clouds, that is where it should be. Now build the foundation underneath it." My attempt is to frame the dream and offer some building blocks for the foundation. This book is as much for the rebel and the dreamer as it is for the goal-oriented pragmatist.

For those of you who have ever felt the stirring in your soul to be a true leader, you are in the right place at the right time. You are travelling the path of the everyday hero. May your journey be filled with joy and abundance. May you reap great reward as you seed hope, plant opportunities, and assist those you serve in harvesting change in their lives.

Denise Bissonnette

CHAPTER 1:
RISING TO THE CHALLENGE

Before exploring the territory of job development, the beliefs we operate from, and the strategies we use to reach our goals, it is important to gain a clear understanding of the purpose of our journey and to become familiar with the road we are traveling. This chapter is an introduction to the rest of the book — it examines the realities most significantly shaping our present challenge, including factors such as the economy, the difficulties faced by our applicants and the nature of the competition we face in the open job market. This chapter also introduces the concept of entrepreneurial job development and the characteristics this revolutionary approach requires from and calls forth in the job developer.

NINE REALITIES SHAPING OUR WORK

As a job development trainer I have had the privilege of talking to and learning from thousands of job developers throughout North America. The concerns and challenges voiced by job developers have not varied much from place to place or from year to year. Certainly there are differences, such as the client populations served and the nature of the marketplaces, which range from small rural communities to large metropolitan areas. Even given these broad distinctions, there are many more similarities among job developers than differences. Among those similarities are nine realities that most significantly shape the challenges faced by the profession. As you read them, consider the degree to which they are true in your own experience.

"It is the challenges of a profession which give rise to the artists and creators who play in its field."

Jean-Paul Sarte, French philosopher

➤ REALITY #1: THESE ARE TOUGH ECONOMIC TIMES.

Businesses and organizations are struggling to survive and maintain equilibrium in the midst of what many economists characterize as "permanent white water." Fear, trepidation and financial insecurity are on the doorsteps of anyone and everyone presently in business. The scramble for advantage is ferocious among organizations of all sizes and in every industry. Although the degree of marketplace stability varies from year to year, economists do not expect this general climate to change. The job development strategies offered in this book were designed to be especially effective during recessionary times.

➤ REALITY #2: AS A NATURAL EXTENSION OF RECESSIONARY TIMES, THERE ARE FAR FEWER JOBS ADVERTISED THAN THERE ARE JOB SEEKERS.

Several factors play into this reality. In recessionary times it is not uncommon for the business community to tighten its belt and decrease staff and/or put a freeze on hiring. Organizations are working hard to put workers they have had to lay off earlier into existing job openings. We also see companies contracting out, leasing employee services, or using temporary employment agencies to fill jobs. (Fortunately for the job developer, these need not be the only responses, as we will discuss in Chapter 3.)

➤ REALITY #3: THERE IS TREMENDOUS COMPETITION FOR THE JOBS THAT ARE AVAILABLE.

It is clearly an "employer's market." People at all levels of skill, and in all vocational fields, are willing to accept employment for less money and in positions offering less challenge and personal satisfaction than they would have in the recent past. Statements like "It's tough out there, you're lucky to get any work at all!" are heard as frequently as the songs at the top of the chart. Securing employment using traditional job search methods is proving to be a humbling and discouraging process for today's eager job seeker. This book presents several alternatives to traditional placement and job search methods.

➤ REALITY #4: BUSINESSES ARE REQUIRING MORE QUALIFICATIONS THAN THE PEOPLE WE SERVE TYPICALLY HAVE.

This is especially true for those who are serving individuals who have never worked before or are changing job fields and have no experience in the field they wish to enter. Even in this "employer market" businesses are having a hard time finding employees with the skills they need. Many of the jobs available require training and education that few people have.

In Chapters 2, 3, and 4 we will look at how to help employers turn a profit by hiring employees with varied levels of skill, even those who do not typically meet their minimum qualifications.

➤ REALITY #5: WE ARE IN THE MIDST OF A JOB MARKET REVOLUTION.

New technology is changing the very nature of our work. Jobs that exist today may not exist two years from now. As jobs become more complex and challenging to the worker, machines are assuming more of the mundane and repetitive functions. As those who work with dislocated workers know too well, the person who has worked several years in an industry or field that has undergone tremendous change is not necessarily at an advantage over a new entrant to the job market who has the ability to learn.

The ideas in this book will assist the job developer who needs to find a new application of people's skills during a job market revolution!

➤ REALITY #6: THE INDIVIDUALS WE REPRESENT FACE
   SITUATIONS OR BARRIERS THAT MAKE IT MORE DIFFICULT
   FOR THEM TO COMPETE WITH OTHER JOB SEEKERS.

We serve many individuals whose lives have been rich in experience, who have unique talents and potential and hold many hopes for the future. We represent people whose vocational aspirations and gifts range from carpentry and bricklaying, to data entry and accounting, to cosmetology and nursing, to art and music. We represent people who offer both significant value and profit to potential employers.

These same people are those who, even in the best of economic times, have experienced tremendous difficulty entering the economic mainstream. It is no mystery to us why this is so. We are working with people who have what society considers to be serious, and sometimes multiple, barriers to employment. To list just a few, we are working with individuals who are challenged by:

◆ An industrial injury
◆ A physical, mental, emotional or learning disability
◆ Illiteracy or a low level of literacy
◆ A substance abuse problem
◆ Lack of financial and personal resources
◆ Little or no transferable work experience
◆ A criminal record
◆ Lack of English proficiency
◆ Receiving welfare or other social assistance
◆ The responsibilities of being a single parent
◆ The need for temporary shelter

In addition, we are serving people of many ethnic and racial minorities, people who span all age levels, women entering non-traditional roles, and seasoned professionals laid off because of plant closure or obsolete skills.

In response to this reality, we will look at ways of taking people who have barriers out of competition with those who do not and creating opportunities that highlight their skills and abilities rather than putting focus on their limitations.

Job developers will also be quick to note that many of the situations and factors listed above do not in and of themselves constitute "barriers," except in the minds of employers and society in general. In Chapters 9 and 10 much attention will be given to resolving the concerns of employers and changing their perceptions of people of various target groups.

➤ REALITY #7: NOT ALL OF THE INDIVIDUALS WE SERVE
   WANT TO WORK, AND OF THOSE WHO DO, NOT ALL HAVE
   THE FAMILY, FRIENDS OR PERSONAL NETWORK TO SUPPORT
   THAT DESIRE.

The people we serve face a variety of difficult and complex life situations, many of which we may be unaware of. How the idea of becoming employed fits into their larger life picture is not always predictable.

Many of the people we serve suffer from low self-esteem, vocational insecurity, anger toward the system, and real fear about the changes we are suggesting or asking them to make in their lives.

How different our job would be if everyone we served came to us of their own accord and really wanted to work! We know that if a goal is to be achieved, it must be embraced by the person him/herself. As we have learned from futile attempts to break down walls of resistance, the gates of change only open from the inside. The job development challenge is that much greater when you have to sell the idea to both sides!

We can empower and motivate our applicants through the use of the employment proposal, a strategy which is introduced in Chapter 2 and described in greater detail in Chapter 3.

➤ REALITY #8: JOB DEVELOPERS, MANY OF WHOM NEVER INTENDED TO ENTER THE PROFESSION, LIKE WHAT THEY DO.

I ask participants in my job development workshops to raise their hands if they like their jobs. Very rarely do I have less than a unanimously positive response.

Job developers like what they do! What's amazing is that few job developers meant to become job developers. Most of us were counselors, teachers, or social workers in the past, while others came from marketing or sales backgrounds in the private sector. Few come from a job development background because the profession is simply too new.

The fact that job developers like what they do is not insignificant. Most of the good that is accomplished by job developers has more to do with their passion for and commitment to their work than any other single factor.

➤ REALITY #9: JOB DEVELOPERS HAVE RECEIVED VERY LITTLE, IF ANY, EDUCATION OR TRAINING ON HOW TO DO THEIR JOB.

We stand aghast in the face of statistics reflecting an increasing number of citizens who cannot read, are addicted to drugs, have not finished high school, are victims and/or perpetrators of violent crimes, and are unemployed. One of five children in our society lives in poverty. And we, a tiny fraction of the social service profession, as I heard at a recent job development conference, "are assigned to tackle the unemployment problem for the troubled masses!"

Perhaps this would not be such a disturbing thought if the job developers of the nation received some kind of bonafide training about how to create employment opportunities. I have often thought to myself, "Thank God the people who depend on us to give them guidance don't know that we're not trained to do it!"

Perhaps we would feel more confident to meet the challenge if there was a college degree in job development, or even a two-year training course which covered the basics of vocational counseling, business, marketing, negotiating and human resource management. In contrast, the typical job developer is hired from a completely unrelated field and receives minimal training. When I was hired as a job developer, I didn't have the slightest idea how to approach a business, make a marketing presentation, analyze a job, evaluate skills and abilities, or ask good questions of employers.

Another question I ask of every group of job developers is, "How many of you have basically learned to do your job by the seat of your pants?" The response is typically a nervous giggle and another unanimous showing of hands. As interesting, and often effective, as training by fire can be, it is far from ideal. We've been put in the game, but no one has actually taught us how to play and win.

In summary, it is in the context of these realities — a challenging and changing economy — and in view of the barriers and difficulties faced by the people we serve, compounded by the limited training and resources made available to us as job developers, that I would like us to consider our roles and how we play a game in which the cards seem to be stacked against us.

This book is about changing the game from "applying for openings" to "creating new opportunities." It suggests that since no other sector of our society takes credit or responsibility for maintaining the way in which its citizens prepare for and secure employment, we can propose a new game: a game in which the people we serve can play and prosper, a game that takes people who have barriers out of competition with those who do not. I am proposing a game where there are no losers; because it will take advantage of each player's abilities and bring profit to those who can benefit from them. The task involved in this revolutionary endeavor is what I call *entrepreneurial job development.*

In order to play this new game, to operate from a new paradigm, the days of the job developer as a social working salesperson are over! This is the dawn of the entrepreneurial job developer, encompassing the skills and qualities expected of a visionary leader, a supportive manager, an effective supervisor, an agent of change, an artisan, an engineer, a designer, a consultant, a teacher, a student, and a humble guide. Rather than approaching employers to ask for something, we approach employers with something to offer — an ongoing partnership characterized by an equal exchange of resources and opportunities. This book is, among other things, about the redefinition and expansion of our roles.

This book provides detail about the whys, wherefores and how-tos of entrepreneurial job development. First, we will examine the kinds of thinking and acting required of this revolutionary approach.

"Everything can be taken from a man but one thing: to choose one's attitude in any given set of circumstances, to choose one's own way."

Viktor E. Frankel, author, survivor of concentration camp

EIGHT CHARACTERISTICS
OF THE ENTREPRENEURIAL JOB DEVELOPER

There are volumes of material available about how to increase one's personal effectiveness, achieve results in sixty seconds and maintain peak performance levels (you catch my drift). The thrust of these books is quick-fix techniques, power strategies, and slick communication skills. I don't claim that these approaches do not have a place, but they are not the focus here.

As job developers we build working relationships with and between people. These relationships are sown and reaped through fundamental character traits like trust, honesty, sincerity and integrity. As Stephen Covey eloquently expresses throughout his book *The Seven Habits of Highly Effective People*, human relationships are natural systems based on the law of the harvest. We cannot learn to cram a relationship (like we crammed information for college exams) any more than we can learn to cram a garden or a field of corn the week before harvest. The seeds of our endeavor are in our own character and in the principles and values we uphold through and in our work. The following eight themes summarize the necessary qualities of character that provide the sustenance for the journey of the entrepreneurial job developer. As you read them, consider the degree to which you already practice these qualities in your work.

CHARACTERISTIC #1: YOU ARE ON THE PATH OF RIGHT LIVELIHOOD AND HAVE A MISSION.

The popular way of thinking about "work" is as a means of "making a living." But it seems to me that, since we spend forty hours or more a week at it, work has just as much to do with "making a life." Work can provide the opportunity for social, vocational, personal, spiritual and financial growth. If it doesn't, don't you think we are wasting far too much of our lives on it?

Much has been written in the last ten years about finding one's "right livelihood." This concept of work couples vocational fulfillment with a sense of mission or purpose. There are four key dimensions of this inner-directed sense of right livelihood noted by many authors:

YOUR WORK SHOULD BE A FOCUS OF GREAT PASSION.

You should feel similar excitement for your work that you do for other areas of your life that bring you joy (otherwise considered "play"). The great poet, Kahlil Gibran, writes *"Work is love made visible. And if you cannot work with love but only with distaste, it is better that you should leave your work and sit at the gate of the temple and take alms of those who work with joy."*

"There's a test to find whether your mission on earth is finished: If you're alive, it isn't."

Richard Bach, author

WORK IS A SOURCE OF CONSTANT LEARNING, GROWTH AND ENJOYMENT.

Your work is where you make your mark. Therefore, it should have room for your constant curiosity, growth, and learning, and offer you challenges that appeal to you time and again. Social theorist, Michael Phillips, writes *"All work has the potential to engross and hold the worker, whether it is garbage collecting or systems programming, because the range of subtle and delicate refinements to one's work is always present."* When one senses that everything to be reaped from a particular endeavor has been reaped, it is time to move on to more fertile ground.

"Make no small plans for they have no power to stir the soul."

Anonymous

WORK SHOULD BE APPROPRIATE FOR YOU AND SERVE AS A VEHICLE OF EXPRESSION FOR YOUR SKILLS, TALENTS, INTERESTS AND PERSONAL STYLE.

Humans have an unparalleled potential to become many things. Buddha taught that your work is to discover your work and then with all your heart to give yourself to it. The true task of job seekers is to hire themselves the right employer. What qualifies as the right employer has as much to do with the opportunity for self-expression as it does with employment conditions.

One aspect of "right livelihood" is doing what comes naturally. I like to point to the animal kingdom as an example of this. Birds have wings, and they have no question that they are here to fly. Fish instinctively know how to swim, and the gophers in my backyard know exactly where to find the best of the garden. There is such a nice sense of order about the animal kingdom. Everybody has their place and their role in the forest, in the jungle, in the swamp. It all works so well and so smoothly. (And all without management seminars or team building workshops!)

I believe there is an order to the human world as well. The problem is that we humans can do so much that we are confused about where and how to put our natural abilities to work. In our culture, we have let the needs of the economic community dictate human potential rather than the reverse.

"What lies beyond us and what lies before us are tiny matters when compared to what lies within us."

Ralph Waldo Emerson, poet

Much of what happens in the world of employment is focused on what one can do. Typical questions of the job seeker are: "Do I qualify for this job which is available?" or "Could I present my skills and abilities in such a way that I will appear to fit that job description?" The problem with these questions is that they leave out the basic need of the job seeker to invest him or herself in the employment endeavor. There is a great deal that each of us is *able* to do that we would never *want* to do for a living! The job seeker needs to ask the following questions: "What do I care about?" "What do I like doing?" "What do I find meaningful, fulfilling and satisfying?" "What comes naturally to me?" "Where do I feel an instinctive belonging?"

I don't know when the perceived needs of the community began to dictate what people did with their lives. Was there ever a time in human history when people's lives dictated what happened in communities?

Whether or not it existed in the past, there is a movement towards meaningful work today. Our lives are not for sale.

WORK SHOULD SERVE SOME GREATER PURPOSE WHICH IS CONSISTENT WITH ONE'S VALUES AND PRINCIPLES.

"We're on a mission from God."

The Blues Brothers

It is truly wonderful when you are paid to do something you would be doing even if you weren't being paid to do it! This is what Joseph Campbell refers to as *"following your bliss."* He says, *"If you follow your bliss, you put yourself on a kind of track that had been there all the while, waiting for you, and the life you ought to be living is the one you are living. When you can see that, you begin to meet people who are in the field of your bliss, and they open doors to you. I say, follow your bliss and don't be afraid, and doors will open where you didn't know they were going to be."*

An exercise I enjoy doing with applicants is called "Making a Difference." People are asked to identify the causes, problems or issues which matter most to them in their lives. The next step is to identify the kinds of organizations or businesses which directly or indirectly deal with those issues. We then identify the types of jobs which exist in each of those organizations. What we discover every time we go through this exercise is that there are few, if any, jobs which cannot contribute in some way to the larger issues or concerns of every person in society. Here's the point: As long as you are going to be selling (or renting) your time, talent and energy to an organization or business, why not invest it in an effort you care about?

Many applicants come to us wondering what we are going to do for them or what the world of work has to offer. I think a more important question (and a much more empowering one) is, "What are you going to give and where do you want to give it?" I am always amazed and delighted to watch what happens when people make that paradigm shift. It puts them in touch with their power, their choices and their control of the situation. Have you ever met anyone who didn't want his or her efforts to make a difference to someone or something else? The need to achieve, accomplish and make a difference in our environment is what distinguishes us from the animal kingdom.

"A different world cannot be built by indifferent people."

Anonymous

I have yet to meet an effective job developer who was not on a mission. This mission takes many forms and is always in the process of change, because we are. As a job developer my mission has undergone many changes. When I began working with refugees, my heart was with all people living behind barbed wire in camps, awaiting entry into the United States. It seemed to me that the best way to help them was to assist the new arrivals to become self-sufficient so they could sponsor their families. In later years my mission changed to helping people who were on welfare to become self-sufficient in spite of the disincentives built into the system. In recent years, my attention has turned to being part of the movement to change the course of history for people with disabilities, to incorporate them as valued members of the work world and larger community. Isn't it wonderful that life offers us continual

8

opportunity to grow, change and choose our purpose?

Do you remember the dialogue from *Alice in Wonderland* when Alice comes to the junction in the road that leads in different directions and asks the Cheshire Cat for advice?

Alice: "Cheshire Puss,...would you please tell me which way I should go?"
Cat: "That depends on where you want to get to."
Alice: "I don't much care where."
Cat: "Then it doesn't much matter which way you go!"

Entrepreneurial job developers set their courses and reach their destinations using maps of purpose and direction. We're on a mission.

CHARACTERISTIC #2: YOU TREAT JOB DEVELOPMENT AS AN ART AS WELL AS A SCIENCE.

Throughout my career, I have viewed job development as both an art and a science. It is a science because a technical body of knowledge and basic scientific principles are applied to the activities of vocational assessment and evaluation, job analysis, and contract development. But job development is also an art in that there is no formulaic way in which you are expected to make these tools and knowledge work for you. Job developers adopt their own styles in order to achieve their ends. In fact, to a great extent the profession is not only an art, but a performance art.

This view of things came to me as I was reading a wonderful and insightful book by Peter Vaill entitled *Managing as a Performance Art.* In his book, Vaill encourages managers to view their job as performance art. He asks readers to think about what a director of a play says to the actors or a conductor of an orchestra says to the musicians. "Here is your instrument," or "Here is your part in the play. Given this basic structure or frame, express yourself fully. Give it life. Make it art, make it music. Celebrate yourself through your work."

Think about how the same acting role or the same piece of music can be interpreted differently by each artist. Can you imagine the various versions of Amazing Grace we would hear performed by Elvis Presley, Nat King Cole, Joan Baez, or Mick Jagger? Have you heard Jimi Hendrix's version of the Star Spangled Banner?

LET'S LOOK AT THE JOB DEVELOPER'S TASK THROUGH THE ARTIST'S PARADIGM:

Here are your applicants. Here is your community. Here are the businesses in your community. Here are the resources available to you. Take them and express yourself. Use your style, personality, values, principles, intelligence, creativity, and imagination. Within the basic frame or structure of the job development position, celebrate yourself through your work!

"We should each be professionally unique in a personal way."

Bellman, business writer

"Creative work is play. It is free speculation using the materials of one's chosen profession."

Stephen Nachmanovitch, writer

A co-worker of mine once commented that I made job development look like street theater. I didn't know at the time to accept this observation as a compliment!

To borrow Vaill's words, *"An artist possesses competence with respect to such things as the nature of the raw materials, the tools, the perspective (past present and future) on the art, methods of working etc. But all these are subordinate to something else: the expressiveness of the artist, creativity, insight, inspiration. The artist is after more than what one ordinarily tries to deal with, determined to find coherence and meaning embedded more subtly and deeply in experience that those around them see...The artistic enterprise is a celebration of one's specialness."*

Dennis Jaffe and Cynthia Scott in their book, *Take This Job And Love It,* consider one's job (any job) as an empty house. You move in and look at its form and structure. Then your creativity takes root. You design your space, decorate, and make the house your home. You personalize it by putting your stamp on it. Just doing what is expected at work is like living in a bare house — there is no "you" there. It becomes fertile ground for job burnout.

One aspect of performance art I find appealing is the lack of an automatic or formulaic notion about what constitutes "quality" art. My partner, Milt Wright, responds to most work situations with the words, "Go with whatever works." If ever there was a profession where the "whatever works" mentality has a perfect fit, it is in the field of job development.

Entrepreneurial job developers enjoy and express themselves through their art. (Although we are far too seldom asked to take a bow!)

CHARACTERISTIC #3: YOU CHOOSE TO OPERATE OUT OF THE ABUNDANCE MENTALITY RATHER THAN THE SCARCITY MENTALITY.

The abundance mentality isn't about having a "positive mental attitude" or viewing the glass as half full rather than half empty. It has more to do with expectations than with our attitude. In his brilliant book, *Guerrilla Tactics in the Job Market,* Tom Jackson discusses the difference between the abundance and the scarcity mentality: *"Most people are deeply scripted in the scarcity mentality. They see life as a finite pie: if someone gets a big piece of the pie, it means less for everybody else. It's the zero sum paradigm of life. The abundance mentality, in contrast, sees that when someone gets a piece of the pie they have more with which to make more pie in order to feed others. It's an endless abundant cycle."*

Now for someone who grew up in a family of eight with a mother who baked great pies, I was not spared the scarcity mentality. It took me a few years of being on my own before I relaxed at the dinner table and realized that I did not have to compete (okay, fight) with siblings to get my fair share of the pie. That lesson has not been as easy to apply to other aspects of my life.

We live in a society that believes accomplishment means climbing the proverbial ladder. And yet, we know there are only so many rungs at the top. If someone is occupying those rungs, there is less room or opportunity for us. Most of our games, athletic and otherwise, have winners and losers. If I win, you lose, and vice versa. Competition thrives on the scarcity mentality.

Do you remember the saying, "Hands that give also receive?" The abundance mentality supports the idea that interactions with people can be synergistic, win-win propositions. The abundance mentality says there is more than enough to go around in life and the more you give, the more you receive. It urges us to share and to work towards the best interests of everyone rather than being concerned about receiving reward, credit or ownership. It means fully participating and giving unselfishly to meet others' ends as well as our own. It means relaxing at the table and enjoying the meal without comparing your slice of the pie with everyone else's.

This story speaks to the difference between these two kinds of thinking.

> There once was a woman who sat on her porch at the edge of town. One day a young man approached asking, "Can you tell me about the town just up ahead? I understand it's quite run down, economically depressed and a very difficult place to make a go of it." The woman nodded in agreement and said, "I'm sure you're right."
>
> A little while later a second man approached asking, "Ma'am, what can you tell me of the town ahead? I understand it is on the edge of renewal, holds great economic opportunity and would be a great place to make a go of it." The woman again nodded in agreement and said, "I'm sure you're right."
>
> Just then the woman's husband walked out on the porch and said, "Dear, make up your mind. I heard you telling one person that the town offers nothing and in the next instant you are agreeing that it holds great opportunity."
>
> The wise woman responded, "That's because they were both correct. I have no doubt that they will each find exactly what they expect to find."

The scarcity mentality attracts scarcity, the abundance mentality attracts abundance. Job Development trainer, Richard Pimentel, tells the story of a co-worker who, during the peak of the recession in the early 1980s, was making placements hand over fist. Everyone was amazed by his ability to do so well during such hard economic times. One day Richard asked him, "How are you able to experience such success in the midst of this recession?" The young man looked up in dismay and replied, "What recession?"

The entrepreneurial job developer expects to find abundance and is not discouraged or slowed by evidence to the contrary. When told, "Hey,

"To experience true prosperity we have to change our thinking from 'getting' to 'giving'."

Lynda Jean Groh, marketing consultant

"We can never exceed our own expectations."

Lao-tzu, philosopher, founder of Taoism

it's a jungle out there!," the entrepreneurial job developer responds cheerfully, "Oh, you mean that beautiful foliage out the window?"

CHARACTERISTIC #4: YOU BELIEVE IN YOUR POWER TO AFFECT CHANGE.

"O God, thy sea is so great and my boat is so small."

Prayer of Breton fisherman

"God grant me the serenity to accept the things I cannot change, the courage to change the things I can, and the wisdom to know the difference."

The Serenity Prayer

One of the greatest roadblocks to personal power is to do nothing because one can do so little.

We are smart enough to know that on a grand scale our effect on the world is relatively insignificant. Hopefully, we are also wise enough to know that who we are and what we do with our lives can be very significant where we live and work and relate to fellow human beings.

I feel the truth of my own insignificance as I take my daily walk along the beautiful, tumultuous shores of the Pacific Ocean. It doesn't matter what has happened that day, in my life, in the news, or in the world, the sea storms the rocky cliffs and lays out white sheets on the shore in the same way every day, as it always has and always will. I know that in the grand scheme of things here on earth, my life will have no particular import or significance.

Fortunately, I don't live moment to moment and day to day in the realm of the grand scheme. Rather, I'm living my life in my tiny corner of the universe, with my family and friends and neighbors and co-workers and fellow community members. In this corner of the world, at this place in time, what I think and how I act matters. It matters in my immediate circle and so it matters in the world.

We have tremendous power to control our destinies. We each have everything it takes to change our world. A friend of mine recently argued this point saying, "Denise, you've got to be kidding. What control do any of us really have in life?" I responded, "We control our perceptions of the world, our values and beliefs, our goals and aspirations, our actions and non-actions, our decisions, our relationships and communications, and our time and place. Most importantly, we control our responses to the events that take place in our lives! How much more control do you want?"

I am a firm believer in the equation E+R=O: Events + Our Response to Those Events = Outcomes. While we do not have control over the events in our lives, we can directly affect the outcomes of those events by controlling our responses to them. To focus on our lack of power to control the events or conditions in our lives is to invite helplessness, discouragement and powerlessness. To focus on our responses is empowering and invites our resourcefulness and power.

"A little axe can cut down a big tree."

Jamaican saying

Hugh O'Brian is an actor who founded the HOBY youth program, an inspirational four-day leadership conference for tenth graders. He wrote the following credo of the organization:

"I do not believe we are all created equal. Physical and emotional differences, parental guidance, varying environments, being in the right place at the right time, all play a role in enhancing or limiting development. But I do believe every man and woman, if given the opportunity and encouragement to recognize their potential, regardless of background, has the freedom to choose in our world. Will an individual be a taker or a giver in life? Will he be satisfied merely to exist, or will he seek a meaningful purpose? Will he dare to dream the impossible dream? I believe every person is created as the steward of his or her destiny with great power for a specific purpose to share with others, through service, a reverence for life in a spirit of love."

"You need to get up in the morning and say, 'Boy, I'm going to - in my own stupid way - save the world today."

Carol Bellamy, businesswoman

One of our basic choices in life is to accept conditions as they exist or to accept responsibility for changing them. A significant portion of our population chooses the first option because of the dangerous illusion that the problems of the world are too vast and too complex for one individual to make a difference. Perhaps they forget the power and divine spirit inherent in every person's capacity to exercise justice, mercy, charity, grace, service, humility, sacrifice, faith, trust, hope and love. Doesn't even the mightiest of oak trees come from a tiny acorn?

In the inspired words of Robert F. Kennedy:

"Few will have the greatness to bend history itself, but each of us can work to change a small portion of events...it is from numberless acts of courage and belief that human history is shaped."

Entrepreneurial job developers act as if what they do makes a difference. We may be but a drop in the stream. But as a drop we make a difference.

CHARACTERISTIC #5: YOU ARE WILLING TO BE A LEADER.

"We must be the change we wish to see in the world."

Mahatma Gandhi, Indian leader

Many people are turned off by the term "leader" and do not care to liken their influence in the world to leadership. The word conjures up a range of images, from a striking figure on a white horse to a riveting speaker at a lectern. Others identify Abraham Lincoln, Cesar Chavez, Mother Teresa, Martin Luther King, John F. Kennedy, Malcolm X, Gloria Steinem, Rosa Parks, Lee Iacocca, Arthur Ashe, Maya Angelou and other famous persons as leaders. They define leadership as the great courage, power, authority, wealth or charisma needed to command the attention or actions of others. The kind of leadership I am referring to is very different.

"It is impossible to avoid leading by example. Someone is always watching."

Jim Cathcart, business writer

The leadership offered by the entrepreneurial job developer is rooted in the everyday expression of conviction, purpose, and integrity in the work and in the job developer's communication with other people.

Warren Bennis defines leadership as *"the natural outcome of a person who is expressing him or herself fully and authentically."* Like love, leadership is an action, not a word. And like beauty, it is hard to define but you know it when you see it. It is based in desire and belief, not in power or drive. True leaders don't have to work to prove themselves and their greatness to the world because they are more interested in leading people to recognize their own greatness, individually and collectively.

Peter Block in his book *The Empowered Manager*, talks about working "in conservative ways but with a radical heart," focusing on a vision of the future rather than on risk. While we respect the need to be practical and goal-oriented, we should not lose sight of our dreams and purposes.

I read that President Eisenhower demonstrated his view of leadership with a piece of string. He'd lay the string on the table and say, *"Pull it and it'll follow you wherever you wish. Push it and it will go nowhere at all. It's that way when it comes to leading people."*

We are not the kind of leaders who push; we are servants to the cause, living our beliefs and communicating our desires, and through our vision and actions, finding beauty where others do not, seeing opportunity where others find problems, identifying answers when others haven't yet recognized the questions.

Entrepreneurial job development asks us to accept our identities as leaders. Such acceptance does not come easily. M. Scott Peck in *The Road Less Travelled* writes about humans' desire to want others to be the heroes, rather than to want to be leaders ourselves. In many ways it is much easier to think of ourselves as merely ordinary. As ordinary people we aren't expected to speak up when it's unpopular to do so, to suggest change where it is sorely needed, or to pick up a burden when someone else might pick it up. Now I am not suggesting anything as dramatic as "picking up the sword of justice" each day. Rather, I am suggesting doing all you can whenever and wherever you can. As the simple proverb says, "If you would get ahead, be a bridge."

Entrepreneurial job developers are leaders.

CHARACTERISTIC #6: YOU ARE WILLING TO QUESTION THE STATUS QUO AND SEEK CREATIVE SOLUTIONS TO PROBLEMS.

Entrepreneurial job developers operate from the spirit of exploration and discovery as opposed to fixed notions about what is. We are not afraid to continually rearrange and reinterpret our understanding of the world, particularly as it relates to ways of better serving our applicants and the community. When some of our cherished ideas are not good maps for the actions we need to take, we look in strange, unexplored places within ourselves for new direction. Entrepreneurial job development depends less on ready-made maps for guidance and places more trust in the compass of our own understanding and intuition as we explore uncharted territory in the community, in individual businesses, and in the realms of individual and collective capabilities.

"There are two ways of spreading light: be the candle or the mirror that reflects it."

Edith Wharton, writer

"It is better to light a candle than to curse the darkness."

Chinese proverb

For example, if an applicant cannot lift the 40 pound box that must be carried from one table to another, the entrepreneurial job developer asks, "How else can we get the box from point A to point B other than by carrying it? Would the use of a dolly enable this applicant to work in this position? Could the applicant move from one table to another rather than moving the equipment?"

Similarly, if an employer states that they only have three or four hours of work a day for someone who needs a full-time job, the entrepreneurial job developer explores the possibility of sharing the employee with other offices in the same building to create a 40 hour a week job.

In other words, entrepreneurial job developers do not take the world at face value, they turn a challenge on its head and inside out before they give up on finding a creative solution.

Warren Bennis in his inspiring book entitled *Leaders,* refers to this as *"conquering the context."* To me, this means the entrepreneurial job developer will recognize the difficulties in a situation for what they are, but will not alter the course because there is a roadblock. We are willing to declare our independence and claim our autonomy from the circumstances which limit what we do and what we can become. When we hear about an employer laying off workers because business is poor, the entrepreneurial job developer looks for the opportunity to help the employer improve business rather than avoid the employer because there are no current job openings.

Deciding not to be a victim of difficult circumstances is a lot easier said than done. Willingness to take responsibility for our actions in a situation can trigger deep ambivalence because it means we stop blaming circumstances (e.g., the economy, the "system," the clients, the bureaucracy, the society, the regulations, the times, the geographic area) for what we can or cannot accomplish.

In the words of Erika Jong, *"Take your life into your own hands and what happens ? A terrible thing, no one to blame."*

Every time you hear yourself saying, "Well, under the circumstances..." ask yourself what you are doing underneath your circumstances!

CHARACTERISTIC #7: YOU ASPIRE TO REACH YOUR FULL POTENTIAL AND REFUSE TO SETTLE FOR LESS THAN WHAT IS POSSIBLE.

Anthony deMello, author of *Awareness: The Perils and Opportunities of Reality,* often began his spiritual conferences with the following little tale:

> A man found an eagle's egg and put it in the nest of a barnyard hen. The eaglet hatched with the brood of chicks and grew up with them.
>
> All his life the eagle did what the barnyard chicks did, thinking he was a barnyard chicken. He scratched the earth for worms and insects. He clucked and cackled and thrashed his wings to fly a few feet into the air.

"When what you want doesn't happen, learn to want what does."

Surely a pragmatist

"The important thing is this: To be able at any moment to sacrifice what we are for what we could become."

Charles Du Bois, educator

Years passed and the eagle grew old. One day he saw a magnificent bird above him in the cloudless sky. It glided in graceful majesty among the powerful wind currents, with scarcely a beat of its strong golden wings.

The old eagle looked up in awe. "Who's that?" he asked.

"That's the eagle, the king of the birds," said his neighbor. "He belongs to the sky. We belong to the earth — we're chickens." So the eagle lived and died a chicken, for that's what he thought he was.

Initially, I wished for an uplifting ending for this tale, something on a par with "The Ugly Duckling." In that classic fable, as soon as the criticized, misunderstood, maltreated duckling discovers he is a swan, his identity crisis resolves and justice prevails. The difference between these two tales is simple; the eagle didn't even notice he was different, and as a result, experienced no real discontent. Dying a chicken was not his tragedy, the tragedy was his failure to discover his own greatness.

Am I likening us to barnyard chickens? No. But I do believe that we spend far too much time on the ground, unaware of the heights to which we can soar. Perhaps it's not what we are that holds us back, but what we think we aren't!

Entrepreneurial job developers put great faith in their own power and influence in the world regardless of their limitations. Each one of us has an internal voice which prompts (or nags) us to do better, to do more, to look further, and to never cease to grow and learn. One of the characteristics which separates a leader from a follower is the propensity to listen to that inner voice and not to disregard it.

> "Come to the edge," he said.
> They said, "We are afraid."
> "Come to the edge," he said.
> They came.
> He pushed them...And they flew.
>
> Guillaume Apollinaire

CHARACTERISTIC #8: YOU GLADLY REMAIN A BEGINNER AND A FRESH LEARNER.

I recently heard someone on the subject of cross-cultural awareness state that we are all "unfinished" when it comes to understanding and relating to people who are different from ourselves. I liked that way of seeing it. It's not that we haven't learned a lot, or that we haven't acquired our own share of expertise or wisdom, but we are forever "unfinished" in our human understanding of things and our means of expressing ourselves in the world. As the saying goes, "The road to success is always under construction."

I am uncomfortable when someone introduces me as an "expert" in

"Ah, but a man's wish should exceed his grasp, or what is a heaven for?"

Robert Browning, poet

"An expert is one who knows more and more about less and less."

Nicholas Butker, educator

job development. Any experienced job developer would know that there is no such thing as an "expert" job developer. Since every new applicant and employer presents a brand new situation, we can never be sure that what we once did or how we once responded will have any carryover in the future. We are always beginning, always learning.

This aspect of job development demands openness and a willingness to stretch, learn, and grow. The ways in which we work and the approaches we take should result from a growing, dawning comprehension of what is going on and of what is needed. As entrepreneurial job developers we never stop questioning our methods, goals, expectations, and our ultimate purpose.

Do you remember the story of the student who visited his Zen master asking, "Master, have you anything to teach me this day?" His teacher responded, "I don't know, it depends on how full your cup is." Perplexed, the student asked, "What cup, Master?" The master explained, "If I were to pour tea into an already full cup, it will simply spill over for there is no room in the cup for more tea. Such is the way of the mind. If you come to me knowing everything already, I will have nothing to teach you. If you come to me empty, there will be room for new knowledge and increased wisdom."

Here's to an empty cup. Cheers!

"When the sun rises, I go to work.
When the sun goes down, I take my rest,
I dig the well from which I drink,
I farm the soil which yields my food,
I share creation, Kings can do no more."

Ancient Chinese Proverb, 2500 B.C.

APPLICATION: AN ASSESSMENT OF RIGHT LIVELIHOOD

What is the mission of your work?

Which skills and abilities do you most enjoy using in your job?

How does your work allow you to express who you are and your personal style?

How can you express your values and principles through your work?

Which area of your work allows for the most growth and challenge?

Do you feel as if you have found your "right livelihood"? If not, how are you going to go about discovering what it is and how to get it?

Imagine your job as an "empty house." What was the framework you were given when you started? How have you interpreted and built on it? What are the sources of light and heat for the job that is your home? How have you decorated? What are your most creative contributions? How can you continue designing your job so that you are able to use your greatest gifts?

What is your favorite artistic activity? How is it a metaphor for your approach to job development?

If you could change your job in one way, what would it be?

Think about the last time you observed someone who was demonstrating a kind of "greatness" that you truly admired. Consider the barnyard chicken and the eagle story. Were you recognizing untapped potential in yourself?

Think about the E + R = O equation. (Event + Response = Outcome.) What are the most significant events or situations that you deal with regularly in your work? What are your choices for responding? How does each choice affect the outcome?

What does being a leader mean to you? What do you consider to be your three finest leadership qualities?

CHAPTER 2:
QUESTIONING CONVENTION –
NEW PARADIGMS IN JOB DEVELOPMENT

The way you see the problem *is* the problem.

The fundamental objectives, challenges, and efforts brought to bear in job development are conceptual in nature. As artisans, our raw materials are the talents, dreams and abilities of individuals and our own ability to speak to the needs of the business community. As craftsmen, we weld ideas rather than steel and build bridges of agreement and mutual benefit between people. Job development is perceiving, conceptualizing, and articulating a vision for people on both sides of the employment relationship. The extent to which we are able to envision and create success in our work directly relates to how we perceive the world. Our thoughts and perceptions direct our actions and behaviors. While the balance of this book deals with behaviors — specific strategies, methods and techniques — this chapter considers our assumptions and the mental maps we use in approaching the job development endeavor.

"Every man takes the limits of his own field of vision for the limits of the world."

Arthur Schopenhauer, German philosopher

THE POWER OF PARADIGM

The concept of "paradigms" (pronounced like pair-a-dimes) is popular in fields of study which question the whys and wherefores of human behavior. Originally a scientific term, today it is frequently used to describe a model, theory, assumption or frame of reference. In a global sense, it's the way we see the world, our perceptions, understandings and interpretations.

Imagine a group of applicants at an introductory orientation of the services provided by your program or agency. One applicant might see new opportunities for her future. Another may view one or more threats to her basic security. A third may perceive differences between this program and the other four programs he's been through during the past five years. Some people won't hear anything you have to say. All are sitting in the same room, listening to the same words, yet each hears and sees different things. Our paradigms, based on our beliefs and basic assumptions, have a profound influence on our experience of the world.

Let me paraphrase Stephen Covey's book *The Seven Habits of Highly Effective People* with this simple illustration of the importance and power of one's paradigm and one's actions:

Imagine that you wanted to arrive at a specific location in central Chicago. A street map would be a great help. But suppose you were given the wrong map. You might work on your behavior — you could try harder, be more diligent, or even double your speed. But your efforts would only succeed in getting you to the wrong place faster. You could

"The difficulty lies not so much in developing new ideas as in escaping from old ones."

John Maynard Keynes, economist

"*I think I can,
I think I
can...*"

*The little engine
that could*

work on your attitude — think positive thoughts and try to see the best in the situation. You still wouldn't reach your destination, but perhaps you wouldn't be as discouraged. The point is, you would still be lost. The fundamental problem has nothing to do with your behavior, your attitude or your effort. It has everything to do with having the wrong map.

Each of us has many maps in our head, which fit into two categories: maps to determine what is (realities), and maps to determine what should be (values). We interpret everything we experience through these mental diagrams, and we rarely question our maps because we're usually unaware that we even have them. We simply assume that the way we see things is the way they really are. Our attitudes and behaviors grow from these assumptions. In effect, we see the world, not as it is, but as we are — or as we have been conditioned to see it. Trying to change outward attitudes and behaviors does very little good in the long run if we fail to examine the basic paradigms which shape our attitudes and behaviors.

The way we see things is the source of the way we think and act. Thoughts are powerful. All the spectacular and terrible creations of humanity began as thoughts and the paradigms which supported them. Every war the world has known began with thoughts. So did art, poetry, culture, free enterprise, the civil rights movements and family celebrations. Every invention and every business started as a thought, notion, concept or an idea. From the idea came the plan and from the plan came the action and from the action came the reality. Somewhere between the idea and the plan was a stretch or shift of a basic paradigm about what is, to what can or might be.

"*Your mind
will be like
its habitual
thoughts for the
soul becomes dyed
with the color of its
thoughts.*"

Marcus Aurelius

The more aware we are of these assumptions, the more we can take responsibility for them, examine and test them against reality. Ultimately, we may consider adopting a new map (or paradigm) more accurately resembling the territory we're traveling. Since our basic paradigms set the stage for our thinking — not just what we think but how we think, perhaps a paradigm shift is in order to set us on a new and more effective way of doing business.

A paradigm shift is a change in perception. Facts do not change, but their meaning does. To determine whether the glass is half empty or half full does not require facts; it is our response to the facts.

Questioning our basic world view can be disturbing. The shifts we will be examining require change. If you feel resistance to such change, know that your reaction is natural. *"Our dilemma,"* says columnist Sydney Harris, *"is that we hate change and love it at the same time; what we want is for things to remain the same but get better."* But as the saying goes, *"If you want to keep getting what you've been getting, keep on doing exactly what you've been doing. If you want to get something different, do something different."*

We will explore several of the central assumptions directly affecting the way job developers see, perceive and operate in their roles. We will examine the existing paradigms, consider alternatives, and look at the implications of each shift. True learning is often preceded by unlearning. Join me on a journey to explore and discard some existing beliefs as we consider new ones. This is a journey taken by everyone who has ever set out to create something better, and succeeded. The questions we must examine are:

◆ What are the underlying beliefs and assumptions of our current job development operations?

◆ Are our mental maps correct and up-to-date?

◆ How are our thoughts about what is possible affecting our outcomes?

◆ Can we create a new paradigm that is more beneficial in terms of the outcomes we seek and the people we serve?

Change your thoughts and you will change your world!

EXAMINING NINE POPULAR BELIEFS

Bear in mind that the following popular beliefs and assumptions build on one another. As you see the natural progression of these concepts you also will grasp the evolution of our present circumstances. Note too, the natural progression of the entrepreneurial approach to job development.

1. THE EXISTENCE OF A JOB MARKET

The idea of a "job market" is a dangerous abstraction. The use of the term reflects a picture of a single, free-standing entity in our communities containing a fixed amount of worker capacity at any given time. We hear comments like, "the job market is extremely tight right now — there just aren't any openings available," or, "How's the job market for someone with an MBA?" This concept fits right in the scarcity mentality discussed earlier — there is either room in the job market or there isn't. The result is acceptance, by both the job seeker and job developer, of artificial walls, constraints and boundaries that needn't be there.

"Though this be madness, yet there is method in it."

William Shakespeare

Wouldn't it be great, though, if there really was such a place as a job market? Job developers could just pull up every Monday morning to find employers putting out their jobs, like bakers with their bread, farmers with produce, or florists with fresh bouquets. As deceptive as the concept is, it is also a tease.

Wegmann, Chapman and Johnson in their book *Work in the New Economy* describe the job market as *"... the net effect of actions and decisions made by thousands of uncoordinated, independent employers."* They continue, *"The American hiring process is a strikingly decentralized operation. Unlike a centralized market, for example, the New York Stock Exchange, there is no uniform reporting of job openings, no composite list of what is available at any given time, and no central meeting place. It is, to mix metaphors, a market of ships passing in the night."*

Richard Bolles in *What Color is Your Parachute?* makes the same point, suggesting that the number of businesses in your community is equal to the number of job markets existing in your local economy. If we wish to use the term "job market" at all, its definition must be totally re-worked.

The "job market" as we have traditionally thought about it, does not exist. It is a limiting concept. We need not limit our thinking about the quantity or quality of employment possibilities by imagining that there is a finite, preordained "job market." There are no boundaries, rules, regulations or prerequisites about who can or cannot participate in the economic mainstream.

The world is our pearl of possibility.

2. THE ORGANIZATION AS AN ENTITY IN AND OF ITSELF

Have you ever heard or voiced some of these comments?

✦ "There's no influencing the powers that be!"

✦ "It's almost impossible to buck the system."

✦ "Job developers have no say when it comes to changing company policies and procedures."

✦ "There is very little common ground between the world of social services and the corporate world."

"It is the anonymous 'they,' the enigmatic 'they,' who are in charge. Who is 'they'? I don't know. Nobody knows. Not even 'they' themselves."

Joseph Heller, author

If these statements and the attitudes they express sound familiar, have you ever wondered who "the system" is, where policies and procedures come from, or who or what constitutes the "powers that be"?

When we think of organizations and corporations, we often regard them as if they exist outside human systems, endeavors and relationships. An organization (e.g., business, hospital, university, firm, bureaucracy) is no more than a structure where its human members meet and work for a common cause. Human beings produce the systems, structure, and style of an organization. Organizations serve the useful role of bringing us together, providing a vehicle for cooperative activity and providing a sense of community. They are created to serve people to reach their goals, not vice versa.

If you think about it, one must make an enormous simplification to abstract a collection of people and physical objects out of the total flow and call it "an organization." Our notion of the organization is a mixture of a physical differentiation and a conceptual distinction. We often forget that a corporation is a human system, and like the people who comprise it, is growing and changing. An organization may actually have more in common with a process than a fixed entity.

Warren Bennis in *Leaders* writes about the danger of the myth of the organization: *"One block to our understanding is perpetuated by the myth of organization as monolith, a myth reinforced almost daily by the media and the temptation of simplicity. The myth is not only grossly inaccurate but dangerous as well. When the evening paper, for example, announces that the Defense Department or the University of California or IBM (or any corporate body for that matter) will pursue this or that course of action, the said action is typically consigned to a single, composite body, the administration. This administration whose parts vibrate in harmony and whose acts, because we are denied a look at the human drama that leads up to them, take on an air of superhuman detachment - is as mythical as the griffin."*

We must be aware of and attuned to the fact that every step taken by an "administration" or a "business" is the result of a complicated pattern of meetings, disagreements, conversations, personalities, and human emotions. A parallel process is responsible for our foreign policy, the quality of public schools, and the scope and treatment of the news the media choose to deliver to us each day.

Think for a moment about how the policies and procedures in your office came to be, what they are and how they change. To those outside your office, it probably appears as if your organization runs more uniformly, rationally and logically than it really does.

This is true of nearly every corporate policy, from hiring criteria and job descriptions to minimum qualifications and recruitment efforts. All of these products of decisions may be manipulated and changed because the human forces behind them are subject to change. We want to believe and trust that actions, movements, and decisions are parts of a systematic, mechanical process which identifies perceived problems, weighs alternative solutions and results in rational decisions. Given human nature, however, that is almost never the case.

Here are just some of the implications of viewing an organization as an ever-changing human system in constant flux, rather than as a static institution:

✭ Since organizations are really the confederation of the people who are hired and work within them, our title could just as easily be "organization developers" as "job developers"!

✭ It is important to remember that every organization was started by a real person who bet the farm to offer a new product or a new service — an entrepreneur. Regardless of the type of organization (e.g., store, theater, candy shop), it was started by an instinctive act of greatness, courage and autonomy mustered by real people. Perhaps at some point the seeds of bureaucracy were sown or a corporate image took over. How easy it is then to lose sight of the roots of the original endeavor. Keeping those roots in mind may prevent us from being intimidated by the magnitude of an organization in its present, more mature form.

✭ While we may feel powerless in the face of corporate or organizational constructs, systems or policies, we are not without power and influence with the people behind them. I can't help thinking of the man behind the curtain masquerading as the all-knowing and powerful Oz. How much of the corporate world is smoke and mirrors appearing to be

"A company is known by the people it keeps."

Anonymous

"A corporation cannot blush."

Anonymous

"Small opportunities are often the beginning of great enterprises."

Demosthenes, Athenian orator and statesman

magic to those operating outside it? This perspective also gives us greater appreciation of the human investment and human resources at the heart and the helm of what happens in the marketplace.

✭ To translate this shift in perspective to our advantage, we must become aware of the substructures all organizations contain, no matter how small. We must sensitize ourselves to the nuances of organizational cultures and the deep human dilemmas just below the surface of the apparently well managed organization.

✭ Given the other statements on the list, our power to create relationships, affect change, and to make and act on propositions in businesses is in direct proportion to our ability to influence and work with the people who make up that organization.

3. ORGANIZATIONS MAKE SENSE

Have you ever wondered:

✦ Why business practices are not always consistent, uniform and predictable?

✦ Why business people don't always seem to know exactly what they are doing? And even less about what their colleagues are doing?

✦ Why some businesses are constantly undergoing changes in management?

✦ Why the average rate of staff turnover is high?

✦ Why 80% of new businesses go under within the first 5 years and other businesses experience tremendous success in a very short time?

The answer is obvious. In this imperfect world full of imperfect people, we try to get things done through large, imperfect organizations. Why would we assume that a twelve-tiered organization of ten thousand people across fifty states and twenty product lines is without strife? Or even a three-tiered structure of fifty people? Should we expect even ten human beings in the same room, delivering the same service, to get along and agree so the operation runs smoothly?

As we've discussed, organizations are basically large, awkward and unwieldy. During the past fifteen years, an entire profession of organizational consultants has experienced a tremendous increase in demand for services. Businesses seeking assistance hope that someone understands how organizations are supposed to work, and can make it happen. As one consultant, Geoffrey Bellman, writes in his book, *The Consultant's Calling*, "*The assumption underlying our discomfort with organizations is downright laughable. It's as if we expect them to work smoothly or rationally and we are astonished when they don't. What is truly astonishing is*

"For God so loved the world, that he didn't send a committee."

Clearly someone who has dealt with bureaucracy!

"When policy fails, try thinking."

American Business Maxim

that we get so much done though these awkward systems and structures. That reality is a testimony to the human spirit and the need to find meaning in our lives. What I have as a consultant that those who hire me don't have is an appreciation of the fact that what goes on in most organizations just plain old does not make sense.... I help the people who make up the organizations accept the idea that what they call rational is really just rationalization."

For the job developer this means that what we take as givens in organizational life are anything but that. We needn't be discouraged if an organization, up to this point, has never utilized services like ours or has never been open to hiring people from the population we are serving. Every organization simply forms its structure by using information that made sense to a given group of people, with given skills, at a given time. We can influence future policies by appealing to the people who are making decisions today. Chapters 4 through 11 provide ideas and strategies to influence positive decisions about using employment services.

4. THE EXISTENCE OF "THE DECISION MAKER" IN AN ORGANIZATION

It is a popular notion in the field of sales and marketing that there exists in every organization "the decision maker," the key person to whom we should direct our attention. This assumption creates three distinct errors in thinking for job developers:

First, there is more than one decision made in relation to hiring. There are at least four separate decisions:

(a) The need to hire
(b) The criteria by which applicants will be screened and interviewed
(c) The strategy to recruit applicants
(d) The final hiring decision

Second, these decisions rarely rest with one person. In fact, in most companies each of those four decisions is shared by many, each of whom has their own idea about what they want in an applicant and what is necessary to perform the job.

Third, rarely are these decision-making responsibilities a regular part of the job description. They are usually a marginal function or one of those "other duties as required." The hiring function is often passed around the company like a hot potato.

We are at great advantage if we are informed about, or better yet, can influence any or all of these decisions. They are not made in a vacuum and should not be treated as if they were. Influencing any of them can greatly enhance the ultimate responsiveness to and acceptance of our services and our applicants.

This perspective may seem disheartening since it follows that there is no formula by which to contact the right person. That's the bad news. The good news is that because the hiring process is so multifaceted and

*"*B*usiness is people. Expect the unexpected."*

Paul Hawken, CEO, author

*"*Y*ou can take my factories, burn up my buildings, but give me my people and I'll build the businesses right back again!"*

Henry Ford

shared by so many, it is likely that anyone you contact is involved in making one of the four decisions and/or can lead you to others who are.

You cannot immediately assume which, if any, of these four decisions the person you contact can influence. One way to find out is to assume that the person is involved in every decision and comment on it. If you are wrong, the person will correct you and volunteer the right information. Sample questions or statements you might use include:

"Far too much reorganization goes on all the time. Organizitis is like a spastic colon."

Peter Drucker, business philosopher and writer

✦ "So you do the hiring for all the departments?"

✦ "You have quite a responsibility doing all the hiring yourself!"

✦ "How do you decide when to hire?"

✦ "How did you recruit the last employees you hired?"

✦ "Out of 10 applicants, how do you decide which people to interview?"

It is also important to remember that a "no" from one person in a company isn't necessarily the company's answer. There are often several people involved in the recruitment and hiring process. If a meeting with one person does not get you anywhere, don't give up on working with the business. Make contact with others in the organization.

Given the perspective of an organization or business as an ever-changing, ever-evolving human system and the fact that the process of hiring is rarely assigned to any one person in the organization, the next issue we need to examine is the concept of what "an employer" really is.

5. EMPLOYERS ARE EXPERTS IN HIRING

"Management is now where the medical profession used to be when it decided that working in a drug store was not sufficient training to become a doctor."

Lawrence Appley, President, American Management Association

Examining this belief begs the question of whether or not there really is such a person as an employer. I don't think there is. Have you ever met anyone who when asked, "What do you do for a living," answered, "I'm an employer"? No one identifies him or herself primarily (or even secondarily) as an employer. This would be almost as silly as the answer, "Well, I'm an employee."

When we speak of working with employers we are really talking about working with hotel managers, beauticians, accountants, restaurant owners, drafters, engineers, or insurance salespeople. Except for the human resource specialist in large organizations, most "employers" do not have expertise in the area of hiring, screening, recruiting, or interviewing; their expertise is in what they do for a living!

We know this is true because most people in a position to make hiring decisions are supervisors or managers in the department where the new employee will be working. So let's look at how people come to be supervisors and managers. Most will tell you that they were so good at whatever they did for a living that they were promoted to supervise that activity. With the promotion came the responsibility to hire and train others to do what they had previously been doing. The problem with this practice is that the ability to perform one function does not always mean the inherent ability to perform the functions on the next rung of the ladder.

I am reminded of the Peter Principle: "In a hierarchy every employee tends to rise to his or her level of incompetence." While I do not wish to imply that everyone you meet is a victim of overpromotion, clearly being a supervisor does not in itself qualify an individual to make good hiring decisions, effectively recruit or screen, or provide sound training.

You might assume that people who are made supervisors and assigned hiring responsibilities would be provided training on how to do it. Positive, useful employment training is rarely offered to business managers and supervisors. More often the training that is provided deals with what *not* to do in the hiring process so as to avoid a potential lawsuit.

It is no small wonder, then, that many supervisors and managers lack confidence in their hiring abilities and that so many "employers" opt to sticking with fixed, traditional ways of recruiting and hiring. They are simply borrowing the methods of the person who preceded them, crossing their fingers and hoping that nothing will go wrong!

Resistance from people in business to our programs or applicants may be as much a lack of confidence in their own ability to hire as it is a lack of confidence in us. If we can show them we're on their side, they are likely to be far more open and responsive to our ideas and counsel than we might assume. As we will discuss in Chapter 6, skilled job developers have far more to bring to a business than qualified applicants; they can offer human resource skills, knowledge and insights to the organization to improve its "human resourcefulness"!

The implications of employers receiving little training in hiring do not end here. As we all know, employers seek to minimize their risks. To that end, they seek a set of tightly structured definitions for what a job is and what it will take to get it done. If I could I would ask for a drum roll here because this leads us to the conventional notion which has most shaped traditional job development and the typical job search.

6. A JOB IS BEST DEFINED BY THE DUTIES WHICH DESCRIBE IT AND THE QUALIFICATIONS NECESSARY TO PERFORM THEM.

This belief powerfully influences the way in which employers hire and people go about becoming employed. There is a three-step process that most employers naturally follow to create job descriptions and qualifications. Job developers and job seekers respond to these job specifications as if they were law, divinely ordained, and central to the work to be performed.

Beginning on the following page is an example of this three-step process:

"Business is no different than learning to play the piano or ride a surfboard - there is no presumption of excellence in the beginning - in fact, just the opposite! We're punting!"

Tom Hawken, CEO, author

(1) EMPLOYER IDENTIFIES A NEED OR A PROBLEM TO BE SOLVED

Imagine that you run a bookstore, and one of the services which contributes most to building customer loyalty is your quick response to requests for out-of-stock or hard-to-find books. Recently, however, the magnitude of these requests has become cumbersome and your staff has not had the time to make follow-up calls. You decide it is worth your while to hire someone who will be solely responsible for this function.

YOUR NEED AS AN EMPLOYER IS TO HIRE SOMEONE WHO WILL:

- Make calls to customers to inform them that their books have come in;

- Place calls to book distributors to track orders which have not come in;

- Look up customer requests in the computer system; and,

- Place new customer orders.

(2) EMPLOYER CONSIDERS WHAT IT WOULD TAKE TO DO THE JOB

Once the problem has been identified, the question becomes, what is required to perform those tasks? This step brings together the employer's understanding of the job to be done as well as a healthy bit of guesswork about what it would take to do it.

JOB REQUIREMENTS:

✓ Must be able to communicate well over the phone;
✓ Must be able to read and write the titles of books and their authors;
✓ Must have basic computer skills to access and enter data into the system;
✓ Must have good organizational skills; and
✓ Must be able to work independently.

Notice how subjective these requirements really are. How good is "good"? How much is "basic"? What exactly are "good organizational skills" and what does it mean to "work independently"?

(3) EMPLOYER APPLIES THE MINIMUM QUALIFICATIONS EQUATION

Your needs in this situation seem simple and straightforward enough. As a manager, however, recognize that you are at risk of hiring the wrong person. What if you hire someone who does not meet your requirements; who in fact places orders incorrectly, forgets to call customers, or misses information on the computer?

You also know there are thousands of unemployed people in your community, and if you ask for the skills stated above, hundreds might apply. To reduce the number of applicants and minimize your risk, you are likely to develop minimum qualifications for the position based on the following equation:

MINIMUM QUALIFICATIONS EQUATION

+   What it would take to do the job in objective, measurable terms
+   What it would take to decrease the risk of getting the wrong person
+   What it would take to cut down the number of people applying for the job

---

=   Minimum Qualifications

Given the equation above, the job order may ultimately look like this:

Job Title: Special Order Clerk

Employment Conditions: $10 per hour.   25 hours a week.

Minimum Qualifications:

Must have an A.A. degree.
Must have 2 years work experience in customer service or
    related field.
Must have 6 months experience working with Bookusers Software.
Previous experience in bookstore preferred.

The problem for job developers is that while the individuals we typically serve may not meet the minimum qualifications as specified, many do meet the employer's basic needs — the very same needs that generated the job!

We have forgotten what creates a job: a problem to be solved or a benefit sought. We have forgotten that a job seeker is not hired on the basis of qualifications, but rather for his or her ability to solve a particular problem or meet a specific need of the employer.

People don't hire others because they have an A.A. degree or because they have three years prior work experience. People hire people to do the job, to answer phones, build walls, fix carburetors, communicate, sell products, clean floors and design plans. Helping employers identify what is needed to improve the effectiveness, productivity and success of their business should be the subject of our conversations, not the criteria used to define present openings. This brings us to two important points:

◆ A job is an opportunity to meet a need. Just as there is an unlimited number of needs in businesses and organizations as well as society at large, there is an unlimited number of jobs to be identified, developed and performed. The measures of a good job match are the results produced, not the list of duties and qualifications which describe it. Job descriptions reflect the reality of a job about as effectively as a flow chart reflects the reality of an organization. The challenges of the entrepreneurial job developer are to identify the needs addressed by classifications, define additional needs distinct from the job description, and market their applicants' abilities to meet these needs.

◆ In response, I propose taking the individuals we serve out of the qualifications game. It's a game they rarely win since they generally can't

"Job classifications do not describe humans any more than song titles describe the music you hear, or a city's name describes its climate."

Tom Jackson, author

31

compete equally. I propose we play a new game based on the following process:

(a) Identify the needs an applicant can fill given his or her skills and abilities.

(b) Identify businesses who have that need, and either don't know it or
haven't acted on it yet. Businesses with either or both characteristics
represent the applicant's potential job market.

(c) Propose employment to potential employers by defining the needs
and presenting the value and benefit of hiring someone to meet them.

(Chapter 3 is entirely devoted to ideas for job creation and writing
Employment Proposals.)

7. THE UNEMPLOYMENT RATE REFLECTS THE LACK OF
OPPORTUNITIES EXISTING IN THE JOB MARKET AT ANY
ONE TIME.

Before we deal with the issue of the "lack of opportunities in the job
market," let's look at what is meant by "unemployment."

Socio-economists talk about three different kinds of unemployment:

(a) During a recession there are simply too few jobs. This is called cycli-
cal or demand deficiency unemployment;

> "*The rate of unemploy-ment is 100% to the person who is unemployed.*"
>
> *David Kurtz,*
> *Business writer*

(b) Others are unemployed because of a mismatch in the economy for
the jobs available and the qualifications of the unemployed workers
or the interests of the worker and the availability of the jobs. This is
called structural unemployment;

(c) The third category of unemployment is referred to as frictional unemployment in which an individual is looking for work, jobs of the
appropriate kind exist and are available, but the worker and one of
these openings have not yet come together. This is often dismissed
or denied as an inevitable phenomenon relatively unaffected by government policy.

I suggest that there are two other kinds of unemployment that are not
discussed by sociologists, economists, politicians, or the general public.
The first I call discriminative unemployment. I use this term cautious-
ly lest readers think that I am pointing an accusatory finger at a malicious
"they" who are consciously discriminating against people who face one
challenge or another (e.g., disability, prison record, history of receiving
welfare). It is not my intention to lay blame but to simply shed light on a
reality of our society. Hundreds of thousands of individuals clearly do
not get a fair shake when considered for jobs because of factors other

than their abilities to do the job.

The fifth form of unemployment I term <u>attitudinal unemployment.</u> Victims of this form of unemployment include everyone who accepts the scarcity paradigm of employment. The scarcity paradigm promotes the belief that there are only so many jobs to go around and there will always be people who are not employed as a result of one of the economic conditions described above.

Let's consider a different paradigm with a quote from Tom Jackson in *Guerrilla Tactics in the New Job Market: "Unemployment is not a condition that rises out of the cranberry bogs and wafts across the land like pollution. Unemployment is a reflection of a society in transition. There is no shortage of jobs to be done in the world, and there are enough jobs to fill several lifetimes for each of us. ... Unemployment is simply the measure of the imbalance between what tasks need to be done in society, and the time it takes to recognize and mobilize the resources that are needed."*

I hope you agree with Tom Jackson because to my way of thinking he is right on the button. Much of what we are going to consider in the balance of this book is based on this paradigm. The abundance mentality views work, jobs and the realm of employment can offer unlimited potential and opportunity for every member of society. Consider the following figures from Tom Jackson's book:

✓ In the late 1980s the U.S. job market expanded at the rate of over 2 million new jobs each year.

✓ Several million people retire from the labor force every year.

✓ Even with a minimum turnover rate of 20%, an additional 22,000,000 people change jobs each year. Total job openings per year: over 25 million.

✓ The 1990s offer a diversity of jobs five times greater than those offered in the 1970s. About one-half of today's twelve-year-olds will hold jobs for which names have not yet been invented.

John Naisbitt writes in *Megatrends, "I do not believe that the United States is, or has recently been in a recession. In the U.S. we have parts of the country that are in prosperity and parts that are in depression, some business sectors that are doing very well, and some that are depressed. Economists have averaged the two together and declared the nation in a recession... But we lose all intelligence by averaging: To understand the U.S. economy today, we have to look at the economic health of each of the states and each of the business sectors within each community within each state."*

Tom Jackson contends, *"All human endeavor exists in the context of problems to be solved. There is not a piece of legislation, technology or major weather pattern change that does not potentially offer new opportunities for people to use their skills and abilities in the community."* In this

"The final solution for unemployment is work."

Calvin Coolidge,
30th U.S. President

"There are all kinds of employers wanting all sorts of servants, and all sorts of servants wanting all kinds of employers, and they never seem to come together."

Charles Dickens,
English novelist

context, it is difficult to believe that there is limited employment opportunity in our communities today. Limited job openings, perhaps. Limited job opportunity, never!

In Chapter 3 we will examine the specific needs and benefits which enhance employer willingness to hire. Chapter 8 discusses the kinds of questions to ask an employer to uncover their particular needs. Chapter 4 offers you the opportunity to examine many of the factors affecting organizations today as well as forces influencing the general economy.

Before we proceed, let's look at another misconception that has profound impact on the work we do and the attitudes of the people we serve.

> *"From each according to his ability, to each according to his needs."*
>
> *Karl Marx, philosopher*

8. THE CHALLENGE OF JOB SEEKERS AND JOB DEVELOPERS IS TO IDENTIFY EXISTING JOB OPENINGS WHICH BEST MATCH SKILLS AND ABILITIES.

Do you somehow suspect that this paradigm is not for the entrepreneurial job developer? (Or entrepreneurial job seekers for that matter?) If so, you're right. "Openings" speak to me of three things:

(1) Minimum qualifications our applicants either do not meet or for which they are over-qualified;

(2) Competition from job seekers who do not necessarily face the same kind of barriers as our applicants; and,

(3) Preconcieved notions on the part of employers about what the job duties will be, what it's going to take to get the job done, and the rate of pay.

Opportunities are much more interesting and promising than openings will ever be. As job developers we are in search of opportunities, not openings. In fact, when I hear an employer say, "I'm sorry, we're not hiring," my response is, "Great! That gives me lead time. How soon can I come down and meet with you to learn about your business and tell you about mine?"

THE HIDDEN JOB MARKET

If you're wondering why it's good news when an employer says, "We're not hiring," consider this rendition of the hidden job market I learned from my partner, Rich Pimentel. The hidden job market is best understood by asking, "How do employers go about filling a job opening?"

1. THE SUPERVISOR HIRES SOMEONE HE OR SHE KNOWS.

This is a logical and attractive first step because it minimizes risk. It does not involve recruiting, screening, lawsuits or headaches and only requires minimal time and cost. It's as close to failsafe as you can get.

If the supervisor doesn't know or cannot identify an appropriate applicant, the business proceeds to step 2.

2. THE SUPERVISOR HIRES SOMEONE A CO-WORKER KNOWS.

This is the second most attractive hiring option since it still involves minimal time, money and risk. The co-worker knows the job as well as anyone and has a good basis for discerning whether or not the person is a good fit for the position. When there are no co-worker recommendations, the business continues to step 3.

3. HUMAN RESOURCES HIRES SOMEONE THEY HAVE ALREADY INTERVIEWED.

(Note that most small to medium-sized businesses do not have a human resource department and the supervisor assumes the personnel functions.)

This is the third most attractive hiring option since it does not require effort or resources to recruit and screen possible candidates. No turning people down. No potential lawsuits for discrimination. No headaches.

If no one has applied who fits the job description, the business proceeds to step 4.

"The closest to perfection a person ever comes is when she fills out a job application form and interviews for the job. It's all downhill from there."

Everyone in Human Resources

4. THE BUSINESS CONTACTS PRIVATE EMPLOYMENT AGENCIES AND/OR NON-PROFIT EMPLOYMENT PROGRAMS.

You got it, that's us! If the business has a working relationship with a private or public agency, they call for potential applicants for the job. This step is far more labor intensive than the first three and almost guarantees the risks associated with rejecting applicants.

(Hopefully it has not escaped your attention that we are only one step up and about fifty cents less than the newspaper, the fifth and final option!)

5. THE BUSINESS ADVERTISES THE JOB OPENING IN THE NEWSPAPER AND/OR ON JOB BOARDS IN THE COMMUNITY.

It is no mystery why this option is at the bottom of the list. It is the most labor intensive since there is no screening device for persons responding to the ad. This option is the riskiest and requires the greatest investment of time and money for applicants who, relatively speaking, have not been screened.

It is estimated that anywhere between 80-90% of all jobs are filled using steps 1, 2 and 3. As a result, only 10-20% of openings ever reach the open job market.

It is interesting that despite widespread agreement that a great number of businesses hire using the sequence of steps described, most job seekers begin a job search by looking in the newspaper! They start from the bottom up rather than from the top down. Many job developers work in a similar way; relying on the classified ads, waiting for job orders called in from employers, and phoning Human Resources to ask, "Do you have any openings?" Let's look at the implications of the hidden job market for the entrepreneurial job developer.

✱   We want to be someone the supervisor knows! That places us on the top rung of the hiring hierarchy. So it is vital to make contact with the supervisor *before* there is an opening so that when an opportunity does arise, we immediately come to the supervisor's mind.

✱   Our applicants are people the co-workers should know! If an applicant wants to be a baker, he or she should meet every baker in town! This is called networking — knocking at opportunity's door. (Whoever said "opportunity knocks" was misinformed, people knock!)

✱   We want our applicants interviewed by Human Resources before there is an opening, so when one arises, they are already lined up for the job.

✱   We should remember that when we approach Human Resources for information about existing job openings, they may only be aware of positions which have not already been filled using Steps 1 and 2.

✱   If a business is advertising in the newspaper, it is probably in great need of an employment resource like your program. Call the business after they have successfully filled advertised openings. (Make contact a week or two after you see the ad.) When you phone consider using the following approach:

"I noticed you were advertising for production workers a couple of weeks ago. I assume you were able to fill those positions." (Wait for confirmation and then continue.) *"Do you mind my asking how many people applied for those positions?"* (After they have responded, continue.) *"And how many did you interview for each position?"* (Wait for their response and then continue.)

"Your experience was not unusual. I speak to business people every day who are seeking an alternative to the labor-intensive process of advertising in the newspaper to fill their openings. I would like to meet with you for 20 minutes or so, at your convenience, to inform you of an alternative offered through our program. Should you find that our program meets your organization's needs, the next time you have a job to fill, we will send you two or three pre-screened applicants to choose from rather than the crowd of 30 you just dealt with. And let me add, you will not get the bill for these

services. We are funded through the Community Colleges."

(Note that this is only one of numerous ways to get your foot in the door to develop an ongoing relationship with an employer. Chapter 6 describes a wide variety of approaches and strategies for initiating contact with employers.)

Remember, any time you hear the words, "I'm sorry but we're not hiring," you need to add the words "yet" or "now" to that statement. "We're not hiring" is another way of saying, "You've just entered the hidden job market"! If they are hiring, and their positions have been advertised, you're probably too late.

Now, last but not least, the ninth commonly held belief to be dispelled:

9. Job Development is a Reactive rather than a Proactive Effort

The way we traditionally go about competing for jobs and hiring in this society reminds me of the story I once heard about a young bride who cooked a ham for her new husband. Before putting it in the pan, she cut off both ends. When her husband asked her why she did that, she replied that her mother had always done it that way. On a later occasion, when they were having baked ham at her mother's home, he asked his mother-in-law why she cut both ends off the ham. The mother shrugged and said she really didn't know, except that her mother had always done it that way. Finally, he asked the grandmother why she always cut off both ends of the ham before she baked it. She eyed him suspiciously and replied, "Because my baking dish is too small, of course!"

The foundation of the employment/education structure operating today was designed to support a factory job-oriented system during a period when the prime motivation of business was to increase production and maximize profits, rather than demonstrate concern about worker satisfaction. During the Industrial Revolution, policies, procedures and corporate structures were created for the sole purpose of supporting the machines and mechanical processes which enabled businesses to thrive. Little attention and even less thought was devoted to supporting the human beings who composed these organizations. Today, many of our fundamental attitudes about employment remain unchanged. Now, we have baking dishes big enough to hold two hams, so we need not persist in trimming off the ends of what can be the most fulfilling and satisfying activity we as human beings can partake in — work.

Today many businesses realize that it is not enough to employ labor and engage workers in physical or mechanical work. The most successful businesses not only rely on the hands, eyes and backs of their employees, but also their hearts, minds and spirit.

"The intangible bonds and connections among human beings are not measurable but they pervade the heart and fiber of every business and of every community."

Paul Hawken, CEO, author

"Being good in business is the most fascinating kind of art."

Andy Warhol, painter and movie producer

The Industrial Revolution is over. It's time to abandon reliance on outmoded systems and procedures. Work has taken on new meaning in our lives. The ways in which we develop and compete for employment need to reflect and support the new definition. Job developers can take a leading role by showing business and the community how to do just that. We can work from a different paradigm, one that puts us in a proactive rather than a reactive role.

The job development endeavor should center on Tom Jackson's fundamental principle of work — *Human resourcefulness is both the end and means of corporate enterprise*. Meaningful work is our birthright, a natural activity of the human species. We are inherently versatile and innovative, changing and growing. We are artists and need not spend our lives in paint-by-number jobs. We are ancestors of courageous, inspired and hopeful people who compared themselves to soaring eagles rather than barnyard chickens. Their spirit and hope still live within us. Our relationship to the world of work, employment, and "the job market" must change. It must affirm, support, encourage and celebrate our potential and the unique contributions we make to our world. Think back to one of the opening quotes in this book from Mahatma Gandhi, *"We have to be the change we wish to see in the world."*

I invite you to reflect on the differences between the traditional beliefs and assumptions presented in this chapter and the entrepreneurial view of job development. Consider what those differences mean to you and then answer the questions at the end of this chapter.

"That all things are possible to him who believes; that they are less difficult to him who hopes: that they are more easy to him who perseveres in the practice of these three virtues."

Brother Lawrence, writer and teacher

Summary of Paradigm Differences

Traditional Job Development	Entrepreneurial Job Development
Sees a limited job market	Sees a world of possibility
Views the corporate world as impenetrable, inhuman	Views the corporate world as a frame for approachable, human systems
Sees organizations as static institutions	Sees organizations as ever-changing processes
Expects organizations to make sense	Expects the unexpected from the people who make up the organization
Focuses on the decision to hire, wants to talk to the decision maker	Focuses on the need to hire, the screening and recruitment process, and the decision to hire; will talk to anybody
Recognizes employers as experts in hiring	Recognizes employers as experts in the business they are running but possible amateurs at hiring
Defines a job by the duties and minimum qualifications	Defines a job by the results produced or needs met
Works to give applicants the best edge against competing job seekers	Works to remove applicants from competition with other job seekers
Seeks openings in the open job market	Seeks opportunities in the hidden job market
Responds to job orders for existing positions	Proposes to create new employment
Utilizes resumes	Utilizes employment proposals and resumes
Sees scarcity of identified employment opportunities	Sees abundance of as yet unidentified employment opportunities
Hears, "We're not hiring."	Hears, "We're not hiring *yet*."
Reacts to the whims of employers	Proacts to the needs of the business community

APPLICATION: PARADIGM CHOICES

What are your thoughts about the paradigm differences as presented?

Which side of the chart are you more inclined to embrace?

How would these shifts in perspective change your day-to-day activities, thoughts and behaviors?

What would you have to give up to become an entrepreneurial job developer? What would you gain?

Is there a way for you to test the waters of the entrepreneurial paradigm without jeopardizing your present way of doing business?

Please return to these questions after you have read the rest of the book.

CHAPTER 3:
CREATING JOBS WITH
EMPLOYMENT PROPOSALS

T o achieve greater success as job developers we do not need more resources, strength, ability, or better qualified applicants. What we need is to use what we have! There is more opportunity within our grasp right now than we could possibly take full advantage of in a lifetime. This section is about making better use of these opportunities through job creation.

The purpose of this chapter is to introduce the concept of the employment proposal, a strategy that has proven successful for me and hundreds of job developers throughout North America who have attended my seminars. It is an innovative approach for taking people who have barriers to employment out of competition with other job seekers and creating new opportunities. This approach does not preclude the use of other job development methods. It is an additional approach you may wish to add to your repertoire. This chapter guides you through the step-by-step process of creating new job opportunities by making employment proposals to businesses. It is my hope that you are ready to embrace the philosophies, strategies and tactics of a truly entrepreneurial job developer.

> *"A true definition of an entrepreneur comes closer to: a poet, a visionary, or packager of social change."*
>
> *Robert Schwartz (The School for Entrepreneurs, NY)*

"Do not follow where the path leads. Rather, go where there is no path and leave a trail."

Nicaraguan saying

APPROACHING AN EMPLOYER
WITH A PROPOSAL

Imagine you have an applicant who wants to be a security guard. Compare the following two ways of approaching a business to consider him for employment:

SCENARIO #1

The job developer contacts a security service firm where an opening might exist and states,

"Good morning. My name is Joe Martin and I work for Project Hope, a community-based organization serving individuals who have disabilities. I'm working with an applicant named George who is very interested in becoming a security guard. I believe he has the skills and abilities that

people in your business look for, and from what I have learned by talking to others in your field, those skills are not always easy to find. I wonder if you have any openings George could apply for. I have his resume with me and could leave it for your consideration. Would you mind taking a quick look at it and telling me what you think?"

SCENARIO #2

The job developer approaches a hotel which has never hired a security guard and says,

> *"A wise man will make more opportunities than he finds."*
>
> Francis Bacon,
> English philosopher

"Good morning. My name is Joe Martin. I would like to make a proposal to your business and think you will find it an interesting proposition.

As I am sure you are aware, in recent months there has been mounting concern in our community about tighter security measures. This concern is very likely shared by your customers, since they are away from home and do not have the security of familiar surroundings.

I am a job developer presently working with a security guard whose name is George Hannely. His qualifications are outlined in this proposal. What I am suggesting is that you hire George to provide security services on your premises during evening and nighttime hours. His services will be appreciated by your staff and customers alike. He also can provide the services of a bellperson when needed.

While the going rate for security services contracted through an outside firm is approximately $15.00 an hour, George is willing to start at $8.00 an hour. If after 3 months you find his work is as valuable as I think you will, you agree to hire him as a permanent employee with full benefits.

Please take this employment proposal and share it with others who may be involved in this decision. I will call you tomorrow afternoon to answer your questions and/or to arrange an interview for George.

By the way, it is only fair to tell you that I have presented this proposal to three other hotels this morning. If you're interested, please get back to me as soon as possible because I have a feeling he's going to be hired quickly!"

While there are many differences between these two approaches, some of the most important distinctions include:

SCENARIO #1	SCENARIO #2
The job developer is asking for something.	The job developer is offering something.
The employer's question is: Do I want this person to fill the position?	The employer's question is: Are these services of value to me?

Focus is on the differences between the person who is applying and the other applicants.	Focus is on the person's ability to meet one of their needs.
Job developer is seen as advocate needed by the client.	Job developer is seen as consultant matching the needs of the business with the abilities of applicants.
Job developer looks to employer to set wage and minimum qualifications.	Job developer names the employee's price and helps develop standards and criteria for the job.
Resume is used which reflects what the person hasn't done as well as what the person has done.	Employment proposal is used reflecting only what the person has to offer.

While responses from employers vary, employment proposals are typically met with surprise and interest. Most employers find them a refreshing alternative to traditional job development methods because employment proposals anticipate and address their needs and interests, as well as the needs of the applicant. Here are frequent responses to the employment proposal:

❋ The employer shows interest in hiring the person in a pre-existing position and assigns additional responsibilities over time.

❋ The employer is not interested in creating a new position but inquires about whom else and what else you have to offer.

❋ The employer decides to create the new position, typically with the condition of a three-month trial period.

"Ask not what employers can do for you, but what you can do for employers!"

John F. Kennedy (paraphrased)

TWO KINDS OF JOB CREATION

We are going to examine two ways of approaching the employment proposal process: first with an applicant focus (developing opportunities for each person) and then with an employer focus (responding to businesses by matching their needs with the skills and abilities of your applicants). I have yet to meet the job developer who doesn't, to some degree, approach the job from both angles. The art of the job developer is to see connections between people and the opportunities they offer business for increased growth and prosperity. It is not important which side of the equation receives our initial focus. Notice that while the first steps of each process are different, they both lead to the same final steps.

APPLICANT-FOCUSED	EMPLOYER-FOCUSED
(a) Assess the needs a person can meet given their skills, abilities and total life experience;	(a) Identify hiring needs of business in response to problems, trends and issues of the local community;
(b) Identify organizations which have those needs;	(b) Look for a match between the business' need and the abilities of the applicants;

(c) Identify how the employer will profit from hiring the person(s); and,

(d) Make a verbal or written employment proposal.

We will examine each of these approaches to job creation. The following ideas and examples are intended to inspire creative thinking about job creation. Remember as you consider this non-traditional approach, job development is as much a way of thinking as it is of doing. We cannot create what we cannot imagine, and vice versa. With an open mind, new frontiers will always appear.

APPLICANT-FOCUSED JOB CREATION: THE TWO-STEP PROCESS

STEP 1: Assess the needs the applicant can meet and the benefit he or she can bring to a business.

"The people who get on in this world are the people who get up and look for the circumstances they want, and, if they can't find them, make them."

George Bernard Shaw, British playwright and social reformer

We are so accustomed to relying on the employer to dictate what is needed to qualify for openings, that we are usually at a complete loss when asked, "What problems can you solve?" or "What value or benefit do you see yourself bringing to the workplace?" People are much more comfortable with the question, "What are your skills and abilities?" which immediately translates to "What are your qualifications for employment?"

But we are not as interested in knowing about qualifications as we are abilities, for a couple of reasons. First, as discussed in Chapter 2, employers do not hire people for their qualifications, they hire people to meet their needs. Second, many of the people we serve either have little work experience, and as a result do not believe they have any skills and abilities, or have extensive work experience and have pigeon-holed themselves. Asking people what needs they can meet or problems they can solve helps to expand their ideas about who they are and what they have to offer potential employers.

Here are some tips to help job seekers identify the needs they can meet or the benefit they can bring to a workplace:

◆ Discover not only what the person can do, but also what the person enjoys doing. (There is a lot each of us can do but would never care to do for a living!)

◆ Look at an individual's abilities in terms of total life experience, not just work experience. Remember, one's work history says more about past opportunities (or a lack of opportunity) than it does about one's potential, talents, and unique gifts. To illustrate this approach, I am including sample assessment questions from *Crossroads*, one of my previous publications. In this activity participants are asked to complete each sentence with the first idea that comes to mind.

> I think I was born to...
> I have always had a keen sense of...
> My favorite way to spend time is...
> The kind of situation in which I show my truest colors is...
> My best friend would describe me as someone who...
> If I were to receive an award, it would probably be for...
> What some people find hard to do that I find easy is...
> A time when I felt really glad to be me was when...
> I am known in my family for...
> A place that I really enjoy being is... because...
> Some of the things I treasure most in my life are...
> I am very good at...
> Three things I care deeply about are...

"If you were a member of Jesse James' band and people asked you what you were, you wouldn't say, 'Well, I'm a desperado.' You'd say, 'I work in banks' or 'I've done some railroad work.'"

Ray Blout, Jr., American author

◆ If the person has a hard time translating their skills and abilities into workplace applications, for each skill ask, "Why would someone pay you to use that skill?"

For example, someone who has the ability to communicate well over the telephone might be paid to:

- Sell or market a product or service
- Make reservations or appointments
- Confirm appointments
- Conduct a survey or gather information
- Do fund-raising
- Remind customers or clients of obligations

Here are other examples of the distinction between skills and their workplace application:

Skill or Qualification	Workplace Application
Files alphabetically	Will organize patient files for billing
Knows basic word processing	Will create a mailing list of past customers

Is able to stuff envelopes	Will prepare 40 marketing kits per hour
Has a driver's license	Will provide valet parking for customers
Can lift 50 pounds comfortably	Will prepare a house or office for painting or moving

STEP 2: Identify businesses which have that particular need.

This is the fun part! Once you have a good understanding of the skills or abilities the person would most enjoy using and the workplace application of those skills, the next logical question is, "Who has that problem?" or "Who could benefit from this person's abilities?"

For example:

The person's qualification or skill: Can tune-up a car

Workplace application: Will maintain and repair cars

"The entrepreneur sees the world from the perspective of his/her idea!"

Tom Hawken, CEO, author

Businesses with this need include those which use a delivery service, employ an outside salesforce or deliver products or services to the community. They include, but are not limited to:

Military	Rental car agencies	Taxi companies
Hospitals	Police stations	Fire stations
Corporations	Moving companies	Hotels
Pizza parlors	Furniture stores	Exterminators
Public utilities	Cable television	Manufacturers

Once you have identified the businesses or organizations which could benefit from the skills and abilities of your applicant, you are ready to put together an employment proposal. Before we delve into the employment proposal process, let's look an alternate route for arriving at the same destination — employer-focused job creation.

EMPLOYER-FOCUSED JOB CREATION: SIX SIGNPOSTS TO NEW JOBS

This approach to job creation considers the needs of industry and the community by identifying possible hiring needs which they themselves have not yet identified. We then assess whether we have the human resources to address those needs available in the pool of people we serve.

You may be wondering how to gather information about the potential hiring needs of a business when they are not advertising. Here are just six of the many tip-offs to this kind of information Tom Jackson recommends in his book, *Guerilla Tactics in the Job Market*. These heralders of employment require ongoing attention from the entrepreneurial job developer.

✤ Social Trends

Social trends beget hiring trends because they create a market of consumers asking for a particular product or service to satisfy a new need or desire. Social trends offer so much opportunity for job creation that an entire chapter (Chapter 4) of this book is dedicated to them. While I cite numerous examples in Chapter 4, here are some useful examples which illustrate their importance:

We see what we're looking for. Look for good, you'll see good. Look for problems, you'll see those too. The work of the Job Developer is to look for opportunity. Then we'll see it.

* When concern about physical fitness became a trend, the world of health clubs, spas and fitness centers exploded, generating increased demand for trainers, teachers, day care providers, food stands, as well as pool and equipment maintenance personnel.

* When it became a trend for high tech firms to provide child care on site, we researched which companies were *not* providing child care. We proposed to assist these firms to develop centers with the agreement that they would hire day care workers from our program. Although opening the initial center required an enormous amount of work and research, we then had a blueprint for opening centers for other businesses.

Consider this example:

Trend: Growing interest in healthy living and eating creates the need for making, marketing and distributing health food to cafeterias, lunch wagons, special events and workplaces.

Job Developer's Questions: Who is not responding to this trend? Who should be? Which delis, bakeries and restaurants offer the kind of food people want, but is not presently available from catering or delivery services? Do we have people who could provide food prep services, packaging, delivery or presentation of food to special events or workplaces? To which businesses might we propose expansion to include catering services?

✤ Social Problems

Social problems often create the need to hire people to address their causes and/or symptoms. Problems range from strange weather patterns to the economy to local social issues. Can you imagine how much employment was created to rebuild communities after the California earthquakes of 1989 and 1994, the 1992 Los Angeles riots, or the flooding in the Midwest during 1993? These problems created a need for everyone from clean-up crews, engineers and construction workers to social workers, health care workers and insurance investigators (and in my case, stress management counselors!)

"A problem is an opportunity in drag."

Paul Hawken, CEO, author

✳ A five-year drought in my community resulted in a need for car wash facilities which recycle water, innovative and safe ways to maintain the appearance of a "green" golf course, as well as employment of hundreds of park rangers throughout the state exclusively devoted to fire prevention activities.

✳ Increasing reports of gang violence in large and small communities has created an incredible boom in the security industry in recent years. *Newsweek* reported that the security industry tripled nationwide within six months of the Los Angeles riots!

Consider this example:

Problem: A recent *USA Today* poll showed that only one in five people in America feel they will be able to afford to buy a home in their lifetime. This problem generates the need for renovation of old buildings, maintenance and expansion of mobile home parks, and conversion of old houses into apartments.

Learning to ask new questions is the beginning of creating new opportunity.

Job Developer's Questions: Which businesses in the community could benefit from addressing the need for affordable housing? Are there contractors who have not sought additional business in this realm? Are there vacant buildings in the community which could be renovated?

❖ New Products and Services

The creation of a new product often brings about the need to hire people to make, distribute, market, service, transport, and repair the product. When the VCR was first introduced I remember my supervisor commenting that an entire industry would be born from that one machine. How many entrepreneurs have invested their savings and talents in the video rental industry? How many clerks have been hired in the last ten years to check out videos and beg the autograph of customers? How many kinds of software have been created to organize and simplify the video rental industry? How many free-lance video photographers have launched careers in response to demand for this new product?

The introduction of any new product or service in the marketplace should be accompanied by a list of questions including:

Who is going to make it?   Who is going to distribute it?
Who is going to sell it?   Who is going to stock it?
Who is going to service it?   Who is going to want it?

When people started sending balloons rather than flowers, I called florists who did not yet stock them and offered information about where to get the helium tanks. Of course I always added that I also had the perfect delivery person — someone who loved to dress as a clown!

Two additional questions to ask about a new product or service are: What other products or services will dovetail with this one? Who does not have a hand in this business who should?

❖ Societal Changes and New Demographics

While this topic is covered in depth in the next chapter, consider the following examples:

✴ The growing population of people in their last third of life has produced the need for a new spectrum of products and services including home health and long-term care, housing, cleaning, gardening, maintenance, and delivery services;

✴ There is a tremendous need for products and services which cater to two-career families who have precious little time to attend to daily upkeep of their homes;

✴ With more people working from their homes, there is a growing need for services catering to the "home office" user. These services include printing, mailing, marketing, graphic arts, computer installation, computer programming, and catering services;

✴ The downsizing of many major corporations and the rapidly expanding number of home-based businesses brings increased need for businesses which contract for services ranging from direct mail and advertising to security, travel, accounting and editing.

"As society changes so must we. As we change so must society."

Anonymous

❖ Legislation

Many laws, bills, ordinances and referenda create the need for hiring in order to initiate and enforce them. Take the following examples:

✴ Recycling ordinances have created opportunities for not only entrepreneurial ventures in the recycling business, but also for the employment of thousands of drivers and sorters.

✴ A local bill requiring routine maintenance of state beaches, created funding for the hiring of a crew of four people to maintain them. I made a call to the city planners as soon as I saw the issue on the ballot and our plan for training the workers was in place before the bill passed.

✴ Consider the Americans with Disabilities Act (ADA) enacted in July of 1992. The law prohibits, among other things, the discrimination of people with disabilities in every aspect of the employment process. Further, it requires accommodation of people with disabilities in all places of public service. The ADA requires affirmative steps by businesses to remove physical barriers and prohibits discriminatory policies and procedures when providing goods and services to the public. The job developer's questions should include:

What will the reality of this law mean for individual businesses?

What barriers will have to be removed or rebuilt?

Who will need to be hired so businesses can provide equal access of services to people with disabilities?

✤ Paying attention to your surroundings

Perhaps this last category carries more potential for job creation than all the others combined! We come by a tremendous amount of information about the needs of our community every day; the trick is to see those opportunities! Consider the following scenarios:

> *" As is your sort of mind,*
> *So is your sort of search; you'll find what you desire."*
>
> *Robert Browning, English poet*

✱ You wait 20 minutes at a restaurant to be seated but you notice that half of the tables are empty. What do you know about the needs of this restaurant? Do they need another waitress, cook, busperson, or hostess?

✱ You drop off your film at a photo developer, requesting the one-hour service they advertise. The clerk tells you it is impossible because they have so many backed-up orders. You suggest they hire a trainee from your program to help handle the work overload.

✱ At a toy store you request to purchase a doll house which has already been assembled. The manager responds that while they receive this request regularly, they do not sell the assembled sample. You propose that they offer the service of assembling their toys for a fee. You suggest they hire a handy young woman whom you just happened to interview the day before!

✱ You ask your friend who is a school teacher how his job is going. He responds that he loves the teaching but does not enjoy all of the behind-the-scenes copying, stapling and collating that seems to come with the job. He also comments about recent press coverage berating public schools for failure to give students individual attention. He wonders how he can possibly make the time to meet with individual students. You know his experience is a common one when he characterizes it as the curse of the teaching profession. Being a believer in solutions rather than curses, you put together an employment proposal for a Faculty Assistant who takes care of all of the teachers' time-consuming paperwork, freeing them to devote an afternoon hour to individual students who need extra help. The principal gleefully announces the investment in this new position at the next staff meeting and the upcoming Parent Association Meeting!

Here is a parable from which the entrepreneurial job developer has much to learn:

> One day an aspiring person heard that a certain Zen master knew the three basic secrets of life. Determined to learn what they were, he traveled far and wide until he finally arrived at the top of the right mountain and stood before the infamous Zen master.
>
> He approached the sage and said, "Master, I have come many miles to hear the three secrets enabling me to live a rich and full life (and make my placement quota for the month). Would you tell me those secrets?"
>
> The master bowed in return and said, "Yes, I will tell you. The first secret is pay attention. The second secret is pay attention. And the third secret is pay attention."

"The quality of life is in proportion to the capacity for delight. That capacity is the gift of paying attention."

Julia Cameron, author

SUMMARY OF EMPLOYER-FOCUSED JOB CREATION

As you can see from the preceding examples, employer needs are easy to identify once you are trained to look and listen with the eyes and ears of an entrepreneurial job developer. Let me remind you here of the Universal Hiring Rule from Tom Jackson's book, *Guerilla Tactics in the Job Market:*

"Any employer will hire any applicant so long as he or she is convinced that it will bring more profit than it costs."

We can bring a fresh outlook and a crisp new perspective to an employer's business keeping this rule in mind.

Some job developers respond to the idea of job creation by questioning whether it is presumptuous to think that a job developer could identify a need of the business which the employer had not already recognized for him or herself. To believe that employers are able to see all existing and future opportunities for profit or improvement is to believe they can always tell the forest from the trees. They cannot.

At this point you may be wondering how you will gain information about relevant social trends, problems, changes, and legislation for job creation ideas. Consider these sources:

"Opportunity is a bird that never perches."

The one who got the worm

- ✎ Every section of the local newspaper, not just the classified ads;
- ✎ Local television news and radio broadcasts;
- ✎ Meetings and conferences hosted by trade associations, rotary clubs, chambers of commerce and other local groups and;
- ✎ Magazines and newsletters containing relevant industry news.

Ask questions and pay attention everywhere you go!

Now Let's Translate The Job Creation Idea Into A Practical Proposal!

Writing Employment Proposals

Once you have identified the way an applicant can meet the needs of a potential employer, you need to organize your ideas and communicate them effectively. Employment proposals can take many forms: a letter, an outlined proposal, or a detailed memo. You may also present your ideas verbally without anything in writing. Regardless of the form, an employment proposal should contain the following:

(a) a statement of the benefit of the proposal for the employer;
(b) a brief summary of how the service will be provided;
(c) a brief description of the potential employee; and
(d) desired employment conditions.

EMPLOYER BENEFITS

Let's examine the first step — identifying the benefit of the proposal for the employer. Here are several ways creating a new position might provide value for and benefit a business.

It saves the employer money.

"The entre-preneur lives outside the mainstream. She is in the society but is able to step back and gain perspective on it."

Paul Hawken, CEO, author

Is it possible to better capitalize on the income-producing abilities of highly paid employees by hiring someone to pick up the lower-salaried, time-consuming duties and obligations of the job? For example, could an employer cut staff costs by hiring an assistant for a painting crew who will do the prep and clean-up work for $8 an hour so the painters who make $16 an hour can spend their time doing work worth $16 an hour?

Would it be possible to cut costs by hiring someone in-house to do the work the company is paying almost double (sometimes triple) to contract out? For example, wouldn't it save money if the firm hired a person to do collections in-house at $10.00 an hour rather than pay $30.00 an hour or a 50% contingent collection fee for the same services done by an outside collections agency? How about saving money in gardening, security, moving or accounting services? The list is endless.

It makes the employer money.

Are you proposing something the employer can charge for, such as adding child care services on site, valet parking for a restaurant, a delivery service for a video store, or catering services for a bakery?

It will expand the employer's client or customer base.

For example, a dry cleaner would gain more customers by adding a delivery service (even though the customers will pay for this service) if they are the only dry cleaner in town offering the service.

It helps employers use old things in a new and profitable way.

I once assisted a very artistic and handy young man to get a job as a helper at a woodshop. Within a few months of employment, he called me and expressed dissatisfaction in his job because he was not able to use any of his artistic abilities on the job. He explained that he had worked with wood during time spent in a state correctional facility. After much consideration and creative brainstorming, we designed an additional task to be accomplished during his workday which served his artistic need as well as the economic motivation of the business: to construct Christmas tree stands from scrapwood accumulated at the woodshop. When we last spoke he was going into business for himself, making and painting the stands as well as picking up the scrap wood from other shops, cutting it, and bundling it attractively to sell as kindling. This example demonstrates how an employment proposal can be used to creatively upgrade a present job!

It reduces lag time in production or in rendering of services.

A woman who attended one of my workshops told me later, "Denise, this stuff really works! I was at a deli/bakery in the food court of a local mall and noticed the person working the cash register also had to run back and forth from behind the counter to clear away and wipe customers' tables so other people could sit down. I saw they were losing business because of the prolonged wait suffered by customers at the cash register. I approached the manager and asked if it wouldn't make more sense for her to hire someone who just kept the tables clean at all times so she could have quicker turnaround at the tables without lag time at the cash register? The woman went for it and hired one of my students!"

It will organize or improve the ways things are being done now.

I once accompanied an elderly friend to a large medical clinic. Along with several other patients, she was asked to fill out long, complicated insurance forms. She did not understand most of the questions. I wondered what misinformation the clinic might have been provided had I not been there to assist her. I noticed other patients having difficulty with the forms. Later, the clinic accepted my proposal to hire a person to assist patients to complete paperwork so there would be less confusion for patients, and more timely payment by insurance companies.

It takes advantage of a built-in market.

Airports are becoming more like shopping centers because the average wait in an airport is 85 minutes. It would be foolish not to take advantage of this captive audience. I can't count the number of books I have read in the last three years purchased from an airport bookstore, and my daughter has every trinket available in the typical concession stand. Recently, I have observed "real" stores opening in the airports and standard airport fare replaced by concessions offering "real" food. What

"Some men go through a forest and see no firewood."

English Proverb

personal services could be offered in an airport to indulge and meet the needs of the busy traveler?

It improves employee morale.

I frequently ask employers to imagine walking into their next staff meeting and announcing to their employees, "Given your complaints about time constraints and too much paperwork, I have just hired someone who will be taking care of all of your printing, collating, copying and filing needs."

I explain that while this would be a cost-saving venture affording staff more time for income-producing activities, it also acts to improve employee morale. It is favorably received as a gesture of goodwill and a response to their concerns. (This kind of proposal is a safe bet in almost any business since nearly everyone has staff members who complain about excessive paperwork!)

It attracts positive press or favorable publicity.

Job developers, by the nature of their jobs, are also community developers!

I once responded to a newspaper article about our increasingly dirty downtown neighborhood and the city's inability to invest money to clean and maintain the area. Since ours is a tourist town, I knew this issue would most affect the merchants. I gathered a large group of local business owners at the local library and proposed that they, together, deal with the problem head on by hiring a clean-up crew of three full-time people to keep the downtown area clean. I also added that the press would eat up a story about downtown businesses taking the lead to solve a community problem. At that moment the owner of the largest department store in town stood and said, "Forget it. I'll take care of it. I'll hire the crew myself." He paused a second and then, with one eyebrow raised and his head cocked in my direction, added, "And I want a lot of press!"

Suffice it to say that I learned quickly how to make contact with the writers of feature stories in the local papers. I also learned that the press likes to have inspirational, human interest stories available as "filler" to print on days when there has been little ground-breaking news.

I must add that while the department store owner did not hire the cleaning crew from my program, I had countless placements from him and the other merchants who attended that meeting for many years. It was a great context from which to draw their first impressions of me and of our program — they saw me as a business person who had their interests at heart! I also felt immense pride at having had a hand in the creation of three new positions in the community.

It improves their reputation in the community.

If a grocery store begins to cater to people who are unable to leave their homes or hospital beds by hiring someone to pick up and deliver their grocery orders promptly, what message is sent to the community about the business? The store may charge for these services, but it also earns and receives a big pat on the back for accommodating the needs of community members.

It assists them to gain or keep the competitive edge.

I recently stayed at a hotel featuring complimentary room service breakfast on weekends. When I asked the manager why they added this service he replied, "This is a service two of our local competitors have offered for months now. For what it costs me to employ two extra people on the weekends to extend this service, I couldn't afford not to do it! It's not easy keeping the competitive edge today."

It is a natural extension of their business.

What if a carpet store was to add carpet cleaning services for customers, signing them up at the time of purchase of their carpet? This value-added service for customers, and the addition of a profit producing activity, would be a natural extension of the existing business.

Along these lines, how about adding a cleaning service to a drapery store, or to a window or screen supplier? What if a hardware store had a crew of four or five people customers could hire to help put up the fence, deliver the bricks or build the children's tree house? What if your local nursery offered to prepare your soil before planting the bulbs you purchased from it?

Any business which has access to used automobiles (e.g., service stations, auto shops, used car lots, rental car agencies), might be receptive to a proposal to add any of the following services (and to the employment of people to provide them):

✓ Reconditioning batteries	✓ Quick oil change
✓ Auto-detailing	✓ Shuttle service
✓ Auto-painting	✓ Glass tinting
✓ Pickup and delivery	✓ Auto cleaning

Every business has natural, logical extensions of its product or service. This realization alone should keep you busy with job creation ideas!

This brings us to the next step in preparing an employment proposal: describing the work to be done.

DESCRIBING THE WORK TO BE DONE

One of the particular advantages of the employment proposal is that you can design the job to fit the skills and abilities of each person. While it's important to have a clear picture in your mind of the tasks the person will be hired to accomplish, it is equally important to have the employer's input into the position so it is tailored to meet specific needs.

There is much information the employer is privy to (which we aren't) about tailoring a position for a specific business situation. Once you begin to discuss the employment possibility with the employer, you may find the position dramatically different from your original idea. Encouraging the employer to imagine how they see the position is a crucial step in getting the employer to buy into the proposal.

To assist you in preparing the initial outline of the job for an

"Everyone in business wants to believe that once they have a market, it will be theirs forevermore. It is an old dream that dies hard, yet no one can control a market that has decided to go somewhere else. All the king's horses and all the king's men are helpless in the face of a better product."

Walter Wriston, Chairman of Citicorp

employment proposal, consider calling businesses where like positions exist and asking questions about what the job entails. Gather job descriptions from other businesses who hire for positions similar to the one you are proposing. Ask for feedback about proposals you are preparing for other businesses from employers you work with regularly. In my experience, employers respond very favorably to this request and have at times bought into the idea of the proposal themselves!

DESCRIBING THE POTENTIAL EMPLOYEE

"If a man does not keep step with his companions, perhaps it is because he hears a different drummer. Let him step to the music which he hears, however measured or far away."

Henry David Thoreau, writer

Although it is vital to describe the person in a way that inspires employer confidence, I find that the less detail given about the person, the better. When great detail is provided, the employer is less motivated to set up an interview because he or she feels that the proposal has answered most of their questions.

I am often asked whether we should include information about a person's disability or other factors such as time in prison or an extended period of unemployment on the proposal. In my view, this kind of information is simply not relevant to the employment proposal, unless you have reason to believe it will affect the individual's performance on the job.

Observe that when you propose employment, you are doing so in a positive light, emphasizing what the person can do and has to offer. Some job developers respond saying, "It's great that we're presenting the applicant's glass as half full rather than half empty." The purpose of the employment proposal, however, is to simply present a full glass, because we only propose a job which the person can do completely, not partially.

One of the exciting differences you will notice when using employment proposals instead of resumes is the effect of this approach on the self-esteem of the applicant. The employment proposal is written to highlight the person's strengths, while a resume merely offers a chronological history of work and educational experience. For persons with very little work experience or those entering a new field, resumes often say more about what they haven't done than what they have done! This is unfortunate, since people tend to pre-judge future possibilities based on what they know about the person's past. We know that the past is more a reflection of opportunities (plentiful or lacking) than it is an indication of talent, potential and ambition!

STATING EMPLOYMENT CONDITIONS

On numerous occasions, I am asked how to develop better, higher paying opportunities for people with barriers to employment. My response is, "First you identify which employment situations the person does not have a barrier to, and then you propose it where it doesn't already exist, and name your own price!" While it is nearly impossible to persuade an employer to increase the wage of an existing position, if the position doesn't exist, there is no wage precedent!

Some job developers and job seekers prefer to put "negotiable" when it comes to the employment conditions. Recognize that you may be missing an opportunity by not naming a price. Once you name a person's price, it often becomes the value of the person's time in the employer's mind. (Not unlike an item's price tag dictating the value of the item to the customer). If the employer finds the stated employment conditions unreasonable, he or she will say so. At that point you can negotiate, but at least you will have made the opening bid.

Here are some sample employment proposals to expand and focus your creativity. Don't let these formats limit your thinking about the forms an employment proposal might take.

RECIPE FOR CREATION OF A JOB

"Take the obvious, add a cupful of brains, a generous pinch of imagination, a bucketful of courage and daring, stir well and bring to a boil."

Bernard Baruch,
American financier and statesman

SAMPLE PROPOSALS

EMPLOYMENT PROPOSAL FOR A "FULL-TIME AUTO-MECHANIC"

Samantha Travis
1424 Windswept Ave., Apt. #2
Carson, CA. 95032
(304) 354-6654

BENEFIT:

With a fleet of 30 cars, your business is currently paying the rate of $35-$40 per hour to have an outside auto mechanic maintain and perform simple repairs on your automobiles. I propose that you hire a full-time auto mechanic to perform the same work for one third the present hourly rate. An added benefit of having an auto-mechanic on duty will be appreciated by your outside salespeople who will not have to wait for repairs from "the shop" or call a towing company to have a battery recharged, tires changed, or minor repairs.

QUALIFICATIONS:

Samantha Travis is an ambitious and hard-working auto-mechanic who finished in the top third of her class this fall from the Carson College Auto-Mechanics Training Course. She has worked on and off for several years in a family-owned gas station, and enjoys working with cars and contact with the public. Samantha looks forward to becoming part of a team where she can utilize her fine-tuned mechanical abilities.

EMPLOYMENT CONDITIONS: 40 hours a week, $12 per hour

REFERENCES

Deborah Callohan, Manager
Union 76 Station, Carson
(304) 654-3324

Gerald Smith, Instructor
Carson College
(304) 656-7435

Robert Wright, Counselor
Carson College Employment Project
(304) 654-7654

(The following employment proposal was designed for an applicant who loved to talk on the phone, had very basic clerical skills and desired some contact with the public. She wanted an alternative to a telemarketing career. She presented this employment proposal to businesses that do not make money unless their customers/clients show up for appointments. These included the offices of doctors, photographers, massage therapists, hypnotherapists, and financial analysts.)

EMPLOYMENT PROPOSAL FOR
"CUSTOMER RELATIONS REPRESENTATIVE"

RATIONALE: Increase your profits by improving the rate of customers who keep their appointments by having a staff person who will primarily serve the following functions:

(a) Organize customer files and create a customer information bank;
(b) Contact customers prior to scheduled appointments;
(c) Keep customers informed of special sales and events and keep an up-to-date file on each customer which will include referrals of friends and family to contact for developing new business; and,
(d) Serve as a customer advocate by inviting feedback on improving and/or expanding services.

WHO: Marcia Williams is an independent self-starter who recently graduated from clerical skills training at Altmont Adult School. She offers keen organizational abilities, excellent communication skills and a highly cooperative and cheerful attitude.

HOW: Marcia needs access to a basic data-entry computer system, a filing cabinet and a telephone. She can work 20-30 hours per week, afternoons or evenings, depending on the needs of your business.

CONDITIONS: Marcia will provide these services for $8.00 an hour for the first three months. If after this period of time you find her work to be as profitable as we expect, she will continue as a permanent employee for $10.00 an hour.

EMPLOYMENT PROPOSAL FOR A "PAINTER'S ASSISTANT"

BENEFIT:

Your business could save money and increase profits by hiring an assistant to do prep work and clean-up at $8.00 an hour which your professional painters are presently doing at $16.00 an hour!

SKILLS AND QUALIFICATIONS:

My name is Thomas Lee and I bring hard work and determination to every endeavor. Having worked at a variety of summer jobs during the last three years of high school, I have also proven to be a quick learner. (Please see attached application for references.)

I aspire to become a professional painter and would like to learn my trade with your company. I spoke with someone at your company who informed me that you do not have an assistant on staff at this time. Having researched other businesses like yours, I can give you the names of others who find such a person to be of tremendous value to their painting crews.

I would appreciate a personal interview to discuss this proposal. I will contact you again early next week to schedule an appointment at your convenience. Thank you in advance for your time and consideration in this matter.

Sincerely,

Thomas Lee

EMPLOYMENT PROPOSAL FOR "SECURITY SERVICES"

BENEFIT:

Given recent media attention about the high incidence of car theft and burglary in our community, I propose that you reduce customer fear (thus raising your occupancy rate) by adding nighttime security services on your premises. Your business will also be recognized for being one of the first in the hospitality industry in our community to take residents' need for greater security seriously.

SUMMARY OF EXPERIENCE:

I served eighteen years in the military in a variety of positions which required me to make on-the-spot decisions, exercise good judgment and handle high stress situations. I have basic mechanical abilities and could serve as maintenance person as well as a security guard. I am good with people and would enjoy making myself available to meet the needs of your guests. As a member of this community, I have always appreciated your hotel and would be proud to be a part of your team.

I would like to work full-time and am available on weekends as well as week nights. I would like to discuss salary and benefits with you in person.

I will call you on Friday to discuss this proposal in more detail. Please feel free to contact the people who are on the list of references that I have attached. Thank you for your attention in this matter.

Sincerely,

Henry Miller

Summary Of Ideas On Job Creation

★ Every job that exists today started as someone's idea!

★ A great many employers are themselves entrepreneurs and relate well to the entrepreneurial approach.

★ A business is the most unencumbered institution in society. No institution in North America is freer to do what it wants to do than a business, and that includes *creating its own jobs.*

★ Most people are not aware of their own potential. They come to us with limited vision and preconceived notions about what they can and want to do. In fact, most people have a pretty serious case of tunnel vision. One of the challenges of the entrepreneurial job developer is to help people destroy the walls of their particular tunnels. Before we can do that, we have to get out of our own tunnels about what is possible for our applicants!

★ In addition to using traditional methods to identify the skills and abilities of applicants, consider assessing their hidden talents and traits which they have not had the opportunity to utilize in the past.

★ There is so much happening in today's world. There are glaring needs for us to respond to and address and seemingly limitless opportunities yet to explore. We have to pay attention, pay attention, and then pay attention some more.

★ We've all heard the saying that some things have to be seen to be believed. Well, there are other things that have to be believed to be seen. We make the road by walking it!

★ Every problem creates an opportunity. It is a trick of our trade to learn to spot needs which can be met with abilities of our applicants. Don't limit your vision to the opportunities which can only be solved with your applicants. Our purpose is to add to the well-being and prosperity of the entire business community. Give your advice and recommendations freely, happily and generously.

★ Here are some further recommendations for embracing the job creation function of entrepreneurial job development:

- Never read the newspaper or listen to the news without considering the employment implications of what is reported.

- Keep a journal of your observations of problems, trends and other happenings in your community which suggest a potential hiring need.

- Hold a weekly meeting in your office where everyone has the opportunity to share their observations. Work together to develop strategies for acting on your good ideas. Make a plan with timelines and tasks for following through on ideas. Begin each meeting with a progress report on last week's plan.

- If possible, ask applicants to keep a journal of their own ideas and observations about job creation.

★ I've heard it said that life is the art of drawing without an eraser. I know people who rarely draw because they don't have erasers. I don't recommend that these people become job developers! Be ready for a large number of ideas that don't work out. As long as you keep risking, learning, and trying, success is inevitable. It won't happen if you put your tools down. Keep your pencil sharpened!

★ Finally, don't wait for extraordinary opportunities. Seize common occasions and make them great! Commit random acts of kindness! Perform senseless acts of beauty! Propose unimagined business opportunities! Be an opener of doors! Be an opener of eyes! Live a little! Live a lot! (Amen.)

APPLICATION: IDENTIFYING OPPORTUNITIES
IN YOUR COMMUNITY

(1) How would the current assessment process of your applicants change if you were to embrace the employment proposal approach of job development?

(2) What are some of the local trends in your community that herald or reflect a potential hiring need?

(3) What are some of the problems in your local community which suggest or reflect a potential hiring need?

(4) Which local bills, initiatives, ordinances or referenda, either passed or under consideration, suggest a potential hiring need?

(5) If you were to consider a job change, what kind of job would you ideally create for yourself? What kind of problems are you good at solving? What benefits could you bring to a workplace? What kind of environment would make best use of your skills and abilities?

(6) What kind of opportunities for employment do you see stemming from the following problems and trends?

HOMELESSNESS   TWO-CAREER HOUSEHOLDS

THE NEED FOR ELDERCARE   BUSINESSES DOWNSIZING

AFFORDABLE HEALTH CARE   PARK AND CITY CLEAN-UP

LACK OF DAY CARE   RECYCLING

ILLITERACY   HEALTH AND FITNESS

(7) What kind of positions can you imagine creating in each of the following workplaces? For each kind of business, ask yourself, "What could my applicants do that could:

✓ Make money?
✓ Save money?
✓ Improve the way things are being done?
✓ Expand the customer base?
✓ Add a new service or product to the business?
✓ Use old things in a new way?
✓ Gain or keep a competitive edge?
✓ Make the boss look good?
✓ Improve the reputation in the community?
✓ Get them press?"

UNIVERSITY	HEALTH CLINIC	COFFEE SHOP
BOOKSTORE	BEAUTY PARLOR	INSURANCE CO.
REAL ESTATE AGENCY	HOTEL	PHOTOGRAPHER
RESTAURANT	AIRPORT	SHOPPING MALL
GROCERY STORE	LAW FIRM	PET STORE
ADVERTISING AGENCY	BUS STATION	NURSING HOME
SOFTWARE COMPANY	TELEPHONE COMPANY	VIDEO STORE
FLORIST	NEWSPAPER	DRY CLEANERS
PRINT SHOP	LUMBER COMPANY	MOVING COMPANY

CHAPTER 4:
CAPITALIZING ON BUSINESS
AND SOCIAL TRENDS

Earlier we discussed how job development is both an art and a science. The artist becomes comfortable with his or her tools and materials before using them as a medium for inspiration and beauty. The musician learns the scales and knows well his or her instrument before attempting to create music. The chiropractor studies biology, anatomy and physiology before attempting to "adjust" the spinal column. We learn what we can in the field of counseling in order to offer more insightful guidance to our applicants. These are examples of applying science to its kindred art. To respond to the needs of employers — people working hard to survive and prosper in the world of business — it is equally necessary for us to grasp the pivotal forces that shape their world before attempting to apply the art of entrepreneurial job development.

Popular books and literature on social and business trends are focusing on the same central issues. These central issues are summarized in this chapter. Although it is beyond the scope of this book to provide exhaustive detail about these trends, they deserve your attention. I recommend that all job developers with an entrepreneurial spirit learn everything they can about these important topics. Deeper understanding of employer concerns equips job developers to effectively operate in their world.

"We cannot expect to solve the problems of tomorrow with yesterday's solutions."

Roger Von Oech, author

FIVE PIVOTAL FORCES
SHAPING THE BUSINESS WORLD

➤ FORCE 1: NEW TECHNOLOGY

"Toto, I don't think we're in Kansas anymore."

Dorothy in The Wizard of Oz

Economists agree that the most significant invention of the last fifty years is the integrated circuit. Forty workers can now produce what it once took twelve hundred workers to produce. The microchip has revolutionized every aspect of our lives. Briefcase-sized and hand-held computers have the same capacity as their gargantuan predecessors that filled entire rooms just a few years ago. We can program our home lighting, heating and security systems from a wall panel smaller than a hand-held calculator.

(They say that as amazing as the impact of the integrated circuit has been, it may pale in comparison with the impact of an as yet undiscovered gene that will emerge in blazing glory in the near future from an obscure bioengineering lab.)

"Ride the horse in the direction that the horse is going."

Anonymous

Wegmann, Chapman and Johnson point out in their book, *Work in the New Economy,* that new technology has only created 15% of all new jobs in the last 10 years. What I have noticed as a job developer is that new technology has changed the nature of work in almost every field. Auto mechanics use computers to diagnose car problems, painters use robotics to do routine spraying of homes, and as a result of ATM machines programmed to deal with the most simple transactions, bank tellers deal almost exclusively with complex, sophisticated transactions. In every arena, technical knowledge and speculation race to stay just one step ahead of obsolescence and irrelevance.

Futurists report that in the fifty years between 1970 and 2020 we will experience change equivalent to that of the last 500 years! The "winds of change" have given way to an "earthquake of change." For example, we can now fly halfway around the world, nonstop from Sydney, Australia to Los Angeles in under 15 hours. Organ transplants are everyday occurrences and cataract surgery is an outpatient procedure, with vision restored in a couple of days. Television programs are viewed simultaneously by millions of people around the world. Satellite dishes dot the suburban landscape, bringing hundreds of channels into many homes.

John Naisbitt, in *Megatrends,* characterizes three stages of technology: (1) new technology or innovation follows the line of least resistance; (2) technology is used to improve previous technologies; and (3) the technological advances themselves suggest new directions and uses. He believes we are currently in the second stage and this stage may last a long time before we are ready to move into the third. When I think about common consumer reactions to the idea of "robotics," I have to agree. Computer technology is to the information age what mechanization was to the industrial revolution. It is a threat because it incorporates functions previously performed by workers.

➤ FORCE 2: THE MOVE FROM AN INDUSTRIAL SOCIETY TO A SERVICE-ORIENTED, INFORMATION SOCIETY

One of the most important distinctions between the industrial economy and the information/services economy is access to being a player. In an industrial society, the strategic resource is capital. One hundred years ago, many people may have known how to build a steel plant, but not very many could get the money to build one. Consequently, access to the system was limited. In our new society, John Naisbitt contends, the strategic resource is information. He says, "It is not the only resource, but the most important. The new source of power is not money in the hands of a few but information in the hands of many."

Ours is a brain-intensive industry rather than a capital intensive one. With the aid of new technology, we now amass and produce information the way we mass-produce cars. R.S. Wurman in his book, *Information Anxiety,* says the amount of available information now doubles every five years. This is the age of information and services. It is said there is more information available than there are things to know! We are drowning in information but starved for knowledge about how to use it.

It is important to realize that the transition from an industrial to an information society does not mean manufacturing will cease to exist. After all, farming did not become extinct at the end of the agricultural society. John Naisbitt observes that 90 percent of us produced 100 percent of the food in the agricultural era; now as a result of industrialization, 3 percent of us produce 120 percent. New technology requires fewer workers to produce the goods society needs. Increasingly, a greater number and percentage of workers will be involved in the "servicing of the society."

Today, services of all kinds, including education, account for a larger proportion of the gross national product than manufacturing. The fastest growing services are those provided by state and county governments, including health and welfare services as well as theme parks and fast-food franchises.

The shift from an industrial to a service economy has not been an easy transition for management. Economists warn that as we move further into a service economy, it is increasingly clear that we can't think of "service" in the same terms as products. Services aren't standardized little packages. Service is a human interaction that unfolds in real time. Service management is not as easy to predict, plan and control as product management.

Peter Vaill notes that *"To really think of oneself in the service business changes the way one thinks of the business entirely. Especially, it changes the way one thinks the 'bottom line' is. What a struggle it is though, to get out of the units-of-output frame and stay out of it. Even fields that have always been service businesses, such as hospitals and universities, are finding themselves increasingly pressured to standardize their services for the purposes of cost control and easier long-range planning."*

> *"In every economy... there is a crucial and definitive conflict...the struggle between past and future, between existing configuration of industries and the industries that will someday replace them."*
>
> *George Gilder, business writer*

➤ FORCE 3: GLOBAL INTERDEPENDENCE

"Business is replacing politics as the world's gossip."

John Naisbitt, author

One of the first things the astute businessman checks daily is the yen-dollar ratio. Fifty percent of downtown Los Angeles is owned by the Japanese. Foreign investment in America in real estate, finance and business continues to escalate. It was predicted that during 1992, when Europe became truly a Common Market, it would serve 330 million consumers, as compared to 240 million in the United States.

Where America used to lead the world in research and development, manufacturing and marketing, Japan and Germany now are the acknowledged leaders in both manufacturing and marketing. Currently, America's hottest consumer item is the VCR. Fifty percent of all VCRs made are sold here and nearly all are manufactured in Japan and Korea.

Futurists predict that the interdependent global economy will spawn a renaissance in cultural and linguistic assertiveness. John Naisbitt writes, *"The Swedes will become more Swedish, the Chinese, more Chinese. And the French, God help us, more French."*

> *"Instead of resisting increased economic interdependence, we should be embracing it wholeheartedly. In my view, it is our great hope for world peace."*
>
> *John Naisbitt, author*

*"The times
they are a
changin'."*

*Bob Dylan,
singer and
songwriter*

➤ FORCE 4: CHANGING DEMOGRAPHICS AND VALUES

It is common knowledge that dramatic demographic changes are taking place in America's workforce. *Workforce 2000*, a report issued by the landmark Hudson Institute Study, projected that from 1985 to 2000, minorities, women and immigrants will account for 85 percent of the growth in the workforce. The working population is aging, ethnic diversity is growing, and more people with disabilities are entering the workforce. A widening gap exists between highly educated persons and the large number of persons who cannot read and write well enough to hold entry-level jobs. Employees' values are simultaneously more personal and more divergent. Consider the following statistics about the marked shifts the workforce will undergo between now and the year 2000.

■ By the year 2000, the bulk of the workforce will be middle-aged, 51 percent will be between the ages of 35 and 54. The number of workers aged 16 to 24 will continue to decline to approximately 16 percent. The senior workforce, those over 55 years of age, will remain fairly stable, fluctuating between 11 and 13 percent (*Human Capital*, 1988).

■ The traditional white majority is becoming a minority in many locales, and U.S.-born people of color and immigrants are expected to comprise 43 percent of new entrants to the workforce between 1985 and 2000 (*Human Capital*, 1988).

■ Women will comprise nearly one-half of the workforce by the year 2000 (*Human Capital*, 1988), when six out of seven working-age women will be on the job. Almost two-thirds of the new entrants to the labor force between now and 2000 will be female, and the percentage of dual-career families will swell from 55 to 75 percent. (Futurists speculate that the changing role of women in our society will prove to be the most significant change in this century.)

■ Another relevant trend is the changing distribution of income. Research conducted by the Socio-Economic Research Institute of America indicates a shrinking middle class, while the lower and upper classes grow. The middle class is moving up and the lower class continues to lose upward mobility, primarily because of deficiencies in education. The income distribution curve is beginning to acquire the shape of a barbell.

Dramatic as these statistics may be, they are not as important for job developers as the reality of identifying and managing the implications of changes in the workplace. While concern about workforce diversity is at an all-time high, industry has been slow to respond to the issues presented by ever-increasing diversity. The number of companies with specific programs to address diversity issues is relatively small. Here are some of the critical concerns businesses will face as they become more and more diverse:

➤ Recruitment and outreach activities
➤ Making job information readily available
➤ Creating alternative job descriptions
➤ Using varied training methods to meet varied needs
➤ Providing career development opportunities
➤ Redesigning jobs to adapt to changing needs
➤ Offering incentives and rewards consistent with varying employee values
➤ Offering flexible employee benefits and services to satisfy varying employee needs and interests
➤ Helping employees take care of family responsibilities
➤ Learning more about job accommodations
➤ Developing effective, integrated work teams of a diverse staff
➤ Offering language and communication training
➤ Providing cultural sensitivity and awareness training
➤ Delivering basic literacy and skill training programs

The successful business of the 1990s and beyond does more than value diversity, it depends on it!

Another significant implication of changing demographics is the very real potential of a labor shortage. Managers should expect increasing difficulty meeting staffing needs. This is primarily because the individuals composing the bulk of workforce growth have been underrepresented in the occupations where the greatest need and growth are projected — the health professions, natural and computer sciences, mathematics, and engineering.

Consistent with current trends, managers of all organizations can anticipate a time when the potential labor force will consist of large numbers of people of minority groups and women. The majority of the emerging workforce is willing and physically able to work but lacks the skills needed to take advantage of occupational opportunities. This scenario has been dubbed the "skills gap." Exacerbating this scenario is the anticipated surge in baby-boomer retirement. Taken together, these circumstances foretell a very real labor crunch.

"The future just ain't what it used to be!"

Anonymous

✷ As job developers we should point out to employers that working with programs like ours is not just a convenience, but very shortly will be a necessity. The sooner a company learns how to work with a diverse workforce, the better. Our programs can serve as transitional bridges, connecting employers to a world of potential employees.

➤ FORCE 5: AN UNPREDICTABLE, CHANGING MARKETPLACE

Tom Jackson asserts in *Guerrilla Tactics In The Job Market* that *"Organizations have had it relatively easy since World War II, enjoying expanding markets, cheap raw materials, enormous infusions of public capital in defense spending and relative political and economic calm. This has ceased to be true in the last 20 years."*

Tom Peters suggests that a company preparing to go to market with a product today may find the following forces at work:

✦ A new competitor from Korea
✦ An established Japanese company that has slashed costs and improved quality
✦ A new American company — or several start-ups
✦ An old-line American company with a new approach
✦ A long-time competitor sold to a company with a great distribution set-up
✦ A firm with an electronically based distribution system enabling it to slash delivery time by 75 percent

"Anyone who says businessmen deal in facts, not fiction, has never read old five-year projections."

Malcolm Forbes, publisher

He goes on to say that today's organization must also accomplish new tasks which include targeting the market in segments, responding to rapidly changing consumer demands and preferences, and negotiating gyrating currencies.

Warren Bennis emphasizes two other phenomena he believes account for the instability of the present marketplace — mergers and acquisitions and the regulation and deregulation of industries.

About mergers and acquisitions he says, *"The takeover fever persists, yet no one knows whether they are economically beneficial. A Harvard Business School study, covering the years from 1950 to 1980, shows that 75 percent of all acquisitions during that period were subsequently divested. Of 116 companies involved in mergers, only 23 percent have successfully weathered the transition."* Certainly this trend in the buying and selling of businesses has decreased employee security and loyalty to the "parent company."

The regulation and deregulation of entire industries have transformed once predictable businesses — utilities, transportation, and insurance — into some of the most volatile. Flung about like a leaf in a windstorm, the airline industry engages in fare wars, route battles and union bashing, while service appears to decline. Failures of savings and loan institutions that took too many risks have cost taxpayers billions in bailouts.

JOB DEVELOPMENT QUESTIONS ABOUT TODAY'S BUSINESS WORLD

In the context of this unpredictable, changing marketplace we are asking employers to increase both overhead and responsibility, take new risks, and trust our job development decisions. Consider these issues and how they relate to the employers with whom you work:

✱ Which economic, demographic and social forces are affecting the business?

✱ How do these issues affect the business in terms of:
  ✓ marketability and competition
  ✓ hiring and employment service needs and,
  ✓ continued viability and growth?

TREND TRACKING

Perhaps the most fertile ground for planting the seeds of new employment opportunities is in the connections we make between current social problems, issues and trends and their impact on businesses. Highly regarded futurist Faith Popcorn believes, "If you can connect the dots between the inception of a trend and the impact it will have on a business, then you can fine-tune your services to fit the trend." As trends build and traverse the marketplace, they increase their grip on consumers. Since trends last an average of ten years, the momentum of current trends will propel businesses, all businesses, to the end of the decade and beyond.

"All things are connected, like the blood which unites us all."

Chief Seattle, 1855

Trends and problems differ from community to community. Businesses respond to trends differently, with varying degrees of urgency. One thing is for sure — the future waits for no man, no woman, and no company.

Futurists from divergent disciplines — healthcare and human services to global communication and transport — cite similar trends. The balance of this section summarizes ten popular trends. It also presents questions entrepreneurial job developers should ask when considering connections between trends and the businesses with whom we develop employment opportunities.

The trends discussed below characterize those which are popular at the time of this writing. Two years from now additional trends may emerge offering new opportunities for job creation. With this in mind, pay as much attention to the thinking process presented here as to the particular ideas generated from today's trends.

TEN SOCIAL TRENDS AND PROBLEMS

#1: People are questioning and seeking personal and career satisfaction, often opting for simpler living. The resurgence and popularity of home businesses are attributed to this trend.

After a decade of greed and years of commuting, people are dreaming of renovating old houses, starting hands-on entrepreneurial businesses and renegotiating their present careers — on their own time and terms. Faith Popcorn describes the 1990s as a period when, *"We are asking ourselves what is real, what is honest, what is quality, what is values and what is really important. We are trading in the rewards of traditional success in favor of slower pace and quality of life."* During the seventies we worked to live. In the eighties we lived to work. Now we simply want to live, long and well.

Partly in response to mergers and acquisitions discussed earlier, there is a new skepticism about the benevolence of big institutions and corporations. We have little faith in "parent corporations" as we witness extensive layoffs and corporations bought and sold like Monopoly properties. Faith Popcorn says, *"Labor's classic mistrust of management had 'trickled up' to management itself. But instead of revolution, we're seeing retreat. Back to home businesses and entrepreneurialism."*

John Naisbitt reinforces the presence of this trend asserting that, *"The transition times between economies are the times when entrepreneurialship booms. We are now in such a period."*

Other sociologists attribute the sharp rise of "home businesses" to the fact that PCs, modems, faxes and cellular phones have made information instantaneously available anywhere. You can have a great laser printer at home. Every member of the family can have an answering machine receptionist. So why go to the office?

According to *Trend Tracking* by Gerald Celente, about 16 million corporate employees work at home, either part or full time. Most work is done after-hours or with informal arrangements, but 3.4 million corporate workers have formal work-at-home arrangements with their employers. Add the nearly 10 million self-employed Americans who operate businesses from their homes, and you come up with a startling 26 million persons working at home — nearly 25% of the total American work force!

I have read conflicting opinions about how this trend will ultimately affect the economy. Some predict a negative effect since, to date there has not been a powerful, affluent nation with an economic base of small businesses. Others disagree, contending that nobody works harder, is happier or more productive than the people who work for themselves. This trend could signal significant economic decentralization of businesses in North America.

" *A s we drive into the future, most of us have our eyes glued to the rearview mirror - a habit that causes accidents."*

Gerald Celente, author

JOB CREATION QUESTIONS FOR TREND #1:

★ What services are needed by the growing number of the home-businesses?

★ Which industries or specific local businesses could expand or extend their services to home-based workers?

★ Are there home businesses in need of part or full time help to carry work overload?

★ Will home businesses contract out services such as printing, typesetting/graphic design, accounting/financial planning, cleaning, or travel arrangements? What type of extra help might these contractors require to service this new market?

#2: People are staying home for entertainment.

A recent poll of adults age 18 to 60+ revealed 57% prefer to spend their leisure time at home instead of going out. The percentage was higher for persons over 60, but at 43%, surprisingly high for persons aged 18 to 29. Some of the factors contributing to this trend are the cost of outside entertainment, technological advances in audio and video equipment, fear of crime and social disease, and less disposable (i.e., spendable) income.

The *Popcorn Report* and *Trend-Tracking* cite statistics reflecting this trend:

▲ Skyrocketing rates of VCR purchase and tape rental. At this writing, more than 60% of Americans have access to a VCR;

▲ Successful marketing of comfort food for the couch (e.g., microwave popcorn sales were a $300 million business in 1989);

▲ Take-out food sales. While restaurant sales plummeted, take-out restaurant sales rose to an astonishing 15% of total food expenditures;

▲ The "echo" of baby-boom babies. During 1990 there were 4.2 million births, the highest number since the big-boom in 1960;

▲ Record numbers of people remodeled, redecorated and restored their dwellings, then watched televised "home repair" programs to relax;

▲ Mail order sales topped $200 billion in 1990, up from $82.2 billion just ten years before;

▲ By February 1991, 18.3 million people were making money in home-based businesses, and 65% were women.

JOB CREATION QUESTIONS FOR TREND #2:

◆ How can a business take advantage of at-home consumers?

◆ Which restaurants are not currently offering take-out food but should consider this line of business?

◆ How can a business market to and communicate with home-based consumers? How will this affect telecommunications (e.g., telemarking, catalog purchases, computer or electronic billboard services)?

◆ Can selected businesses (e.g., cosmetologists, manicurists, tailors, chiropractors) service customers in their homes?

#3: Baby boomers don't plan on growing up.

Perhaps partly because aging baby boomers represent a full third of the population, the saying "Don't trust anyone over thirty," has been replaced with "Life begins at forty." We're listening to our old music and watching reruns of "Leave It to Beaver." We're even learning how to bungie jump and sky-dive. (Well, some of you are!)

Says Faith Popcorn, *"Modern age whets our desire for roads untaken. We see it in video rentals and aggressive foreign cuisines, perfumes named Safari, and mountain bikes you ride to the mall."* The cultural inclination toward all things adventurous is evident in popular music, decor to fashion and leisure activities.

This trend bodes well for any business that offers a service or product promoting longevity, youth, dexterity, or the appearance of youth. Americans spend $2 billion a year on products to ward off aging. Forty percent of women between the ages of 25-43 color their hair, and Retin A (an anti-aging prescription skin preparation) sales rose to $60 million in 1990.

The "trend literature" predicts that opportunity will abound for almost anything that makes us feel better, makes us laugh, or makes us feel like a kid. Savvy marketers know the baby-boom generation will grow old with a stylish vengeance.

JOB CREATION QUESTIONS FOR TREND #3:

✶ How can a business improve or change its product, service, or presentation to capitalize on this trend?

✶ Can the business offer consumers products, services or illusions of adventure, youth, longevity and fun?

✶ Have you heard about hotels that offer various kinds of room decor to suit the fantasies of guests? How about shopping malls that incorporate amusement or theme parks? Consider restaurants and bars with costumed employees who entertain diners, or establishments where guests sing karaoke style.

#4: People want personalized products and services.

The computer era has bred a consumer who wants assurance that he or she is important. We want to buy things made especially for us! The more personal the better. Profits will accrue to businesses catering to the consumer demand for personalization — in terms of concept, product design, "customizability," or personal service. One of my favorite department stores now offers custom cosmetics to complement individual skin tone and coloring. Fast food restaurants boast "you can have it your way!"

JOB CREATION QUESTIONS FOR TREND #4:

✶ How can the business offer customized services or products?

For example, can a business add an engraving, embroidering or painting service to personalize the product? Can furniture stores, car dealerships, or real estate agencies add special features to a chair, auto-mobile, garden or kitchen window for a price?

★ Could fast food restaurants offer table service?

My first job was as a car-hop at an A&W in Kankakee, Illinois. During the humid summer months the parking lot was filled with hungry patrons enjoying hot dogs and root beer in their air-conditioned cars, listening to AM radio. Years later when the establishment stopped the car-hop service, they nearly folded because business decreased so dramatically. They learned the hard way that a little extra service goes a long way!

#5: People are willing to hire other people to attend to the things they no longer have the time to do.

The *Popcorn Report* summarizes this trend quite well:

"We have so many crusades. To stay young, get fit, live healthy. Achieve self-fulfillment and conquer self-doubt. Win friends and influence people. Get rich, get smart, get ahead of the crowd. Accumulate toys and trophies, the badges of having lived. Save the planet, save ourselves. Test out the theory that nothing is impossible. So many goals, so little time!" (Does this sound familiar, or what?)

She goes on to say, *"Too fast a pace, too little time, causes societal schizophrenia and forces us to assume multiple roles and adapt easily. Life's arithmetic used to be simpler: one job per family, one marriage, one house, one community for a lifetime, one crop of kids. Today these statistics get multiplied over and over."* (Does this sound even more familiar?)

Multiple work and family roles have certainly complicated our lives. So have the effects of living in the "age of high tech" and the "information society." For example, do you remember when you could get away with saying, "I will put that in the mail to you tomorrow" before faxing was a possibility?

Information management and communication technology not only make information instantly accessible to us at all times, but also make us accessible to information. We carry our cellular telephones with us. One quarter of American homes have cordless phones (more than 9 million sold in 1989 alone!) and 3.5 million of us have car phones. (Hertz plans to install 45,000 car phones in its fleets by 1995. Avis has them too.)

Answering machines, voice and electronic mail, as well as call forwarding/call waiting features contribute to instant accessibility. There's just no reason or excuse for being unreachable. (I love the feeling of inaccessibility on an airplane. I know, having seen the debut of in-flight phones, that this "freedom from information" is short-lived.)

We are not only "out of time," but also find the time we have is moving faster. We expect to accomplish more during the average business day than ever. Witness the mounting sale of microwave food products, take-out dinners and snack food.

Cluster marketing is a new response to this trend. It is the idea of bringing together products and services typically offered by separate businesses, — one-stop-shopping, e.g., parking lot valet services (with pickup and delivery), coffee shops located on the ground floor of office buildings, daycare centers in commuter train stations. In my town there is a new Laundromat-Cafe-Bookstore. I recently read in *Entrepreneur Magazine* about new "Speed Service - Automated Tellers" which dispense stamps, metro tickets, bus passes, even shopping mall gift certificates at locations across the country. Another company started a "drive-through" morning newsstand service that enables consumers to pick up the daily paper, coffee and cigarettes without ever leaving their cars. But then, why not have it washed while you wait for your coffee?

JOB CREATION QUESTIONS FOR TREND #5:

✶ Which businesses have products or services that could buy the consumer some time?

✶ Is there a way to make the product or service more convenient for, or accessible to the consumer?

✶ Is it possible to extend business hours (add weekend or evening hours) so working people do not have to take time off to receive the service or buy the product?

✶ Could the business save customers time by offering multiple products or locations which serve multiple purposes, enabling them to accomplish two or three activities simultaneously? Why should we have to make one drop at the cleaners, one at the tailors, and a third at shoe repair?

#6: The make-up of our households has changed.

Businesses used to be able to market their products to the "average housewife" during the day and the "average working male" during the evening or weekends. Those days are long gone. Let's look at some statistics taken from *Trend Tracking* by Gerald Celente:

"Businesses can't market to June and Ward Cleaver anymore. And Father doesn't necessarily know best!"

New Marketers to their predecessors

■ The number of single-father households has grown 82% in the last ten years, faster than any other type of household unit.

■ One-third of the 91 million American households are headed by single adults, and a fifth consists of one adult living alone. In today's society, with 65 percent of mothers working outside the home, many children are virtually on their own. An estimated seven million children under age 14 are unsupervised while their parents work, and this number is increasing.

■ Although there's no official tally, the number of gay men and women parenting through adoption, foster care, and sperm banking has increased substantially in recent years.

■ In 1990, there were 20 million 18-34 year olds living with one or both parents. "Boomerang families" — where adult children return to the nest (usually in response to economic pressures or dissolution of marriages) are forcing a redefinition of traditional family roles.

■ Millions of people throughout North America hold multiple jobs. Some are working double-time for career advancement. A select few pursue two or more careers simultaneously because of ambition in overdrive or sheer enthusiasm. However, most are forced to do double-duty to pay the bills — plain and simple economics.

■ One out of four children in our society lives in a single-parent family. Single-parent families have increased as a result of escalating divorce rates and an increasing number of births to unmarried women. One out of two marriages ends in divorce, and births to unmarried women now account for 22 percent of all births. That's more than one out of five births!

■ In dual-career families, teenagers are picking up some of the slack in terms of household responsibilities. Teen shoppers select and purchase a substantial portion of groceries and household items. Discretionary spending by teenagers is estimated in the billions!

■ It is estimated that the average family can afford to spend about 10 percent of gross income on child care. The actual cost of most child-care services is higher, consuming about 25 percent of gross family income.

■ By the end of the 1990s about 50 million people in this country will be age 65 or older, and 30 to 50 percent of them will eventually need long-term care. In another era, families would have provided long-term care, but if working adults don't have time to care for their children, how are they going to find time to care for their parents?

■ Estimates of homelessness top 4 million, and this number increases by 40 percent a year. The American Affordable Housing Institute warns that the number of homeless people could triple during a minor recession.

JOB CREATION QUESTIONS FOR TREND #6:

✯ Are businesses reaching and serving the vast variety of households which constitute our society today?

✯ What services are needed by single parent families? Do single-father households have unique needs?

✯ Which organizations could profit by offering urgently needed child and elder care services?

✯ Which businesses could profit by appealing to teenagers' discretionary spending habits?

#7: The country rediscovers a conscience of social ethics, passion, and compassion.

Awareness of the need to save our society is at an all-time high. We're thinking ahead, turning from short-termism to long-termism (another future persuasion discussed by John Naisbitt in *Megatrends*). We've taken from the world, and now we want to give back. In Faith Popcorn's words, *"the prevailing cultural biological clock is beginning to say it's time to be good and clean up our act."*

The best news for the environment (and important news for business) is the growing recognition that decency can be profitable and tax-deductible. Think of the companies that stand out both morally and financially in the past few years: Ben & Jerry's, The Body Shop, Patagonia, Tom's of Maine. Each placed social responsibility before profitability. Consumer demand is the impetus for this change. Corporate and individual business commitments drive it. Consumers want to patronize companies using recycled plastic containers and manufacturers careful to use phosphate-free laundry detergents. They want to purchase biodegradable diapers, bathroom tissue made from recycled paper and coffee filters that don't release chlorine. Consider these statistics from *The Popcorn Report* and *Trend Tracking:*

■ Nearly one half of Americans took some kind of environmental consumer action in 1990. More than fifty percent stopped using aerosol sprays, 49 percent bought products made from recycled materials, 34 percent reduced their use of paper towels, and 34 percent chose not to purchase a product because of concern for the environment.

■ During 1990 alone, more than 800 pieces of recycling legislation were introduced. Curbside recycling is now law in many communities. Voluntary recycling is accelerating.

According to *The Popcorn Report,* the new maxim is this: *"Let the concerns of the nation become the concerns of the corporation. IBM is already giving computers to classrooms. Apple, to ecological groups. But soup companies should run soup kitchens. Clothing companies should donate clothes to the poor. Toothpaste companies should start dental clinics for needy children. The publishing industry should plant trees. Car companies should provide transportation to people who are old, who are young, and who are infirmed."*

Concern about the present and future has spawned a new concept — *cause marketing* — purchases that express a point of view about the environment, social issues or even support for political candidates. Many marketing plans for both products and services include funds and strategies to publicize corporate contributions to admirable causes.

JOB CREATION QUESTIONS FOR TREND #7:

✵ Which businesses have not responded to this trend and might benefit by doing so?

✵ Is there a natural, low-cost service the business could offer to send a message of "cause marketing" to the consumer? For example, could a grocery store advertise its donation of food (i.e., items approaching their final dates for retail sale) to homeless shelters or convalescent hospitals?

#8: There is a market for the purchase of small indulgences.

During recessionary times people use depressionary thinking when it comes to making big-time investments or large purchases. In other words, "No can do." But we hard-working, over-extended, stressed-out folks believe we deserve some small indulgence — a little luxury — to compensate us for our efforts. The trends indicate that we believe in indulgences — just make them small! For example, we are spending exorbitant amounts of money to:

A seasoned job developer always asks questions. A green one will always have answers.

✦ Regularly purchase personal services (e.g. nails, facials, manicures, saunas, hot tubs, mud baths and massage.)

✦ Buy designer products (e.g., athletic gear, perfumes, underwear).

✦ Send $4 artistic greeting cards instead of a gift. When we do purchase gifts, we wrap them in designer gift wrap that costs more than the gift itself!

✦ Indulge in gourmet products, everything from coffee beans to ice cream. We may be eating at home but look what we're eating!

✦ Scoop up potted tulips, daffodils and miniature roses by the dozen, since there is no time to cultivate a garden of our own.

JOB CREATION QUESTIONS FOR TREND #8:

✵ Which businesses have a product or service that fits into the category of a "small indulgence"? How can a business advertise its product in order to capitalize on our desire for little luxuries?

For example, a hotel could advertise "weekend get-aways" to locals as an affordable alternative to a costly Caribbean cruise!

#9: People are taking care of themselves and moving away from institutional care.

Self-help has always been a part of American life. During the 1970s, the self-help/self-care movement cut a sweeping tide, cutting across many institutions and disciplines and including a broad spectrum of geographic areas and political ideologies. Here are examples of the self-care movement throughout North America:

"The more technology we put in our hospitals, the less we are being born there, dying there and avoiding them in between...In a sense, we have come full circle. We are reclaiming America's traditional sense of self-reliance after four decades of trusting institutional help."

John Naisbitt, author

✦ Community groups acting to prevent crime, strengthen neighborhoods, salvage and deliver food for the elderly, and rebuild homes. They act independently, without government assistance or exerting considerable local control over government help.

✦ Churches, apartment buildings and stores are hiring private security guards in record numbers.

✦ Private police work is one of the fastest-growing occupations in the country!

✦ Hundreds of community groups throughout the nation have transformed vacant urban land into flourishing organic gardens.

✦ Grassroots organizations across the country have started volunteer fire departments.

✦ People are assuming increasing responsibility for personal health habits and lifestyles as well as the environment. There is a rising demand for holistic, "person-centered" care, treatment and services. A redefinition of health from "the absence of disease" to "the existence of a positive state of wellness of the whole person" is gaining consumer acceptance.

✦ A Harris Poll found that 19 percent of respondents bought organic produce for the first time during 1990. The same year, a full 30 percent changed their eating habits in response to news and concern about pesticides. Another study reported that 84% of Americans prefer organic foods over conventionally grown produce.

✦ Homeopathy, reflexology, acupressure, acupuncture, biofeedback and holistic medicine are rapidly moving from the fringes to the mainstream of medicine. (Recently, aromatherapy and herbology have gained popularity as "alternative" healing methods.)

✦ People are reclaiming (some are seizing!) personal, individual control over the processes and mysteries of life and death from the medical establishment. The hospice movement, natural (i.e., unmedicated, low tech) childbirth, home births, birthing centers and interest in medical self-care are examples of this phenomenon.

✦ The ranks of the entrepreneurial movement, which rejects large corporations in favor of self-employment and small businesses, have swelled.

In *Megatrends,* John Naisbitt says, *"Of America's 11 million businesses, 10.8 are small businesses. Sixty million of the nation's approximately 100 million workers are in small businesses."*

✦ In the schools, parents have embraced activism, questioning the public school system, and in some cases rejecting it in favor of private or home education. Home-schooling has become an increasingly popular educational option in the last five years.

✦ Self-help and peer support groups address practically every conceivable problem — addictive spending, smoking, single parenting, retirement, widowhood, weight control, alcohol and drug abuse, being an adult child of or partner to a person who has an alcohol or drug abuse problem, mental illness and overcoming the effects of child or sexual abuse. The list is endless.

JOB CREATION QUESTIONS FOR TREND #9:

✱ To profit from the self-help trend, can a business expand its operation to offer "how to" instruction?

For example, can construction companies or contractors offer home-building classes, can auto-service businesses offer classes on rebuilding or reconditioning of old cars, can home furnishing companies offer wallpapering and carpet-laying instruction? These businesses have the expertise, the equipment, the tools and the customers who want to learn to do it themselves!

✱ How can job developers develop employment proposals together with the input, support and ideas of community or neighborhood groups who are taking power into their own hands?

#10: People want to have their say in everything from politics and product development to employee rights.

Let's look at this trend from three interrelated viewpoints — politics, consumerism and corporate involvement.

POLITICS

John Naisbitt in *Megatrends* writes about participatory democracy, which he describes as, *"the need for people to be part of the process of arriving at decisions that affect their lives. Participatory democracy is revolutionizing local politics in America and is bubbling upward to change the course of national governments as well."* Ross Perot gained the

"Mom, shouldn't we vote on whether or not we will have broccoli for dinner?"

Children of the nineties

support of millions of voters in a mere 3 months decrying that "We can take our country back." This trend is also reflected in the success of Clinton Administration "town meetings." People want a close, personal forum where they can speak their minds and ask questions.

Perhaps the most obvious product of this trend is the popular and successful use of local and state initiatives and referenda to control local issues and address local problems and interests. Borrowing John Naisbitt's words, such initiatives are the key instruments for people "to leapfrog traditional representative processes and mold the political system in their own hands."

CONSUMERISM

Faith Popcorn believes, *"This is the day of the Vigilante-Consumer: the corporate aura of power and omniscience has been demystified. For years, consumers couldn't see the person at the top of the corporate ladder. Now we want him out front and held accountable. There will be no forgiveness of huge mega-corporations that hide behind huge and complicated corporate structures. Labels will become more important than ever before. We'll want to know the biography of the product and the ethics of the maker. We'll want to know the company's stand on the environment, how it regards animal testing, human rights, and other issues - rather than a list of the ingredients, a glimpse or an image."*

"Consumers are to economics what voters are to politics."

Jim Turner, author

Tom Peters writes about how "markets are becoming niches, and niches are growing smaller. As this market miniaturization occurs, consumers gain more stature — and they know it." Corporations will have to act promptly to revolutionize packaging and distribution, detoxify their products and set standards for themselves that meet consumer standards.

The marketing implications of the "vigilant consumer" include the elimination of time-honored selling techniques. For example, "new" will no longer be a compelling selling point — an amazing departure for the American marketplace. "New improved" doesn't do much for vigilant consumers, except prompt them to verbalize the nagging doubt about why it was not good enough in the first place.

Futurists predict that we will choose one product over another when we feel we are in partnership with the seller, and the purchase promises a positive impact on the future. Some think that anonymous, impersonal selling — the old style K-mart — is over. To encourage us to warm up to them, many retailers will create an atmosphere of intimacy, complete with personal notes and sayings, suggestion boxes, manager's names, employee profiles, samples, contests and fun. We want to buy from people and we want to trust the people who sell us goods and services.

CORPORATE INVOLVEMENT

There is a growing trend for participatory democracy in the corporations where we spend a significant amount of our time. John Naisbitt writes, *"It is in corporations that we earn our wages, invest our talents, secure our health care, and invest our money. It is where we make our social ties and define our self-esteem and earn something as pedestrian as our daily bread....Just as we seek a greater voice in political decisions, through initiatives and referenda, we are reformulating corporate structures to permit workers, shareholders, consumers and community leaders a larger say in determining how corporations will be run."*

There has been a tremendous mismatch in the American tradition of "personal liberty" and the classic, top-down authoritarian manner in which the American workplace has operated. Today, hands-on, controlling management is out and hands-off, visionary leadership is in.

This trend is reflected by the growing number of companies using quality circles and TQM (total quality management) to obtain employee perspectives and encourage employee participation in the day-to-day decisions about their worklife. Networking is replacing hierarchies. We also see concerted efforts to involve more "outside" board members, invigorated shareholder activism and renewed interest in and attention to employee rights. Enactment of the Family Leave Bill is a clear expression that society is recognizing employees' rights and responsibilities as family members while continuing to include them in corporate culture.

In summary, we want a voice in every aspect of our lives and we are increasingly aware that we have the power to use our voice. The greater the harmony among us, the stronger the power of the song. And as the old African saying goes, "When the music changes, so does the dance."

"Business is like riding a bicycle. Either you keep moving or you fall down."

American business saying

JOB CREATION QUESTIONS FOR TREND #10:

★ How can businesses better respond to the consumer need to have a voice?

For example, would a business profit from instituting "interactive warranties" which could be faxed from the point of purchase to the manufacturer? How about hiring "corporate reps" who telephone consumers to find out if they're happy within days of the purchase? Would this satisfy the need for greater consumer/corporate contact?

★ How can a business create more opportunities to listen to customers?

★ What would enable a business to more fully respond to the consumer's concerns and desires?

★ Could a business which does not already have one, create an 800 number? Could you, the job developer, provide a person to answer the calls?

"The reason a lot of people do not recognize opportunity is because it usually goes around wearing overalls looking like hard work."

Thomas Edison, American inventor

FINAL THOUGHTS ABOUT THE RELATIONSHIP BETWEEN
BUSINESS AND SOCIAL TRENDS

★ How can the typical business owner deal with the daily demands of running a business, managing employees, dealing with the economic, social and political realities discussed earlier, and be prepared to respond to current trends and their implications for the business? Wouldn't it be great if job developers, as part of their service to the employer community, kept a finger on the pulse of the consumer community and offered recommendations and advice about how businesses could prosper and benefit from current trends? What if many of those recommendations took the form of employment proposals, and were accepted? Everybody would win!

★ Businesses are like human beings. A person can keep only so many problems, opportunities and concerns in his or her head or heart at any one time. That's why we need the perspective and participation of other people in our lives. Businesses need the vision and resources of our programs to support and stimulate them!

★ One last thought from Alan Kay, author of *Creating Excellence:*

*"The best way to predict the future
is to invent it!"*

APPLICATION: TRANSLATING TRENDS INTO JOB OPPORTUNITIES

(1) Choose one of the ten trends discussed in the chapter and identify:

(a) The connections you see between the trend and possible employment opportunities;

(b) The kinds of organizations which would benefit from capitalizing on the trend; and,

(c) The names of particular businesses in your locale who you believe could benefit from acting on the trend.

#1: People are questioning and seeking personal and career satisfaction, often opting for simpler living. The resurgence and popularity of home businesses are attributed to this trend.

#2: People are staying home for entertainment.

#3: Baby boomers don't plan on growing up.

#4: People want personalized products and services.

#5: People are willing to hire other people to attend to the things they no longer have the time to do.

#6: The make-up of our households has changed.

#7: The country rediscovers a conscience of social ethics, passion, and compassion.

#8: There is a market for the purchase of small indulgences.

#9: People are taking care of themselves and moving away from institutional care.

#10:People want to have their say in everything from politics and product development to employee rights.

TREND:

Connections between trend and possible employment opportunities:

The kind(s) of organizations that could profit from capitalizing on this trend:

The names of local businesses I could approach with an employment proposal:

(2) Choose one of the ideas brainstormed in the first part of this exercise and put together a marketing plan for making a business proposition to one or more of the identified organizations.

CHAPTER 5:
DEVELOPING PARTNERSHIPS WITH EMPLOYERS

The purpose of this chapter is to examine the quality and nature of the relationships we aspire to develop with employers. Included here is an examination of our goals and objectives, as well as our role as consultants to business. This chapter also discusses what job developers and employers have to offer one another, and how to make the shift from the sales to the partnership paradigm of job development. This shift in perspective provides a foundation for everything we hope to achieve through our work with employers.

THE PARTNERSHIP PERSPECTIVE: OUT OF THE SALES PARADIGM

Job development is often described as "just another kind of sales." Certainly there are similarities between the two professions. In fact, there is an element of "sales" in nearly every job and in every relationship we have with other people. For example, we may sell our friends on going to one particular movie rather than another or sell a co-worker on the idea of making the next pot of coffee. You sell your ideas in meetings, your perspective to supervisors, and your credibility to funding sources. Attempting to bring people around to our way of seeing the world, to valuing our way of thinking, or agreeing to set actions is part of life. Nearly everyone has to communicate, work and negotiate with other human beings. Job development has an element of sales, but there are important distinctions between the two professions.

I ask participants in my job development workshops to tell me what connotations they make with the word "sales." Responses usually include: "sleazy," "slick," "pushy," and "persistent." The underlying assumption is that the salesperson must push something the customer does not really need or want. While there are many salespeople who do not fit this stereotype — people who sell with sincerity, integrity and a real concern for customer needs — the negative connotations of sales persist.

In the world of job development, using an approach which incorporates the stereotypical sales attitude would be setting up everyone — applicant, employer, and job developer — for failure. I would like to present a departure from the existing sales paradigm for job developers and propose the partnership paradigm, based on the following three premises:

(1) In the partnership paradigm we do not confuse the goal of placement with the overall purposes of our programs;

> *"If job development is sales, it's the toughest kind of sales going because we have a product that can refuse to go! Can you imagine a product, that once it's been sold, refused to get on the truck?"*
>
> Richard Pimentel, job development trainer

> *"There are worse things in life than death. Have you ever spent an evening with an insurance salesman?"*
>
> Woody Allen, actor, director, philosopher

(2) It requires us to embrace the role of consultant rather than that of the classic salesperson; and,

(3) It emphasizes the equal exchange of resources and opportunities between the job developer and the employer.

Let's examine each of these premises.

PUTTING PURPOSE FIRST

"He who has a why to live for can bear almost any how."

Friedrich Nietzsche, German philosopher

Let us consider the true purpose of employment and training efforts. Our goals include assisting people in attaining gainful employment, and developing subsidized and unsubsidized training opportunities and/or valuable work experience situations. These are important and worthy goals. It is critical, however, that we do not confuse these goals with our greater purpose. Our goals are what we hope to achieve through our programs, our purpose is the motivation — the reason we want to achieve these goals.

The purposes of employment programs vary according to the individual philosophy and concerns of each program. Obviously, the aims of organizations like community colleges, high schools, vocational schools, private rehabilitation agencies, independent living centers, and community based organizations differ from one another. Nonetheless, there is consensus about the primary purposes employment projects share. These are:

★ To improve the quality of life of the individuals we serve through increased vocational and employment opportunity;

★ To serve the general community by enhancing and expanding opportunities for all job seekers to be productive, valued members of the workforce; and,

★ To offer services and resources which contribute to the growth and prosperity of the business community.

Most people in our field agree that these purposes are equally important, but I think there is far more emphasis and attention paid to the first two than to the third. More time and effort are spent serving individuals and advocating for the target group than for supporting, understanding and serving the business community. This is foolhardy since it is the health and well-being of individual businesses which make it possible for us to pursue the first two purposes! Ignoring the needs of business is as short-sighted as a farmer disregarding the condition of the soil before planting.

Adding to the well-being and prosperity of individual businesses must be as important a mission for the job developer as any other goal or purpose.

Sometimes contributing to the well-being and prosperity of a business means offering employment services, wage subsidies, on-the-job training contracts, job coaching, or other services. Bear in mind, however, that sometimes it means a recommendation that the business *not* hire from you. You may actually encourage employers to hire from someone else, or to use your services down the road, when you are better able to meet their needs.

Our role is to help employers make a good decision, not to convince them that utilizing our services is the best decision.

Some of you may be reading this and thinking, "Well, it's all fine and good to be committed to purposes, but what if you are accountable and must reach certain goals in terms of placements, not purposes?" Our placement goals and our purposes are not mutually exclusive. When you feel pressured by measurable outcomes, remember they are simply indicators. Like road signs, they keep us moving in the right direction. The numbers help us keep track of what is happening. They are not designed to work against our purposes but rather to increase the likelihood we will achieve them.

"There's a big difference between selling and helping people to buy."

Michael Le Boeuf, author

It is easy when faced with quotas, to find ourselves working to achieve measurable results for their own sake, without regard for the "big picture." I remember all too well when the pressure was on to "meet quota." It was altogether too tempting to compromise what I knew was important to an applicant and an employer for the immediate payoff of a placement. On those occasions when I even considered taking advantage of the trust people had in me and my ability to manipulate their decisions to meet my own ends, I learned, first-hand, the definition of the word "sleazy." It means compromised integrity.

This is not an indictment of having and using quantifiable placement goals. It is a reminder to use them effectively rather than being used by them.

EMBRACING THE ROLE OF CONSULTANT

With the purpose of adding to the well-being and prosperity of businesses, our role with employers is three-fold:

(1) To communicate and inform employers about the resources and services available to them through the program;

(2) To help the employer make good decisions about the utilization of these resources and services; and,

(3) In the event the program addresses the needs of the business, to deliver services to the best of our abilities.

Let's look at each of these roles and consider how they relate to the notion of selling.

In the first role, if we consider communicating with genuine enthusiasm as selling, fine. If informing employers in a manner that addresses their concerns is deemed selling, fine again. Still, our purpose is not really to sell. It is to communicate simply and clearly the options and opportunities your program offers. This is more often akin to the concept of consulting than it is to selling.

In the second role, our purpose is to help employers make good decisions about whether to utilize our services. If your services are not needed or relevant to the employer's present situation, the best decision may be not to extend your services at this time. The goal is to develop and maintain long-term quality relationships.

If we convince an employer of something that is not in his or her best interest, in the short run we may get referrals, interviews, job leads and even possible hires. But by opting for short-term gain, in the long run we may be sacrificing our credibility. Using successful persuasive techniques to gain support for a project that does not work or is not needed, may in effect, mortgage our future.

Given the option of not pushing for a job placement, you are liberated from the shackles of the sales paradigm and are genuinely able to work together with an employer. There is no need to manipulate, push your own agenda, calculate your every move, or drive hard for what you want. (You don't even have to worry about dressing for success!) Both parties can be open and examine the pros and cons of moving forward in a business relationship. You can feel the difference when neither party is aiming to push a viewpoint solely to meet his or her own ends.

The decision not to move forward in a "hiring relationship" with an employer at one point in time does not preclude a future working relationship, and it does not shut the door to the possible exchange of secondary resources.

In the event the need for or interest in your services is not present, you can demonstrate your professional integrity by agreeing not to move forward in a "hiring relationship," leaving the door open for other ways to exchange resources. Consider these options for working with employers:

✦ You provide information on job accommodations in exchange for information on training opportunities in the industry;

✦ The employer agrees to speak to a class and schedule students for a tour of the company;

✦ You exchange a task analysis of a training position for a possible apprenticeship opportunity for employer review and request comments about the resumes of three applicants applying for higher-level positions;

✦ The employer agrees to mentor an applicant; in return, you agree to offer a one-hour workshop about communicating with people who speak limited English;

> "*People ask me what 'being professional' means to the role of the job developer and this is what I say: Any one can get someone hired anywhere once. Being a professional means you can do repeat business with the same employer over and over again.*"
>
> *Richard Pimentel*
> *job development trainer*

✦ You offer to provide information about the tax benefits of hiring people from high-risk populations, and the employer permits your applicants to job shadow his or her employees for a day.

There is an unlimited number of possibilities for exchange and unlimited opportunities for continuing relationships between job developers and employers. To focus solely on a hiring relationship is to unnecessarily narrow the scope of possibilities.

The goal of developing a partnership with an employer is inconsistent with the classic sales paradigm in which the job developer goes out to "make a quick placement." Helping employers make good decisions is very different from "making placements" or "persuading them to hire." The commitment to remain true to our convictions and purposes earns the well-deserved trust and respect of our customers — applicants and employers. It is a positive political act in a culture inclined to value outcomes rather than process, numbers more than needs, and quantity over quality.

Traditional selling emphasizes overcoming objections and perfecting closing techniques. The best sales organizations don't worry about closing techniques but focus on helping customers feel supported and understood. If we share the employer's goals, then the objective of our meeting is to assess and agree about the best utilization of each party's resources and opportunities. Good ideas develop naturally. Closing techniques are not necessary nor relevant in this environment.

"Inventing options for mutual gain is a negotiator's single greatest opportunity. Effective negotiators do not just divvy up a fixed pie. They first explore how to expand the pie!"

William Ury
author

CULTIVATING AN EQUAL EXCHANGE OF RESOURCES

Another paradigm shift helps to explain and expand our relationship with employers. The existing paradigm supports the idea that employers hold all the cards — it's their game, played on their turf. We make our best pitch, hoping they will notice that we are on the field or perhaps even allow us to warm the bench, instead of aspiring to being recognized as valuable players.

In his wonderful book, *The Consultant's Calling,* Geoffrey Bellman makes the case that a partnership is truly what we are after. Described in the context of job development, "Partnership is created when the employer's investment in your unique combination of abilities and resources equals your investment in their unique combination of opportunities." This definition emphasizes the power of both parties to give and receive rather than to wield and take. There is no power differential in partnership. Each partner must have something the other wants. You must have abilities and resources the employer wants; the employer must have opportunities you want.

We often hear job developers define themselves as powerless. "Employers dangle job openings in front of us and we compete for them. They accept or reject our services and accept or reject applicants. We don't take it or leave it; we take whatever we can get!" This is not the making of a partner, it's more the making of a puppet!

The entrepreneurial job developer is looking for opportunities, not openings. The agreements we make, or don't make, depend on the opportunities offered. Our power increases when we accept a choice and the choice is in everyone's best interest.

PARTNERSHIPS: HAPPY SAILING

Before summarizing the distingushing features of the partnership paradigm described in this chapter, I'd like to share with you this excerpt from an insightful article written by Nancy Leamen from the Canadian Bankers Association about her organization's partnerships with employment service providers in Canada:

> *A partnership is like any other kind of ship. If it is not seaworthy, it will sink. If it is not balanced, it will capsize. If it is not kept on course, it could end up on the rocks. If a destination is not agreed upon, it will drift. If that destination is not well charted, it will flounder. If there is no fuel, it will not make any progress. If all hands on deck are not working together, it will stall. And if it is not able to adjust course with shifting currents, storms, sands, and seas, it may never make it to its destination.*
>
> *The same holds true for employment equity partnerships. And speaking on behalf of the Canadian Bankers Association, I can honestly say that employment partnerships are not always clear sailing. We sometimes encounter storms, and drift off course. But overall, we have found successful partnerships to be the best vessels available to arrive at our destination — this is, our employment equity and business goals.*
>
> *Different partners in any relationship have different needs, different motivations and different goals. How, then, can we chart a course to arrive at the same destination? The key is to understand that different goals and needs can and must be accommodated — they don't necessarily lead to different destinations.*
>
> *Think of the ship again — three partners of an ocean-going expedition may have very different reasons for wishing to sail to a certain port of call. One of the partners may be looking for an ocean cruise, and like the route to that port of call. Another may want to reach the port itself as a tourist destination. And the third might want to deliver cargo to that port.*
>
> *So it doesn't matter if they have different goals and needs, if they can accommodate each others' needs and*

on a destination and a mutually acceptable and
ficial course.
accomplish that, each partner has to take the time
make the effort to try and understand the others'
als and needs.

better understand the terms of potential partnerships with employ- see what each party in these relationships may offer the other.

Maine Medical Center

Deborah D. Rousseau, B.S.
Employment Specialist

Department of Vocational Services
22 Bramhall Street, Portland, Maine 04102-3175
(207) 662-6131 • TTY (207) 662-4900 • Fax (207) 662-4064
Toll Free (888) 208-8700 • roussd@mmc.org • www.mmc.org

The MaineHealth Family

95

RESOURCES AND OPPORTUNITIES FOR PARTNERSHIPS

WHAT THE JOB DEVELOPER HAS TO OFFER THE EMPLOYER

Primary Resources

Qualified applicants
Financial incentives
On-the-job training
Education and training of potential employees
Pre-screening of applicants
Education or training opportunities for staff
Job coaching
Ongoing support services
Quick response to need

Secondary Resources

Expertise and insight on:
  Looking at an applicant's skills as cost-saving
    or money making ventures
  Occupations across industries
  Job accommodations
  Job sharing options
  Operations of other businesses including hiring,
    training, recruitment, and supervisory methods
  Assessment and evaluation techniques
  Interviewing methods
  Job and task analysis methods
  Building "natural supports" in the work
    environment for people with special needs

Knowledge of and access to information about
  target populations

Knowledge of and access to other
  community resources and support systems

Perspective and objectivity

References for applicants

Community recognition

WHAT THE EMPLOYER HAS TO OFFER THE JOB DEVELOPER

Primary Resources

Employment opportunities
Job interviews
Training opportunities
Informational interviews
Work experience opportunities
Job shadowing opportunities
Apprenticeship opportunities
Mentorship of job seeker

Secondary Resources

Expertise and insight about:
  The Industry
  Occupations in
    The field
    The business
    Related industries

Feedback and advice about:
  Marketing materials
  Approaching businesses
  Placing an applicant

Opportunities to:
  Tour a business
  Set up tour for applicants
  Sit on advisory board
  Speak to class
  Offer feedback on resumes
  Review course curriculum
  Send monthly job listing
  Refer to other employers
  Inform about company or industry
    functions
  Speak to them in person
  Respond to a letter
  Attend a function
  Receive and respond to monthly
    applicant listing

DISTINGUISHING FEATURES OF THE PARTNERSHIP PARADIGM

★ The relationship between a job developer and an employer is a dynamic and ongoing process. It continues to evolve and change as both parties' needs and interests change.

★ The role of the job developer depends on the services or resources the employer wants and needs. It also differs depending on the reason(s) the employer decides to use your services.

Does your program offer a service or benefit which:

- Employers want and can't find elsewhere?
- Businesses don't have time to do themselves?
- Increases their capacity to perform existing tasks?
- Employers are willing to experiment with?

The role of the job developer varies in response to the employer's reason for seeking services. You may be a co-designer, teacher, student, consultant or even a co-worker on a particular project. Employer motivations and decision-making are more fully described in the next chapter.

★ Do not limit your ideas about what you have to offer employers. Among other things, you can provide:

Experience	Friendship	Support
Understanding	Objectivity	Perspective
Research, data	Authenticity	Age
Wisdom	Information	Vision
Values	Skill	Resources
Expertise	Credibility	Assurances
Reputation	Insight	Personality

★ Go out every day saying, "I want to help as many people as possible today," instead of, "I hope that I can find someone who will listen to me," or "I am going to make as many placements as possible today." If you focus on long-term goals, you are less likely to be side-tracked by short-term frustrations.

★ On the next page you will find a summary chart of the differences between the Sales Paradigm of Job Development and the Partnership Paradigm of Job Development. Read it and answer the questions that follow.

SALES PARADIGM OF JOB DEVELOPMENT	PARTNERSHIP PARADIGM OF JOB DEVELOPMENT
Key behaviors:	*Key Behaviors:*
Persuades, Manipulates Convinces, Influences Verbalizes, Negotiates	Understands, Fosters Discerns, Interprets Listens, Communicates
Focuses on placement goals	Focuses on enhancing the growth and prosperity of business community
Sees employer as power-wielding party, holder of primary resources	Sees employer as equal partner in exchange of primary and secondary resources/opportunities
Goal is to convince employer to use services and hire people from program	Goal is to help employer make good decisions about utilization of services
Works for short-term gain in developing employment	Aims for long-term gain by developing relationship with employers
Sees limited options for working with employers, looks for "yes" and "no" answers	Sees unlimited options for with employers, keeps all doors of possibility open
Concerned about closing techniques at the end of the meeting	Concerned about gaining understanding throughout the meeting
Has more answers than questions	Has more questions than answers

APPLICATION: DEVELOPING A PARTNERSHIP PROFILE

Review the list of Resources and Opportunities for Partnerships on page 96. Without limiting yourself to the information provided, identify what you consider to be the most valuable resources and/or opportunities you have to offer an employer.

Identify the most valuable resources and/or opportunities an employer has to offer you as a job developer.

Using your lists, identify at least twenty possible combinations of exchange of resources between you and an employer.

What do you see as your primary purpose(s) as a job developer? What are your primary goals? What are the main distinctions between your purpose(s) and goals?

How would adopting the partnership paradigm of job development change your present approach to working with employers?

What skills, abilities and personal characteristics do you bring to your role as a consultant to business?

CHAPTER 6:
TARGETING NEW EMPLOYERS

*"Look around for a place to sow a few seeds. It is the generous
giving of ourselves that produces the generous harvest."*

Mother Teresa, Great Human Being

Thoughts about sowing seeds may seem an odd way to begin a
chapter about targeting and approaching employers, but it is a fitting metaphor. As job developers we are sowing seeds that, once
firmly rooted and properly nurtured, will eventually blossom. The seeds
we sow bear rare and special fruits — the chance for someone to realize
a vocational dream, an opportunity for a young person to try his hand at
independence, or the occasion when a business opens its doors to people
with barriers for the very first time.

Most job developers agree the work they do is valuable and important
for employers and applicants alike. Paradoxically, many job developers
admit to overwhelming embarrassment, difficulty and timidity when
approaching employers to plant seeds. I presume that you, dear reader,
like myself, have been there.

Initiating contact with employers who don't automatically recognize
the value of what we offer and who employ a person whose job it is to
screen us out, is no picnic. It is this aspect of job development that
requires the most courage, persistence, confidence, discipline and perseverance. There's plenty of room for resourcefulness and a bit of ingenuity
too!

This chapter offers a variety of ideas, methods and strategies for targeting employers and expanding your employer base. It details ways to
obtain exposure to (and from) employers and ways to initiate contact.
This section also aims to expand your present notion of the available
avenues to reach employers, alleviate some of the anxiety associated with
this aspect of our work and encourage you to adopt an adventurous, creative spirit as you contact new employers.

> *" A handful of
> pine seed
> will cover moun-
> tains with the green
> majesty of forests.
> I too will set my
> face to the wind
> and throw my
> handful of seed on
> high."*
>
> *Fiona MacLeod,
> Writer*

ACCESSING THE HIDDEN JOB MARKET:
QUESTIONS, ANSWERS AND A PARABLE

Typically, contacts made with employers in the hidden job market
will bring more benefit, quantitatively and qualitatively, than those made
in the open job market where employers advertise employment needs.
There are many questions about how to best access this elusive and yet
promising business community. This section answers many of those
questions. But first, a parable.

The Job Developer and the Little Fish

One day a young and very enthusiastic job developer approached an old and very wise job developer saying, "Teacher, everywhere I go businesses tell me they have no job openings. I seek the hidden job market. Can you tell me where to go?"

The master smiled kindly and told him the ancient tale of the little fish:

"Excuse me," said an ocean fish, "you are older than I, so can you tell me where to find the thing they call the ocean?"

"The ocean," said the older fish, "is the thing you are in now."

"Oh, this? But this is water. What I'm seeking is the ocean," said the disappointed fish. And he swam away to search elsewhere.

The job developer, with a furrowed brow, walked away to buy the Sunday newspaper to scan the classified ads.

FIVE CRITICAL QUESTIONS
ABOUT ACCESSING THE HIDDEN JOB MARKET

(1) If not through the newspaper, how do we target potential employers?

Any business or organization with employees who do what your applicants are skilled, able and want to do, is a potential employer. Businesses with problems your applicants can solve are also potential employers. Only a fraction (an estimated 10-15 percent) of the businesses in your community actually advertise employment opportunities in the newspaper.

In addition to approaching employers, we will discuss a variety of strategies for identifying and expanding your employer base. They include: networking, presentations to employer and community groups, attending conferences, job fairs, town meetings, professional and civic association events and employer forums, as well as the use of directories.

(2) Responding to an advertisement offers a natural reason to approach employers. How do we approach employers who aren't advertising?

We should approach employers as providers of services and resources to provide qualified people for their businesses and simultaneously increase employment opportunities for the people we serve. We perform more than basic employment services like referring, interviewing and hiring applicants. Job developers are also educators, trainers, mentors, researchers, counselors and even friends to both employers and job seekers.

Entering into a hiring relationship with an employer is just one of many points of exchange that can transpire between an employer and an employment project. As we have observed, there are many other resources and opportunities a job developer can offer an employer. The employer also has more to offer a job developer than unfilled openings. Given this larger context for relating to the employer community, the initial purpose for contacting and meeting with an employer is to determine which, if any, of those points of exchange are relevant and valuable to each party.

Regardless of how you approach a new employer, (letter, telephone call, in-person visit) your initial communications with an employer should contain these two elements:

◆ An introduction stating who you are, and how and why you chose to contact the business.

Your introduction should communicate the relevance of the business to your program and the potential value of meeting or working with you. This kind of introduction sets you apart from "cold callers" who frequently contact employers without rhyme or reason.

◆ A specific request or proposition to which the employer can respond.

There are numerous options for beginning a relationship with an employer other than the referral of an applicant for a job opening. You might request that the employer:

- Schedule an exploratory meeting with you;
- Allow you to send literature (or an employment proposal) and agree to a specified time for a follow-up call;
- Arrange a job interview for an applicant;
- Meet/interview an applicant you have referred to the company and agree to a specified time for a follow-up call;
- Receive completed applications, employment proposals, resumes or other documentation that you will deliver;
- Provide information about the industry or company;
- Refer you to another company or give you advice on marketing a particular applicant;
- Agree on a future date for contact; or
- Attend or participate in a function or event.

Later, we will look at different ways to present yourself to employers who have had no prior contact with your agency and who are not advertising their employment needs.

(3) What are the most effective methods for initiating contact with new employers?

The answer to this question will vary with every job developer you care to ask. That's because what qualifies as "effective" depends on the abilities of the person making the contact, the person being contacted, and the goals, objectives and other variables present in the job development equation.

For example, a job developer with an extremely small caseload, working in vocational rehabilitation, might find the telephone very valuable for initiating contact. On the other hand, the job developer with a larger caseload might identify in-person meetings as more beneficial than phone contact. The job developer working with a class of trainees will probably benefit more from meetings with employers before the training is completed rather than contact with employers after the class has graduated.

Chapter 7 describes strategies for contacting employers and lists approaches and purposes for each strategy. Consider the following factors when deciding which method of contact to use for each employer:

- Your personal style and strengths;
- Your goals and objectives in the situation;
- The size and type of business you are contacting;
- Response(s) from the business to prior contact methods; and
- Available time, money and other resources.

(4) What's wrong with finding people jobs in the open job market?

Absolutely nothing! Finding people jobs in any market is cause for celebration! If you are confident and effective in responding to the classified ads, by all means continue. As they say, "If it ain't broke, don't fix it!" (There are others, of course, who cry, "If it ain't broke, break it!")

While you need not replace what you are doing now, I recommend you consider expanding your job development efforts to include employers who are not advertising for the following reasons:

• You may be losing out on some of the better, higher-paying jobs which never reach the newspaper;

• Your applicants will face less competition for jobs not advertised in the newspaper; and;

• By expanding the ways in which you work with employers, you will be perceived as more than simply a referral source. Opportunities for training, apprenticeship, job shadowing, or work experience may arise as a result of ongoing, mutually satisfying, relationships. Contacting employers for the sole purpose of referring applicants for job openings yields short-term gains. Productive, enduring relationships generate long and short-term benefits.

(5) How do I initiate contact with new employers who are not advertising employment needs?

Follow these four steps.

(1) Conduct job market research to expand your employer base.

(2) Develop a marketing strategy targeting those employers in your community who can most benefit from your services and who have the most to offer your program in return.

(3) Consider all avenues — methods, strategies and approaches — for contact, and choose the one which seems most fitting and appropriate for each business.

(4) Develop a plan which includes:

  - The initial point of exchange you would like to make with the employer;

  - How you will present yourself and your ideas to the employer; and,

  - An alternate strategy, for use in the event the employer is not interested in your original plan.

First let's take a look at twelve innovative ideas for developing and expanding your employer base.

Twelve Ideas For Expanding Your Employer Base

(1) Start with people you know.

While we don't ordinarily view friends, acquaintances, family and neighbors as new prospects, we should. Many of the people with whom you have regular contact are responsible for hiring or know people who hire. A good place to start to expand your employer base is with the people you know and the businesses you frequent.

Draft a list of individual names from the categories below and decide whom you could contact for work purposes (e.g., information, referrals). Your list may include:

"I get by with a little help from my friends..."

George Harrison, the Beatles

  ✦ Friends and family
  ✦ Friends of family members
  ✦ Family members of friends
  ✦ Neighbors and community-based relationships
  ✦ Customers and clients from past jobs
  ✦ School and university acquaintances

- ✦ Church, synagogue or religious fellowship members
- ✦ People you know from support groups, social clubs, athletic teams, your children's school
- ✦ Professionals, such as your attorney, doctor, dentist, accountant, insurance agent, banker, hairdresser, teacher, travel agent, apartment manager
- ✦ Establishments you do business with: shopping malls, markets, restaurants, pharmacies, dry cleaners, book and music stores
- ✦ Your agency's vendors: printers, caterers, recycling company, telephone company, suppliers, building manager
- ✦ Everyone that businesses in the last three categories do business with!

(2) KEEP UP WITH NATIONAL, STATE AND LOCAL NEWS.

There is an easy way to keep up with local news and world events — read the newspaper. If you wish to minimize your time spent reading, scan the index to identify stories of interest. Read headlines and the first and last paragraphs of important stories. (Remember using Cliff Notes for book reports?) The business sections of the newspaper offer valuable information about:

- ✎ Industry trends;
- ✎ Upcoming meetings and events;
- ✎ Changes in local organizations and companies;
- ✎ New businesses in the area; and,
- ✎ Business, civic and community leaders.

Local print and electronic media advertising — newspaper, magazine, television and radio commercials — can provide valuable insight into the concerns of local companies and hot new products, services and businesses.

Some job developers prefer radio or television news programs. If you are a television watcher and have cable, tune in regularly to CNN Business News, CSPAN, the financial network CNBC, the Discovery Channel or local education or community-access channels. Bear in mind, a different brand of news — in terms of emphasis, detail and depth of coverage — is offered by print and electronic media.

Think about the stories aired during a typical local TV new broadcast: police activities, trials, scandals, the weather, sports, cute human interest stories. If you're lucky you will see an occasional brief story about the local economy, or a local business. Newspapers relegate much of the news TV reports to small stories on back pages. Their features and cover stories offer the kind of information you need. Newspapers not only provide details about what happened, but also why it happened, and the implications for those involved. Newspapers also provide pertinent and timely information about the local community like employment trends, interest rates, and city plans.

(3) READ BUSINESS JOURNALS, MAGAZINES, AND OTHER NEWSPAPERS.

In addition to the local daily newspaper, most cities are served by a local business newspaper or magazine. These publications serve specific business markets. They feature articles about:

- Local business news and events
- New businesses
- New products and services
- Calendars of events
- People on the move
- Interviews with local business leaders
- Chamber of Commerce news
- New technology
- Management
- Marketing, sales and customer service
- Business and personal finance
- Advertising
- Special sections on health care, careers, employment and education
- Construction plans and projects in the works for new businesses

Given the new global economy, learning about other parts of the world is important too. Pick up national and industry-specific publications you have never read before.

(4) ATTEND MEETINGS WHERE PEOPLE GET TOGETHER ON A REGULAR BASIS FOR A COMMON PURPOSE.

Consider attending meetings sponsored or hosted by:

- ✓ Chambers of commerce
- ✓ Fundraising groups
- ✓ Political organizations
- ✓ Sports teams
- ✓ Community organizations
- ✓ Professional associations
- ✓ College and alumni groups
- ✓ Religious organizations
- ✓ Social clubs
- ✓ Volunteer groups

To reap networking benefits from a group, you need to become an active member. When joining a new group, plan to attend three or four consecutive meetings to become a familiar face. In addition, consider volunteering to help plan meetings, handle registration, print newsletters, greet guests, any activity that involves contact with people. By helping out, you'll find it easier to meet people, and sooner than you might expect, you'll arrive at a meeting and realize you know half the people in the room! This involvement will be more play than work if you choose groups and clubs you will genuinely enjoy.

Obviously, it is too time-consuming to become actively involved in more than one or two groups. If your program assigns each staff member to an organization, it can increase program visibility and exposure in the community without consuming too much time from any one person.

(5) ATTEND SPECIAL STATE, CITY, TOWN AND NEIGHBORHOOD EVENTS.

Public hearings, city council meetings, community development commission meetings, and other forums provide vital information and insight about issues which affect community employment needs and trends. If you can't attend the events yourself, you might be able to read about them in the newspaper, or obtain a written transcript or report.

Make political connections. Your state senator or local political representatives are good sources of information about the trends and events affecting your local economy. Many have local office hours, and you can call or write them. They should know what's going on politically and economically in their districts and you can benefit from their knowledge.

Check out community events held at your local library, high school or town hall. Event information is usually posted on a lobby bulletin board. Many communities also broadcast a calendar of events on the local public television channel.

If there are colleges or universities in your community take advantage of seminars, lectures, guest speakers series and courses, as well as the faculty and library. Business and vocational schools frequently invite local employers to participate in these events. Place your name on the mailing lists of local schools, chambers of commerce, community and civic organizations to receive notices about special events and programs.

(6) JOIN LOCAL AND NATIONAL ASSOCIATIONS.

For a great networking opportunity, join the local chapter of a national organization. Professional, industry, political and community groups with national affiliations are all good choices. Their local chapters offer a chance to regularly meet new people, without the expense of travel to State or regional association meetings.

One of the advantages of joining an association is receiving a monthly or quarterly journal. Don't just put it on a shelf. Read it! There are newsletters devoted to almost every topic imaginable. Subscribe yourself, or recommend one or several publications to your agency or organization.

To find out about national, State and professional organizations in your area, ask people who work in the industry or profession. Ask employers! (Who knows, you may receive a personal invitation to attend the next meeting or event from the person you ask.) The yellow pages of telephone directories also list those associations large enough to have a local office and a telephone.

Another good source is the Encyclopedia of Associations (Gale Research Co., Book Towers, Detroit Michigan). This two-volume directory can be found at many libraries, and lists most of the national associations in the United States.

The categories listed under Associations in the yellow pages of my local telephone directory include: athletic, business and trade, consumer protection, environmental, conservation and ecological, health maintenance, labor, veterans and military, and women's. Some of the associations listed in these categories are:

Retail Merchant's Association
Meeting Planners International
Small Business Federation
Business/Industry Association
Independent Insurance Agents
Construction Industry Association
Association of Accountants

Bar Association
Hotel/Motel Association
Horticultural Society
Dental Society
American Cancer Society
Ecological Groups
Educational Councils

(7) MAKE PRESENTATIONS TO CLUBS, MEETINGS, CONFERENCES OR CLASSES.

Nearly every club and association has an ongoing need for luncheon and guest speakers. I have met job developers who give regular presentations to business classes at their local universities. Many of those classes are composed of people in business, pursuing an advanced degree or additional professional credential.

Develop a concise, informative and up-beat presentation about your program, services and participants. Contact local organizations to ask for an opportunity to inform members about your program and services during a 10 to 30 minute presentation. Communication and marketing ideas presented in Chapter 9 may assist you in preparing a presentation. In addition, keep the following points in mind when developing your speech:

◆ Whenever possible, ask for an introduction from a member of the group who has had positive experience working with you and/or your program.

◆ Engage your audience in a way that attracts their interest and attention before getting down to business. Then, make the most of your time.

◆ Encourage audience participation in the presentation. Ask questions, brainstorm, role play or conduct a survey or quiz.

◆ Prompt participants to explain the benefits of your program to the group by asking, "What do you see as the potential benefits of a program like this one?"

◆ Request a mailing list of the people present so you can follow-up your presentation with a call, visit or letter.

◆ Distribute information for participants to take with them. Place your business cards on seats, desks or tables.

◆ Follow up with the participants while you (and the name of your program) are still fresh in their minds.

(8) ATTEND JOB FAIRS AND CONFERENCES.

Job fairs and industry-specific conferences are held at hotels, convention centers, schools, colleges and universities. These events are a wonderful way to gather information about a company and secure the name of individuals you can contact at a later date. Job fairs are places to:

✎ Find out about opportunities in the open job market;

✎ Become familiar with the qualifications requested and salary range offered for positions with various companies;

✎ Familiarize yourself with how a company presents itself to potential employees;

✎ Gather information about products and services offered by local organizations;

✎ Solicit input from people in industry about employment proposals you have developed;

✎ Take the opportunity to speak with a representative of a company and request the business card or name of a person you could contact at a later date.

Job fairs are also opportunities for job-ready applicants to practice interviewing skills. Who knows, some of them just might land an offer!

(9) SPONSOR TRAINING OR EDUCATIONAL EVENTS FOR EMPLOYERS.

Sponsor education or training events — speakers, panels or a public forum — about key issues or timely topics with local appeal. For example, invite industry spokespersons, political appointees, elected officials, or a representative from the public sector or a university to discuss topics such as:

◆ Interviewing people with limited English
◆ Accommodating people with disabilities
◆ Working with the prison system to train productive employees
◆ Reducing turnover of teenage employees
◆ Increasing morale among minimum wage employees
◆ Increased productivity through teamwork and synergy
◆ Facilitating upward mobility for employees
◆ Enhancing corporate ability to serve a diverse market
◆ Recruitment and outreach activities
◆ Ensuring availability of job information to diverse segments of the population
◆ Creating modified or light-duty job descriptions

◆ Using varied training methods to meet different needs
◆ Offering a variety of incentives and rewards consistent with varying employee values
◆ Offering flexible employee benefits and services in response to changing employee needs and interests
◆ Developing effective, integrated work teams with a diverse staff

If you are or can become knowledgeable about any topics of interest to employers, offer to conduct on-site workshops for employees. This is among the most effective ways for a job developer to gain access to a business and simultaneously gain credibility with the people inside!

(10) HOLD SPECIAL EVENTS INVOLVING EMPLOYERS WITH THE PROGRAM AND PARTICIPANTS.

This is a wonderful way to introduce your program to a large number of employers at one time. To the greatest extent possible, delegate the planning, organizing, advertising, set-up and clean-up responsibilities for events to the program participants. Give them ownership of the event, allow them to showcase their talents and abilities and recognize their contributions. This is a great way for a printing, food preparation, data processing, or graphic arts class to practice newly acquired skills. It also helps individual participants gain confidence and recognition for newly acquired skills. Here is a list of the kind of events to consider:

✦ Awards banquets to honor both employers and employees for participating in the program.

✦ Graduation ceremonies for participants in vocational training, GED preparation, job search/job club classes, self-esteem or employment preparation workshops.

✦ An Interviewing Day for participants who are job-ready. Organize an industry or occupation-specific interviewing day. Participants sign up or interviews with specific employers and employers gain exposure to the members of the target group. (Advise employers to send supervisors or interviewers who need to hone interviewing skills and/or those who may benefit from increased exposure to diverse populations.)

✦ An Employer Day or an Industry Day such as "Hotel/Motel Day" or "Opportunities in the Automotive Industry." Ask employers to speak to the class or participant group about relevant issues. Alternatively, invite employers from various industries to speak about the work standards and expectations of employees throughout the industry and in their specific business.

✦ Welcome-to-the-Community Reception for employers new to the area. Invite both new and established employers to an event to welcome new businesses to the community. Use the reception as an opportunity to introduce your program and distribute educational and promotional materials. Invite new employers to speak about their business aspirations and encourage established employers to give positive testimonial about your program. If the event is "potluck" it will cost you next to nothing. Event attendance is practically guaranteed — it's unlikely for employers to turn down an invitation to a reception held on their behalf!

✦ Invite employers to serve on an Advisory Board convened to discuss and act on issues of vital importance to the business, industry or local community.

✦ Hold an Observation Day or an Open House allowing employers to observe and become familiar with your program, agency or school.

✦ Invite employers to holiday celebrations such as Christmas gatherings, a Thanksgiving potluck or a cultural event hosted by members of the target population. (I recall tremendous turnouts at several of the events held by members of refugee communities. These events sensitize and educate employers about distinct cultures and customs.)

✦ Hold Organization or Project Anniversary events to celebrate past successes and program or agency contributions to the business community.

✦ Fundraising events are a powerful way to gain exposure to employers and the community. Be creative when choosing your unique brand of a fundraiser and be sure to seek advice and expertise from an experienced, professional fundraiser.

Without professional input, you may not make a penny, and your agency could actually lose money on the event. Themes for a fundraising event include an art auction, silent auction, dinner/dance, casino night, draw-down or 50-50 split event, concert, children's talent show, fashion show, or holiday gala (e.g., Easter-egg hunt, pumpkin patch, Christmas tree lot). I was especially impressed by the success of a Christmas tree lot sponsored and run by clients of a half-way house in our community. They passed out literature about their program and introduced themselves as members of the HOPE program. They not only personalized their program — associating names and faces to a program known to most as an acronym — but also generated goodwill in the community.

(11) INITIATE AND/OR MAINTAIN CONTACT WITH EMPLOYERS THROUGH MASS AND TARGETED MAILINGS.

Mass or targeted mailing of one or more of the following materials introduces your program to employers and prepares them for further contact with you. Some of the most effective direct mail pieces are interactive, requesting a response from the recipient.

Examples of direct mail include:

- ✉ Promotional brochures;

- ✉ Flyers describing selected services, an event or a special offer;

- ✉ Invitations to tour your facility, speak with a job developer or attend a special event;

- ✉ An Exceptional Candidate Listing containing brief descriptions of applicants who are ready to work and meet the qualifications of the specific business or industry;

- ✉ An article or reprint from a newspaper, journal, business newsletter or magazine promoting the attributes of your program and/or applicants;

- ✉ A newsletter published by your agency for employers;

- ✉ An information packet detailing the services, features and benefits of your program. This packet or folder may include items such as resumes, course curricula, quantitative and qualitative measures of the success of your program and reference letters from employers presently using your services;

- ✉ Business or industry specific letters;

- ✉ Employer or industry surveys soliciting employer feedback about concerns ranging from recruitment needs and hiring methods to past experience with job developers, employment programs or the target population;

- ✉ Announcements of interest to employers such as a graduating class in a specific field, new or additional funding for your agency or the availability of new courses, services or personnel to assist them; and,

- ✉ Business or industry specific employment proposals.

(12) LEARN ABOUT LOCAL BUSINESSES BY USING DIRECTORIES, JOURNALS AND OTHER WRITTEN RESOURCES.

There is a wealth of information about businesses in your community available from the local library, schools and universities, chambers of commerce and community service clubs and organizations. Refer to the resources listed on the next page to gather information to answer each of the following questions.

(a) Which companies are nearby?

> State industrial directories
> Chambers of commerce, state and local
> Standard and Poor's Register of Corporations,
> Directors and Executives
> Dun & Bradstreet Million Dollar Directory
> Wards' Business Directory of U.S. Private and Public Companies

(b) What are the high growth industries?

> Value Line Investment Surveys
> Bureau of Labor Statistics Publications
> Moody's Industry Review

(c) Which industries employ various types of professionals?

> Encyclopedia of Associations
> The Career Guide: Dun's Employment Opportunities Directory

(d) Which companies manufacture, distribute or market particular products?

> Moody's Industrial Review
> Thomas Register of American Manufacturers
> Dun & Bradstreet Million Dollar Directory
> Standard and Poor's Register

UTILIZING KEY RESOURCE GUIDES

Dun & Bradstreet Million Dollar Directory, 3 Century Drive, Parsippany, NJ 07054

Five volumes, updated annually. A guide to 160,000 public companies in the U.S. with net worth of $500,000 or more. Fifth volume lists the top 50,000 moneymaking companies. Alphabetical listings by business name, including address, telephone number, and titles of officers and directors, Standard Industrial Classification (SIC) Code, annual sales and number of employees.

Standard and Poor's Register of Corporations, Directors, and Executives, 25 Broadway, New York, NY 10004.

Three volumes, updated annually. Volume 1 contains an alphabetical listing by business name of more than 45,000 corporations, including names and titles of officers and directors, SIC codes and annual sales. Volume II contains biographies of 70,000 individuals who serve as corporate officers, directors and trustees.

Thomas Register of American Manufacturers, Thomas Publishing Company, One Penn Plaza, New York, NY 10019.

Consists of 21 volumes, updated annually. Lists 140,000 product manufacturers, both large and small. Volumes 1 through 11 list firms under product headings. Volume 12 is an index to products and services. Volume 13 contains company profiles. Volume 14 is an index of manufacturers by trade names. Volumes 15 through 21 contain bound catalogs of more than 1,400 manufacturing firms.

Moody's Industrial Review, Moody's Investor Service, Inc., Dun & Bradstreet Company, 99 Church Street, New York, New York 10007.

Annual, with weekly updates of 11 industries per issue. Ranks 4,000 leading companies in 145 industry categories according to standard financial criteria: revenues, price-earnings ratio, net income, profit margin and return on capital. Classified by industry and arranged by company name.

The Career Guide: Dun's Employment Opportunities Directory, Duns Marketing Services, Dun & Bradstreet, 49 Old Bloomfield Rd., Mountain Lakes, NJ 07046.

Lists more than 5,000 companies with 1,000 or more persons employed in sales, marketing, management, engineering, life and physical sciences, computer science, mathematics, planning, accounting and finance, liberal arts and other technical and professional areas. Includes selected public sector employers. Entries include company name, location of headquarters and offices and plants, disciplines or occupational groups hired, company overview, training and career development programs.

Ward's Business Directory of U.S. Private and Public Companies, Information Access Company, Division of Ziff-Davis Publishing Company, 362 Lakeside Drive, Foster City, CA 94404.

Contains 133,000 companies, listed by state and zip code. Lists company name, CEO name, address, telephone, SIC code, number of employees, annual revenue.

Bureau of Labor Statistics (BLS), Inquiries and Correspondence, 441 G St., N.W., Washington DC 20212.

The BLS publishes a comprehensive array of bulletins and periodicals analyzing statistical information about major occupational fields. A complete catalog and order information are available. BLS publications include past employment figures and projections by major sector, selected industry, and broad occupational groups. The BLS publishes salary surveys by industry and geographic location. Suggested BLS publications are:

- ✓ Dictionary of Occupational Titles
- ✓ Monthly Labor Reviews
- ✓ Guide for Occupational Exploration
- ✓ Exploring Careers
- ✓ Occupational Outlook Handbook
- ✓ BLS Update

A Bureau economist is available to answer questions. To obtain "hot-line" telephone numbers for your area, call your local Bureau/Library of Labor Statistics.

There are many other ways of developing and expanding your employer base in addition to those mentioned above. Remain open and attuned to opportunities to learn about potential employers during the normal course of your day.

Let's look now at how you might be able to further incorporate these twelve ways of expanding your employer base.

*"Genuine beginnings begin within us,
even when they are brought to our attention
by external opportunities."*

*William Bridges,
author*

APPLICATION: ACCESSING YOUR HIDDEN JOB MARKET

Here are recommendations for taking greater advantage of each of the twelve ways for expanding your employer base discussed in this chapter.

(1) Start with people you know.

Brainstorm the names of people in each of the categories listed on pages 105 and 106 whom you could contact for networking purposes.

(2) Keep up with national, state and local news.

Keep a daily journal of questions raised, ideas sparked and information gathered by watching the news. Refer to Chapter 3 for recommendations on implementing these ideas.

(3) Read business journals, magazines, and newspapers.

Keep a file on interesting articles, ads, and information in the categories below. Share them in staff meetings and brainstorm ideas for follow-up or implementation.

- ✓ Industry trends;
- ✓ Upcoming meetings and events;
- ✓ Changes in local organizations and companies;
- ✓ New businesses in the area; and
- ✓ Business, civic and community leaders.

(4) Attend meetings where people get together on a regular basis for a common purpose.

Contact at least three local organizations which meet regularly and obtain their meeting schedules and agendas.

Attend at least one community meeting each month.

(5) Attend special state, city, town and neighborhood events.

Call local schools, the chamber of commerce and at least four other community and civic organizations to receive notices about special events and programs. Place your name on the mailing lists. Plan to attend at least one meeting a month.

(6) Join local and national associations.

Discern which associations have the most to offer your program in terms of information and networking opportunities. Call and request a complimentary membership for your program or agency. Inquire about upcoming events or meetings which you may attend. Request to be placed on their mailing list.

(7) Make presentations to clubs, meetings, conferences or classes.

Target three community groups (associations, clubs or civic organizations) to whom you would like to make a group presentation. Call and ask for the person who organizes events and request an in-person meeting. Bring an outlined proposal including the purpose of your presentation, a summary of its key points, and the benefits of the presentation for the audience. If the contact person is not receptive to a personal meeting, offer to mail or fax the proposal and arrange a time for a follow-up telephone call.

(8) Attend job fairs and conferences.

Plan to attend at least three job fairs a year. Ask employers with whom you have a working relationship for advice on which events to attend.

(9) Sponsor training or educational events for employers.

Choose an issue of importance to your employer community and organize an event in which you or someone you recruit will offer an educational or training event. To build your confidence and finetune your presentation skills, offer to make a 30-60 minute presentation to the staff of an employer with whom you have already established a working relationship.

(10) Hold special events involving employers with the program and participants.

Brainstorm with your supervisor and co-workers the next event to be offered to the employer community. Participate fully in planning and recruitment efforts. Decide that it will be one of the best-attended events held by your program, then make it so!

(11) Initiate and/or maintain contact with employers through mass and targeted mailings.

Consider what you can do to improve the quality and quantity of written communication with employers as well as increase the variety of forms this communication can take.

(12) Learn about local businesses by using directories, journals and other written resources.

Schedule time on a regular basis for researching new businesses with the help of written resources. As a team, become accountable to one another to report information and to brainstorm and implement the most effective use of it.

CHAPTER 7:
INITIATING CONTACT
WITH EMPLOYERS

"If you don't put your line into the water, you ain't gonna catch any fish!"

My Grandfather

We have likened job development to farming, design, construction, gardening, music and art. Let's try a fishing metaphor.

Putting the line in the water is important, but making sure the hook is baited with something the fish would like to eat is equally important. There are more varieties of bait than types of fishing. While you may be creative when choosing what goes on the hook, skilled fishing requires the consistent application of established principles. You need to know what is biting and where, as well as when to find it. It also helps to know when to reel in and call it a day.

There are numerous ways to initiate contact with employers. This section summarizes four approaches — events and direct mail (described in the previous chapter) and telephone and in-person contact (discussed below).

Naturally, there is an overlap of methods and their purposes. For example, an employment proposal can be made by phone, in person or through the mail. It is also possible to use all three methods to present the same employment proposal: you may phone for information during the research stage of the proposal, present it in person and then follow-up by mail. Typically, job developers use all of these avenues for various purposes throughout the course of relationships with employers. Further, when job developers are involved with more than one person in a business, they may call upon each with a different approach.

Accustomed as you may be to using particular avenues to contact employers, I recommend you use (or at least attempt to use) the entire spectrum of approaches. Why should you try all of the approaches?

First, because all people do not respond to the same approach. When employers consistently put off or ignore your telephone calls, it may be wise to approach them in person. If there is no response to your letter or fax, then a telephone call may produce better results. Some people learn best by reading, they need to see things in writing. Others learn by doing, they prefer to have things demonstrated or shown to them. For the latter group, a tour of your facilities would be more meaningful than a program brochure.

Second, using a variety of methods challenges your abilities. It keeps you from getting stuck in the proverbial rut. Challenge keeps people alert and on their toes. It lends freshness and vitality to tasks which can become monotonous or tiresome.

*"*B*ehold, I stand before the door and knock. And he who bids me enter, I will sup with him and he with me."*

The Revelation of St. John

I am not proposing that everyone use these methods the same way or to the same degree, because we all have different strengths. Some job developers love using the telephone and others avoid it at all costs. You need to discover your strengths and make the best use of your time by doing more of what you do best.

SUMMARY OF AVENUES FOR MAKING CONTACT: APPROACHES AND PURPOSES

TELEPHONE CONTACT

Approaches:	Purposes:
Employment Proposal	Refer an applicant
Before/After Mailing	Request a tour for applicants
Referral	Request an informational interview
Special Occasion	Invite to a function
Applicant Interest	Respond to an advertisement
New Idea	Present an employment proposal
Reference Check	Gather information about the company
Information Call	Receive advice on placing an applicant
Thank you	Request referrals to other employers

IN-PERSON CONTACT

Approaches:	Purposes:
Employment Proposal	Pick up written materials
Information Call	Obtain name and telephone number of hiring person
Applicant Listing	
On-the-Spot Interview	Make contact with people who work there
Geographic Scan	
Industry-Specific Call	Leave information
	Request to interview staff members
	Have applicants interviewed on the spot
	Present an employment proposal

EVENTS AND PRESENTATIONS

Types:

Graduation
Interviewing Day
Employer Guest Day
Employer Appreciation/Awards Event
Training/Educational Event
Advisory Board or Committee Meeting
Observation Day
Fundraisers
Welcome to New Businesses
Holiday Celebrations/Potlucks
Organization/Project Anniversaries
Presentation to Community Groups
Attending State and Local Meetings
Joining the Local Chapter of Relevant
  Associations

Purposes:

Gain exposure to many employers
Educate and inform employers
Gain credibility
Increase employer willingness to
  work with program
Decrease resistance to
  client population
Equip employers with skills
  and/or tools to work with client
  population
Recognize and reward employer
  participation
Get employer input to improve the
  quality of program and services
Provide opportunity for employers
  to gain exposure to applicants
Increase employer investment in
  program
Take advantage of unique context
  for introducing your services and
  gaining employer participation
Network with business people in
  your community
Learn about the issues, problems,
  and trends affecting local
  business and industry

MAIL/FAX

Types:

Brochures
Flyers
Invitations
Applicant Listings
Articles, Newspaper
Newsletters
Information Packets
Letters
Employer Surveys
Industry Surveys
Announcements
Employment Proposals

Purposes:

Time and cost efficient
  way to get exposure
Reminders to employers
Introduce program
Expose employers to
  quantity of information
Gain credibility
Share information and expertise
Gather information and/or
  elicit feedback
Keep in contact
Prepare employer for
  other forms of contact
Weed out employers

Approaching Employers By Telephone

Introductory Calls Vs. Cold Calls

In my job development seminars I often ask participants how they feel as they make telephone and in-person cold calls to employers. The responses are rarely positive. Inevitably, participants observe that they do not like to make cold calls because they hate getting them! It's a familiar scenario — you toil for hours preparing a meal, only to be interrupted by a telephone from a disembodied voice urging you to take advantage of a special offer for more insurance, a family portrait package or aluminum siding!

When we get these calls, we know the caller does not know us from the man in the moon. Fortunately, job developers are not in the business of making random cold calls to strangers. We make introductory calls to people who need or will likely need our services. In his book, *Relationship Selling*, Jim Cathcart describes cold calls:

"Let's talk for a minute about the term cold call. It doesn't sound friendly; yet we are expected to be friendly. On a cold call one person telephones or walks into the place of business of another person, introduces himself or herself, and checks to see if there's an opportunity to enter a working relationship. Why not call it an introductory call? That's really what it is, because we are there for the opportunity of introducing ourselves and our services and discovering whether or not what we have to offer is relevant, timely or pertinent to the needs of the business. Selling is a very noble profession. In fact, it is selling which drives the entire free enterprise system!"

Here are a few distinctions between classic cold calling and making introductory calls:

Cold Calls:	Introductory Calls
The goal is to persuade.	The goal is to offer services.
Employers must be sold.	Employers will discern the relevance and value of what you have to offer.
One-sided sales pitch.	Two-way dialogue.
You get what you are calling for or you don't.	Multiple options for gain. No such thing as failure, just feedback.
Callers learn to deal with failure.	Callers reap something from every call.

Another important distinction is that the partnership paradigm of job development offers an unlimited number of ways of working with people.

> *"Whether you are a butcher, a baker or a candlestick maker, everyone's a telephone solicitor."*
>
> Gary Goodman, Author

Using this paradigm, the emphasis of an introductory call shifts from sim-ply seeking a "yes or no" answer to establishing the rapport necessary to develop creative responses to employer needs and concerns.

The following techniques aim at increasing your effectiveness, creativi-ty, and success using the telephone to make contact with employers. Let's start at the beginning: dealing with receptionists.

WORKING EFFECTIVELY WITH RECEPTIONISTS

One of the essential duties of a receptionist is to screen the boss' calls. The boss, as life would have it, is usually the person we hope to contact! The primary tool receptionists use to screen and divert callers is a series of questions. Do any of these sound familiar?

"What is your name?"
"Where did you say you were from?"
"What is this regarding?"
"Why are you calling?"
"And where were you on the night of...?"

If these questions sound familiar, then you've been talking to skilled receptionists. They are paid to guard the gate. Unfortunately, each of these questions is intended to weaken the caller's confidence and resolve. After the fifth question it's tempting to say (or think), "Oh well, never mind, I didn't want to talk to anyone anyway!" We hang up and dial the next number on our list of potential employers. While this is an exagger-ated example, I'm sure you recognize the story line.

In the initial approach with a receptionist, it is important to communi-cate three things:

(1) Respect;
(2) Professionalism; and,
(3) Confidence that yours is a call the boss would not want to have screened out!

Your approach should be a straightforward introduction which includes all of the information the receptionist needs to make a decision about the value of your call and ends with a question which will direct the course of the conversation.

For example:

"Hello. My name is Dee Williams. I have prepared a business proposal for your firm's accounting department and would like to speak to the person who is in charge of collections for your company. Who would that be?"

*"*H*ello!* *(snort)* *Is this the party to whom I am calling?"*

Lily Tomlin as job developer

"Hello. My name is Coralee Meyer and I am a vocational counselor with Bay Area Network. I am calling to conduct a labor market survey with Joe Capetelli and hope this is a good time. Is he in?"

"Good morning. This is Jane Conley from UVC. Would you please connect me with Glenn Anderson?"

You may be wondering if the job developer in the third example is giving the receptionist enough information to communicate the value of the call. In fact, the third example may be the most effective depending on how the job developer is using her voice. The value of the call is often communicated not by what you say, but how you say it! Spoken in an assertive, authoritative tone, the third approach might even prove more powerful than the first two.

RESPONSES TO COMMON REPLIES

If you had a nickel for every receptionist's roadblock, how rich would you be?

Let's look at the ten most common responses job developers hear from receptionists. In addition to ideas about how to interpret each response, I've recommended a reply. These approaches and replies are merely suggestions. As you read through them, identify those that are suited to your personal style.

❖ **"We're not hiring now."**

REMEMBER: That's great, it gives you lead time! You're in the hidden job market!

REPLY/APPROACH: Request the opportunity to meet with someone so you can familiarize them to your services and you can become familiar with their organization and its recruitment needs.

❖ **"Why don't you just drop some of your literature in the mail?"**

REMEMBER: Use this request as a first step to develop a relationship with the employer. Call again, after the employer has had a chance to read the literature.

REPLY/APPROACH: Reinforce the necessity and value of meeting in person. Send the literature and make an appointment for future contact with the employer. Attach a note or letter outlining why you think their business might find your services useful. Specify the date and time you will call again.

❖ **"Have your applicants come down and fill out applications."**

REMEMBER: It requires no investment on the employer's part to consider your applicants for the job. Most of the time, applicants responding to this type of request are wasting their time. Your approach will differ depending on the nature of your services and what you want out of the call. If you are simply looking for places job seekers may apply, you may agree to send people to fill out applications. If you are calling with the hope of entering an ongoing relationship with the employer, try the following approach.

REPLY/APPROACH: Express your concern about not wasting time and your need for more information about the business before you can select appropriate applicants. Suggest a 15-20 minute in-person meeting so you will be better equipped to screen applicants to meet their future hiring needs.

✤ "We don't work with agencies."

REMEMBER: Many employers have misconceptions about our programs. This reflexive response is rarely based on genuine understanding of your program. Be persistent.

If you had a dollar for every roadblock you've gotten around, could you retire?

REPLY/APPROACH: Explain that you offer all of the services of an employment agency except that you charge no fees. Offer to send some literature in the mail or deliver it in person. Get the name of the person you should contact. Call again after he or she has had a chance to read your letter.

✤ "We just had a layoff."

REMEMBER: The fact that the employer is experiencing tough economic times does not mean this employer does not have something to offer your program and vice versa. Maybe you will be able to present a proposal that will make or save them money. Just because the business has had to lay off employees in particular positions does not mean it would not make sense to hire others (or bring their own employees back) in new positions.

REPLY/APPROACH: Empathize with the employer's position. Comment about the hard economic times experienced by many businesses in the community. Emphasize that the need for your services and resources may be even greater in times of economic uncertainty. Encourage the employer to meet with you now so you will be prepared to meet their hiring needs when business improves.

✤ "We're working with another program."

REMEMBER: The employer may believe that working with one program means there is no need for the services of another. The employer also may be worried about betraying his or her loyalty to another program.

REPLY/APPROACH: Assure the employer that working with more than one program only serves to increase the company's options. Explain that each program offers different resources and a unique pool of applicants. Stress the fact that programs work cooperatively, not competitively. (Just a little white lie!)

❖ **"The person you have asked for is not available."**

REMEMBER: This may or may not be a way of screening your call.

REPLY/APPROACH: Ask the receptionist to recommend a time for you to call back. Do not simply leave a message.

❖ **"Maybe I can help you."**

REMEMBER: This response may be a true attempt to offer assistance, although it is a common way to screen calls.

REPLY/APPROACH: One response is to accept the person's offer to help, assume they are the person you need to talk to, and sell your heart out! If the person can't help you, your enthusiasm and sincerity will probably motivate him or her to put the right person on the line.

Another approach is to prepare a question that can only be answered by the person you wish to contact. For example, if you want to make contact with the supervisor of the accounting department you might say, "I am working with graduates of an accounting class and I am interested in knowing if they have been trained on the software used by your accounting department."

❖ **"What, may I ask, is this regarding?"**

REMEMBER: Exude confidence. The self assurance conveyed by your voice and in your tone will communicate that this call is one the receptionist should not screen.

REPLY/APPROACH: Here are sample responses to this frequently asked question:

"I am calling to extend a special invitation to Marilyn to attend our open house this Thursday."

"I would like to invite a member of your human resources staff to participate in an employer brainstorming session devoted to finding ways of increasing youth retention in the workplace."

"I would like to meet with Ms. Jones and I am hoping to schedule an appointment at this time."

"I have a business proposal for your shipping and receiving department. I was told to speak with Jim Anderson."

"I represent Kankakee Community College, a school dedicated to training and preparing qualified employees for local businesses such as yours. The college would like to meet someone from McInnes Enterprises to inform you of our services. With whom do you recommend I meet?"

Receptionist: "What may I ask is this regarding?"

Creative Job Developer: "Well, it's a surprise!"

"I am conducting an important survey for the Santa Cruz Older Worker Project. Many of the people we work with express interest in working in your industry, so we would like to learn more about existing opportunities. As you are one of the leading businesses in the community and in your industry, we thought we would start with you. I would appreciate a few minutes of your time, in person, to ask you some questions. Are you the best person to answer these questions?"

Refer to "Eleven Ways to Introduce Your Services to Employers" on page 129 for additional ways to respond to this question.

✤ "We're just not interested."

REMEMBER: This is a standard reaction to anything new. Persist in your efforts to describe your program and communicate its benefits.

REPLY/APPROACH: Express that while it is true that your services are not suited to the needs and interests of every business, given your understanding of theirs (e.g, the fact that they hire for entry-level positions, the size of the company, the wages they pay, their turnover rate) you suspect that, in fact, theirs would be the kind of business which would benefit most from your program.

Go on to explain that in a short meeting with someone from the company, you could provide all of the information needed to make an informed decision about the value of your services. Stress that it is a no-risk, win-win proposition; the services are at no cost to their business, and it is at their discretion whether to make use of them.

Receptionist:
"I'm sorry, we're not interested in working with people who are too young, too old, inexperienced, too experienced, disabled, fresh out of jail or speak with an accent."

Job Developer:
"No kidding. Why do you think they're paying me to call you!?"

TWO ADDITIONAL APPROACHES TO RECEPTIONISTS

◆ Ask for Advice

When all else fails, ask the receptionist for his or her advice about how to proceed. For example,

"I have been trying in vain for about two weeks to get a hold of Ms. Donovan. May I ask your advice? What would you do if you were me? Should I call at 6:00 in the morning, 7:00 at night? Should I try coming by in person? I need to talk to her for about 10 minutes. What do you think I should do?"

◆ Write for a Telephone Appointment

Write a short note to the person you want to talk to requesting a telephone appointment.

Three examples are provided on page 128.

Dear Mr. Unreachable,

I have been trying to reach you by phone for the last couple of weeks to no avail. I would greatly appreciate the opportunity to speak to you about an invitation to a special training event offered through the Marriott Foundation for People with Disabilities. It is important that I receive verbal confirmation of your intent to attend. I can assure you this is an event you do not want to miss! I will be calling again on Wednesday, November, 5th at 3:00 p.m. Please advise your receptionist to expect my call.

I look forward to speaking to you.

Sincerely,

Overly-anxious

Dear Ms. Open-minded,

Is recruiting entry-level employees with the necessary skills, abilities and work attitudes an ever-increasing need of your company? If so, then you may be interested in the services offered through the Evergreen Valley College Youth Program. I would like the opportunity to tell you what we're about and explore aspects of our program I feel will be of particular interest to your business. I will fax you an outline of our services on Thursday and call your office on Friday morning at 9:00. If you like what you read, we will schedule an informational meeting at your convenience. Please advise your receptionist that I will be calling.

Thank you!

Ever-hopeful

Dear Mr. Diversity,

My name is Joe Dimaggio. I am an employment specialist at Project Hire, a local employment program. We are collaborating with Adult Education on a very exciting project to augment their clerical training program with a customer service component. Given the nature of your business, I presume that having access to a resource pool of qualified applicants trained in these specific skills would benefit your recruitment efforts. I would like to schedule a time to meet with you in person to explore the ways we could work together. I also look forward to meeting with you because so many of our several students have expressed a desire to work for your company.

I will call you on Monday to set up a time when we can meet. I would be happy to answer any questions you have at that time.

Sincerely,

Full of nerve

Employer responses to the appointment letter:

Most employers respond to the appointment letter by phoning immediately upon receipt of the letter rather than waiting for you to call them. In the event the employer does not call you beforehand, be sure to call at the time specified in your letter. If the receptionist asks what your call is regarding, you can truthfully say that the employer is expecting your call!

Now let's go on to the next part of the introductory call: talking to the employer.

ELEVEN WAYS TO INTRODUCE YOUR SERVICES TO EMPLOYERS

☎ THE EMPLOYMENT PROPOSAL

This straightforward approach tells the employer what the proposal is about and rather than trying to sell the employer on the proposal, sells the employer on an in-person meeting.

"Good morning Mr. Meyer. My name is Maria Moy and I am calling from Chipps Vocational Services. I have a business proposition for you. I'd like to suggest a way for you to significantly increase your customer pool without having to invest in costly marketing strategies. I have written a proposal for you which outlines the rationale for hiring a part time graphic artist. I'd like to meet with you in person to discuss the details and show you how well it worked in businesses similar to yours. I am confident you will be able to tell me whether this idea is appropriate for your business within ten minutes of our meeting."

> *"If you are looking for needles in a haystack it helps to bring a magnet along to help you."*
>
> *A resourceful telemarketer*

If you do not have the time to meet with employers in person, request a few minutes to discuss the proposal on the phone. Then mail, fax or deliver the proposal in person and schedule a follow-up telephone call to discuss the proposal.

☎ THE REFERRAL

Referrals are powerful endorsements because they reduce perceived risk; a third party listened to you and decided that what you have to offer is relevant and of potential benefit to others. Obtaining a referral from one person to another is great, but not always easy to come by. However, a business-to-business referral can be just as effective and job developers receive this kind of referral all the time. Consider these three examples:

"Hello! My name is Judy Fache and I am an Employment Specialist with Vancouver City Schools. I am working with a bank teller by the name of Jamie Rodriquez. I spoke with people from various banks today who all seemed to agree that Jamie's skills are better suited to work in a credit union like yours."

"I just finished an on-the-job training contract for a stock person in a local grocery store. They recommended that I present this same opportunity to other kinds of businesses who have consistent stocking needs. I've been a customer of yours for long enough to know that you do a great deal of business in this community. I would love the opportunity to speak with someone from your store, in person, about the possibility of participating in our on-the-job training project."

"I am working with a chef who has had no luck securing employment at any of the local two star restaurants. Evidently they think he's over-qualified and suggested he contact an establishment that could truly take advantage of his culinary talents. Naturally, your restaurant came to mind."

We get referrals like this all the time in our business, we just don't always recognize them as such. Remember to finish each call to an employer with the question: "If you were working with this person (or people) with these skills, how would you go about placing him (them)?" Use the information you receive from the employer as a referral from his or her business.

☎ THE INFORMATION/RESEARCH CALL

This approach combines the real need to gather business and industry-specific information with the opportunity to engage the employer in a meaningful discussion about the potential exchange of resources.

"Good morning. My name is Sierra Ashley and I am a Placement Officer for Mare Island Workers in Transition. As you know, the base is closing and many of the workers are looking to apply their skills in the local community. Several of the people I am working with have expressed interest in computer programming. It is my understanding that your business employs a number of computer programmers and I wondered if you would be willing to take part in my research into the field. Could I ask you a few questions right now over the phone? (Or: I would appreciate a few minutes of your time in person.)"

Here's another example for gathering industry-specific data:

"For the first time since I've been in the job development business, I am working with people who have a great deal of experience in agricultural work. Since you are the largest employer in the industry, I know your experience, insight and information could help me to better serve our program participants. I would appreciate a few minutes of your time. Could

you meet with me Thursday or Friday afternoon?"

Refer to the List of Employer Assessment Questions in Chapter 8 for sample questions to incorporate in your employer survey. Consider including the following questions:

✦ What are the specific skills and abilities you look for in employees?
✦ What advice would you give to the person just entering this field?
✦ How could your business benefit from a program like ours?

☎ THE FIRST TIME APPROACH

"Hello. My name is Tim Fischer and I represent the Dayton County Private Industry Council. Our organization has been delivering quality recruitment services at no expense to local businesses for the past eight years. As I was going through our employer resource file this morning I realized this is the first time we have ever been in contact with your operation! Frankly, I was quite surprised and I apologize. I would like to remedy this situation as soon as possible by meeting with someone at your company to tell you about our services. With whom would you recommend I meet?"

This approach communicates three important messages to employers:

★ They are important — or you wouldn't have been surprised that they had never been contacted;

★ They've been missing out on something — why else would you have apologized?; and

★ Everyone else has been contacted!

Caution! Do not use this approach unless you sincerely feel the business is important and has been missing out on services of value. Your sincerity is a critical element to the effectiveness of this approach.

☎ THE NEW IDEA APPROACH

Compare the following two approaches to asking an employer to interview an applicant:

(a) "Hello. My name is Maureen Hamb and I am a Work Experience Coordinator for Project Hire. I am working with young people who have a wide variety of skills and abilities seeking full and part time employment. Given your tremendous hiring needs in anticipation of the summer months, I am confident our program can offer you valuable assistance. I would appreciate the opportunity to meet with you in person to explain exactly who we are, what we do, and how we can meet your need to recruit quality employees."

(b) *"Hi! My name is Maureen Hamb and I am calling from Project Hire, an innovative program linking young qualified workers with employer hiring needs. I have an idea and I would love your comments. Many of the youths I have interviewed recently are looking for part time and temporary opportunities since they will return to school in the fall. I may be completely off base, but it occurred to me there might be a natural link between our participants' skills and availability and your summer recruitment needs. At this point it's just a hunch, but I would love to talk with you in person and let you tell me if this idea holds water."*

Some of the major differences between these two approaches are:

The first caller is confident, professional and quite certain about the benefits her program offers the employer. Still, the employer is left wondering: What if I'm not interested in what she has to offer, how difficult will it be to get her out of my office?

In the second example, the job developer has enthusiasm for her idea but far less certainty about the value of what she has to offer. She invites the employer to judge its value for his or her particular situation. Presenting ideas rather than certainties gives the employer a natural easy out: If I'm not interested in what she has to offer, I'll simply give her the opinion she requested.

Although both approaches have merit, I prefer the second because new ideas are often irresistible, enthusiasm is contagious, and it's flattering to be consulted about new ventures. Further, being asked your opinion about a new idea is more appealing than a request to listen to a presentation about how a program or agency can solve your problems or meet your needs.

Any proposition you make can be presented as a new idea. For another example, compare the following requests for an interview:

"Gerald is a qualified technical writer. I wonder if you would be interested in interviewing him for a position with your publications staff."

— versus —

"When considering Gerald's education and work experience it occurred to me his technical writing abilities may be worth a lot to a business like yours. Obviously, you'd be a better judge of that. Would you be willing to meet with Gerald to help us evaluate whether we're headed in the right direction?"

☎ THE SPECIAL OCCASION APPROACH

This approach is used to make a time-limited or time-sensitive offer. It may be used to extend an invitation to an event, announce the upcoming graduation of a class, or promote an applicant with an ideal combination of skills to an employer. For example,

"How do you do? My name is Michelle Donahue and I am calling from Women's Network. We have successfully trained and placed over 200 computer operators in the last 24 months. I have been in contact with your business before although we have not placed any of our graduates in your business. The reason I decided to get back in touch with your company is because we have a computer operator about to graduate who has outstanding customer service skills. I know these skills are critical in your industry since operators have constant contact with the public. I know Rebecca will not have a hard time finding employment, but I wanted you to be the first to have an opportunity to interview her."

Whenever possible, extend a "special offer" to employers you contact. Urgency is a powerful motivator, especially for employers inclined to make decisions quickly. For those who deliberate over long periods of time, a special offer may inspire a more timely decision.

☎ THE APPLICANT INTEREST APPROACH

Ask employers whom they would rather hire: a person who has applied to the company of his or her own volition or someone referred by a job developer. Nine times out of ten you'll get the same answer: the person who came on their own. This is not hard to understand. Employers want to be chosen just as much as applicants. For this reason, I suggest we credit our applicants for calls to employers. Take the following examples:

"I am working with a manager trainee who is extremely enthusiastic about your company and has asked my advice about how to get his resume to the right person in your business. I told her I would call you directly to get your recommendation."

"Many of the clerk typists I have spoken to recently have expressed interest in your firm. I felt I owed it to them to at least find out more about you."

☎ THE BEFORE AND AFTER MAILING APPROACH

This is a safe, low risk approach because it invites a non-committal response from the employer.

"Hello. My name is Alexis Grant and I work with Vocational Services, Inc. We offer a wide variety of services for employers ranging from training and educational opportunities to employee recruitment and on the job support. I would like to send you some materials about our program and give you a chance to review them. At the end of the week I will call you again, and if you are interested, we can set up a time to meet in person."

When using this approach, be careful not to preclude the need to meet with you by providing too much information on paper. Give them just enough to make them want more!

☎ THE REFERENCE CHECK

If you have applicants who have worked before, place a call to their past employer for the purpose of doing a reference check. An obvious benefit of a reference-check call is that you are immediately connected to a supervisor since personnel departments may only validate dates of hire and termination. Once the supervisor is on the line explain who you are and carry out a classic reference check:

"Hello, my name is Jeffrey Dupree and I am a job developer with the Cook County Rehabilitation Program. I am working with Tom Banks who I understand worked for you last summer. I would like to ask you some questions about his performance and general work practices so I have a better idea about the kind of environment where he will excel."

Pose questions you know are pertinent to a particular business or industry. Once the employer has responded to your questions, continue along these lines:

"Thank you so much for your feedback. I feel more qualified to work with Tom now that I have a better grasp of his contributions to (or, responsibilities in) your department. Listening to your comments, it occurs to me that I am working with applicants who may meet the needs of your company. Would you please give me the name of the person you feel would be interested to hear about the no-fee recruitment services we offer employers?"

Nine times out of ten the response will be, "Well, that's me." since you've been speaking with a supervisor. I like this approach because it's a chance to show your stuff to the employer. He or she will recognize your conscientious assessment of Tom as an indication that anyone you refer will be similarly screened and evaluated.

There are regions of the United States and Canada where reference checking is an obsolete practice. Employers' legal liability and stringent regulation of what may or may not be said during a reference check, limit the utility of this once common practice. Today, most employers are delighted to give a positive reference for a past employee. Employers become concerned when the information disclosed in a reference check is negative. Determine the correct protocol for reference checking in your area before trying this approach.

Ideas for re-establishing contact with an employer

☎ THE "THANK-YOU" APPROACH

Everyone loves to be appreciated, and the thank-you approach communicates our appreciation of employer participation in the program and encourages continued cooperation, allegiance and exchange.

"Hello, Mr. Smith. This is Jenny Grateful. I am calling to thank you for (e.g., attending our training, putting me on your job listing, interviewing Angela, taking the time to read our brochure, recommending our program to your neighbor). Really, it's the generous participation of people like you that drives this program. I also want to suggest a great next step to take with our project..."

☎ THE NON-PARTICIPATORY EMPLOYER CALL

It is not uncommon to meet with an employer who seems enthusiastic about working with you but never responds or follows up. Here are a few ideas for re-contacting an employer.

"Hello, Ms. Bergeron! This is Christopher Jones from Project Surprise. I ran into Jerry Winters last night who worked with you in the summer youth program last year and I realized it has been a long time since I've been in touch with you. I just wanted to call and say hello, update you about what we're doing, and find out how things are going with Auto Enterprises. How is business?"

"Hello Mr. Passive. This is Jeanette Stanford from Jewish Vocational Services. I met with you last year just after you opened your new store. How is it going? (After discussion) Last year we hadn't started our Employer Interviewing Days. Let me tell you about it to see if the idea interests you...."

"Hello, Mary, do you remember meeting me at the Job Fair at the Thunder Bay Convention Center? I am sure you spoke with many people that day, so let me refresh your memory. We discussed several potential ways to work together... I have often thought about scheduling a tour of your plant for some of our students. Would early this spring be a good time for a tour?"

When making a call of this sort, be sure to have an idea — question, favor, request, or proposal — which requires a response from the employer.

A DOZEN TERRIBLY IMPORTANT TELEPHONE TIPS

✆ PAY ATTENTION TO HOW YOU ARE USING YOUR VOICE TO COMMUNICATE YOUR MESSAGE.

Create a completely different mood from the typical one-sided solicitation used by "boiler room" telemarketers. You know them, the ones who don't seem to need to come up for air and sound something like,

"HellothisisDeniseBissonnetteandboydoIhaveadealforyou!"

Avoid:

- Speaking too loudly or too softly
- Speaking much more rapidly than you do normally
- Ending statements with the tone or rising intonation
- Speaking in a monotone as if you are reading
- Exaggerating emotion or attitude in your voice to compensate for lack of facial expression and eye contact

Notice that the habits listed above are triggered by basic nervousness. Being one of those people who finds it hard to communicate by phone, I have found the following suggestions helpful in reducing anxiety:

- Picture the person sitting in front of you and think about initiating a conversation rather than trying to make a presentation;

- Make your calls in private so you are not distracted by other things happening around you;

- Stand up when placing the call. For me, standing adds confidence and assertiveness to my voice.

- Take a deep breath and smile. (You can hear a smile in someone's voice!) Be prepared to like the person you are calling.

ℂ KNOW AND APPRECIATE YOUR OWN VALUE AS A PROVIDER OF EMPLOYMENT SERVICES.

Think beforehand about what you have to offer which will be valuable to the employer. Sell yourself on the benefit of your services so you can comfortably and naturally speak with conviction and confidence. To sell your idea to someone else, you have to be sold on the idea yourself!

ℂ USE ASSERTIVE LANGUAGE.

Compare the following requests for an in-person meeting:

#1: "Perhaps you would consider meeting with me, that is if you have a few minutes. If possible, we could determine how the services provided by our program could be of benefit to your company in some way. I would like to drop by tomorrow, if you don't mind, and if I wouldn't be interrupting something important, of course."

#2: "To determine what our program has to offer your business, I need to meet with you in person. I realize your time is valuable. I am confident you will feel our meeting was well worth your while. What time later this week or early next week would be convenient for you to meet with me?"

Among other things, you probably found the second request more compelling because the language was direct, assertive and without apology. Do not be too tentative in your approach. Avoid words like "maybe," "possibly," "perhaps," "if," "could," "would," and "might." (I mean if you think you possibly, in some way could!)

© *"BE BRIEF, BE BRILLIANT AND BE DONE!"*
Gary Goodman, Author

Pay attention to overall word economy because you are granted less time for telephone visits than for direct personal contacts. Long-drawn-out introductions and/or lengthy explanations motivate people to end calls quickly. Short of referring to a telephone script, know what you are going to say and say it as succinctly as possible.

© IMAGINE THE SUCCESS OF YOUR CALL BEFORE YOU MAKE IT.

"Get the smelling salts for Joe! An employer just agreed to interview one of his applicants!"

The idea of "envisioning it before it happens" is one of the fundamental principles discussed in "peak performance" literature. It is also a common practice in theater. Directors often ask actors to prepare for the stage by projecting their image into the set before their physical body is on stage. Then it's a matter of matching the physical body with the image created for the stage.

© BE WILLING TO DIG BELOW THE SURFACE OF AN EMPLOYER'S FIRST RESPONSE. DO NOT TAKE AN EMPLOYER'S INITIAL DISINTEREST AT FACE VALUE.

Remember, when employers say "no," it usually means "not now," "not yet," or "I don't have the time to understand what you're offering." With this in mind, it is critical for you to communicate the urgency or timeliness of the offer and specify, right from the start, what you want from them. Ask for something easy, as opposed to something that requires a great deal of time, energy or more commitment than the employer would otherwise be willing to make this early in the game.

© BE PREPARED WITH AN "OPTION PLAN" OF REQUESTS OR SUGGESTIONS.

Develop an "option plan" listing the possible requests you might make of a particular employer. If the employer does not agree to your initial request, go on to describe another option and continue until you have found something of interest to the employer. Normally, employers will agree to one of the first three options on your list.

An "option plan" for calling on a particular business may look like this:

Option plan for Myriad Technologies:

Option #1: Schedule an in-person meeting
Option #2: Fax employment proposal and schedule follow-up call

Option #3: Request sample job descriptions of other positions in the
           company and write a letter
Option #4: Request a tour of the company
Option #5: Ask for information about the company

Option Plan for GetLife Insurance Agency:

Option #1: Refer Joyce Evans for informational interview
Option #2: Agree to have Joyce drop off resume and schedule follow-up
           call for tomorrow
Option #3: Request agency Job Listing and advice about placing Joyce

✆ ONCE YOU PICK UP THE RECEIVER, DO NOT PUT IT DOWN UNTIL YOU HAVE CALLED EVERY EMPLOYER ON YOUR LIST.

"The contin-uous drip polishes the stone."

Chinese saying

Most job developers agree it is not the first call you place that is the most difficult, it is call after call that turns our hair white. Perhaps that's because we feel we need "recovery time" after a call that did not end as we had hoped. Since most calls do not end exactly as we had hoped, taking time off after nearly every call accounts for much time spent in *re*covery that could have been better spent in *dis*covery! Have you ever noticed the momentum of activities such as race car driving, mountain climbing, cliff diving and cold calling? Let the momentum work for you!

✆ KNOW THYSELF AND THY MOODS!

Telephone effectiveness is closely tied to how you use your voice. Your voice reflects your state of mind and your spirits. There are times when you should be placing telephone calls and there are times when you should not. Don't waste the precious opportunity of a first contact with an employer when you've got the social graces of a sea slug. If you are in "a mood," call your clients who haven't shown up for the last ten meetings, don't call an employer! If you're sitting on top of the world, take advantage of cloud nine by placing a call you've been putting off. Make your calls during the part of the day when you feel at your best.

✆ REWARD YOURSELF FOR EACH AND EVERY CALL YOU MAKE.

"By going and coming, a bird weaves its nest."

Ashanti saying

It is said the journey of a thousand miles begins with a single step. The successful placement of an individual in his or her chosen field of endeavor begins with the first call. Not necessarily *the* call, but *a* call. Regardless of its outcome, every call you make is an important step toward reaching your goal. If you only reward yourself for the calls which end exactly as you desire, you are bound to be easily discouraged.

I remember hearing that Thomas Edison conducted more than two thousand experiments in an attempt to produce the light bulb. When asked by one of his associates why he would persist after more than two thousand failures, Edison responded that he hadn't failed even once, he'd had two thousand lessons about what doesn't work! Much of the job developer's work is to research where someone shouldn't work and which employers do not provide fertile soil for productive working relationships.

☯ KNOW WHEN TO PERSIST AND WHEN TO QUIT.

"Heroism consists of hanging on one minute longer."

Norwegian saying

Many employers may not fully appreciate the value of your services or the potential of your applicants from an initial phone call. Be persistent. If they do not respond to one approach, try another. If they do not agree to one request, propose another. If one person from a particular business seems closed to your ideas, consider approaching a different person on another day.

At the same time, not all employers will deem our services timely or relevant. Remember, there are employers in your community who genuinely do need your services. Don't spend your time and energy where you feel it is wasted. As W.C. Fields so aptly put it, *"If at first you don't succeed, try, try again. Then quit. No use being a damn fool about it."*

Telephoning new employers trains you to balance the resolve necessary to achieve a goal with the flexibility to recognize and accept when it is time to move on. In case you haven't noticed, striking this balance is critical to our mental health and emotional well-being.

☯ DO WHAT NEEDS TO BE DONE FIRST; DON'T CREATE UNNECESSARY STRESS BY POSTPONING CALLS.

"Procrastination is opportunity's natural assassin."

Anonymous

Are you the type who eats your dessert first and saves the vegetables for last? If so, take this tip: place the calls you least want to make, first. Get them out of the way because you can't afford the cost of the guilt, stress and worry that results when you postpone them. Take it from a world-class expert in procrastination, a little extra self-discipline at the beginning of the day produces a clean slate at the end of the day. The people who use the "mañana plan" still have to get the job done. We just do it with an "attitude" because inevitably, tomorrow is the busiest, most impossible day of the week! To bolster my efforts to combat procrastination, I recently put a sign over my desk which asks, "If not today, when?"

Many of the ideas and practices addressed in this section are equally applicable to direct personal contact — making in-person calls to employers.

So, let's hang up the telephone and turn on the answering machine while we consider one of the most popular and effective ways to approach an employer — live, and in-person!

TAKIN' IT TO THE STREETS —
LIVE AND IN PERSON

"Lights, cameras, action!"

Imagine, if you will, a job developer on a bright and sunny afternoon leaving the office shortly after one o'clock, briefcase and hat in hand, smiling from ear to ear. In an enthusiastic tone, the departing job developer announces to the other desk-bound employees, "I'm off to see employers!"

Some wonder about the mysterious world of corporate intrigue the job developer may be entering. A few gasp in awe of the job developer's courage and valor as she strides to the doorsteps of unknown employers — strangers about whom she knows so little and asks so much. Others silently offer their sympathies to the weary job developer who will once again pound the pavement of the urban jungle, only to face rejection. Meanwhile, in the background of our imaginary scene, are skeptics who assume this bright, sunny afternoon will find the job developer sipping cappuccino at an outdoor cafe with several job developers from other agencies.

"Opportunities come from knocking on doors until they open."

An opportunist

Which of the observers of our imaginary scenario had the most accurate insight into the real world of cold-calling? You will receive a different answer from every experienced job developer. Approaching employers in person can be an exhilarating, intriguing, productive and highly rewarding venture, or it can be a grueling, discouraging and tiresome waste of time. The fact is, in-person cold-calling is only as valuable as the job developer intends and is only as positive as the job developer allows. The inherent value of initiating contact with employers in person is primarily a question of intent and attitude.

Some people argue that calling on employers in person wastes time because a greater number of contacts could be made by telephone in the same amount of time. While this may be true, contacts established in person usually result in more productive, enduring relationships than those initiated by phone.

Surveys have confirmed that while 75% or more of communications are verbal and 25% are written, only 15% of the information retained is received by listening — 85% of what is retained is seen, read or visualized. (Edward T. Hall, *The Silent Language*) In view of this, it is reasonable to assume that you can make significantly more impact in person than as a disembodied voice wafting out of the telephone receiver.

An additional motivation for approaching employers in person is that being out in the business community allows you to keep your finger on the pulse of the ever-changing job market. It is virtually impossible to do this from your office (even if you do have a window!) For example, seeing "opening soon" signs, noting the location and progress of major construction (and destruction), observing trends and problems and discovering small businesses which aren't listed in directories are only possible on the pavement. This is how the little fish discovers the ocean it has been swimming in all along. The job market is a living, breathing community

140

and there is limitless opportunity to feast at the communal table. This opportunity will not arrive at your door; you must seek it out. It is found at the doorsteps and in the alleyways and back rooms of the local business community.

APPROACHES FOR MAKING IN-PERSON CONTACT

There are as many purposes and approaches for in-person calls as there are for telephone calls. Each of the twelve approaches presented in the telephone section of this chapter can be used to introduce yourself to an employer in person. The purposes of making in-person calls, however, may differ from those made by telephone. Here are a dozen scenarios for an unscheduled in-person employer call:

◆ To approach a small business with the intent of meeting with the manager and marketing your program on the spot;

◆ To enter a large business solely to establish rapport with the receptionist and obtain the business card of the person you will be calling later;

◆ To explore a business on a whim, because you are curious to know what the company does and whom they hire;

◆ You are referred by an employer to a neighboring firm;

◆ To investigate opportunities described by posters proclaiming, "New Management," "Now Hiring," or "Opening Soon";

◆ To conduct a cold-calling venture in a certain geographic area, accessible by public transportation and/or in the vicinity of your applicants' homes;

◆ To visit a designated list of companies in the same general industry;

◆ To present an employment proposal;

◆ To meet with someone and gather industry-specific data;

◆ To drop off a listing of applicants ready to go to work who have the skills and abilities needed by a specific business;.

◆ To accompany applicants to businesses and initiate on-the-spot interviews with managers or supervisors; or,

◆ To respond to a referral from one employer to another in the same industry.

There are many possibilities for initiating in-person visits. Use your imagination to choose the approach that best suits your purposes.

"If you think there are no new frontiers, watch a boy ring the front doorbell on his first date (or a job developer walking in the door of a new employer)."

Olin Miller (paraphrased)

TEN TREMENDOUS TIPS FOR STREET SMARTS

★ HAVE A WELL-LAID PLAN WITH SPECIFIC OBJECTIVES AND TIMELINES.

"Don't wait for your ship to come in, swim out to it."

Anonymous

For example, if your intent is to go into the field to generate opportunities for auto mechanics, research the areas of your city where auto service businesses are numerous. Research and map out your cold-calling plan. Arm yourself with industry specific materials, resumes or employment proposals, and dress appropriately for the business.

If you are simply parking your car and researching a certain neighborhood or industrial park, set a definite objective, e.g., the number of people you will contact in a designated amount of time. Commit to follow through to meet your objectives. If your stated objective is, "I will hand deliver the resumes of three applicants to at least five auto shops during the next two hours," pace yourself to meet your objective.

Cold calling without a plan can result in an afternoon spent drifting from one place to another, wasting time and dissipating energy. (And as the afternoon drags on, the idea of relaxing at a sidewalk cafe grows more attractive!)

★ BE PREPARED WITH OPTIONS FOR WAYS OF WORKING WITH EMPLOYERS WHILE REMAINING FLEXIBLE ENOUGH TO ADDRESS THEIR IMMEDIATE NEEDS.

Like the "option plan" suggested for use when telephoning employers, it is important to remain flexible during in-person meetings. While you may enter a business with expectations about what is going to happen, reality may present a totally different scenario. Go with the flow, bend with the wind, and, as one of my favorite sayings goes, "If at first you don't succeed — try to hide your astonishment!"

★ BE CONSCIOUS OF YOUR ATTIRE AND WHAT YOU ARE COMMUNICATING BY HOW YOU DRESS.

One school of thought suggests that job developers should dress in formal business attire when visiting any and all businesses. Another school suggests that you dress in a way comparable to the people who work in the environment you are visiting. For example, there are certain businesses where you would feel comfortable dressed in formal business attire (e.g., banks, insurance companies, high tech computer firms), but formal attire might be out of place in an informal environment like a gas station, machine shop, or wrecking yard.

I adhere to the theory of social protocol which asserts, "When in Rome, do as the Romans do." I would add a minor addendum, "unless it renders you ineffective." As a rule it is wise to dress professionally, even though one of the best darn job developers I have ever known worked his magic wearing a baseball cap on his head, backwards, to boot!

★ **USE YOUR POSITION AND LEVERAGE AS A CUSTOMER WHENEVER POSSIBLE.**

You will never have more power with an employer then as a customer. Whenever possible, approach the employer as a customer first, then as a job developer! Order a cup of coffee or push the vacuum cleaners before you ask to see the manager. You will get better results with this approach because the manager is likely to be more accessible to customers than to roaming job developers. Further, the value of your perspective and opinions is greater when employers know you view their businesses from the inside, as a patron, customer, client or patient.

"God gives all birds their food but does not drop it into their nests."

Native American saying

★ **BE AN EAGER AND ENTHUSIASTIC LEARNER.**

Gather as much information about the business as possible by talking to everyone you meet about their roles and responsibilities in the company. Ask questions and seek advice to demonstrate your desire to learn more about the business. The kinds of information to gather during an in-person visit include:

✎ The name of the receptionist;

✎ The name and business card of the person you should contact later and advice about the best time to call the person;

✎ The nature of the company's product or service;

✎ Any business literature, such as product catalogs, brochures or the annual report;

✎ The employment application used by the business;

✎ Information about the hiring practices of the business;

✎ A general idea of the spectrum of positions that exist in the business at present;

✎ Information about present challenges faced by the business and/or opportunities open to them.

★ **FOLLOW UP IN-PERSON VISITS IN A TIMELY AND PRODUCTIVE MANNER.**

The value of an in-person visit depends on how you use the information obtained from the person you met. Productive ways to follow up an in-person visit include:

➡ A letter describing your observations of the company and how your program can meet its needs;

➡ An employment proposal or an idea which reflects what you learned about the company (e.g., how hiring a person with specific skills and abilities might contain costs, increase profits or productivity);

<ul>
<li>A telephone call to schedule an appointment for an informational meeting with the person whose name you were given;</li>

<li>Delivering completed applications or resumes of applicants with a note attached stating how you selected them;</li>

<li>A fax listing services you would like to make available to the business with an action plan describing how to proceed.</li>
</ul>

★ REAP THE BENEFIT OF EACH IN-PERSON VISIT, REGARDLESS OF THE OUTCOME OF THE MEETING.

"Pray for a good harvest but continue to hoe."

A happy farmer

Every call you make will leave you with more than you started with — a name, an idea, information, a telephone appointment, advice about when to call back, maybe even less anxiety or a new friend! There is benefit to be gained from every call you make, regardless of its outcome. Don't define your success solely in terms of quantifiable outcomes such as job orders, referrals, or placements. Expand your notion of what constitutes success. Your criteria for success should include everything you learned in the meeting — clarity or a new perspective about an applicant's potential, deeper understanding of an employer's needs, or greater insight into how your services meet or don't meet the needs of a particular business.

★ SET GOALS AND OBJECTIVES WHICH ARE IN YOUR DIRECT CONTROL TO ATTAIN.

"I know why there are so many people who love chopping wood, they can immediately see results of their efforts."

Albert Einstein

Don't focus on goals that are not within your power to achieve, like job placement. Rather, focus on the steps you can control which ultimately generate placement, e.g., calling employers, knocking on doors, making presentations to community groups or sending letters.

Setting goals which are realistic and achievable is motivating and empowering. Working toward an end that you cannot directly influence is disempowering and discouraging. If you were in the position to actually employ people, then job placement would be a reasonable goal. Sadly, the only jobs we have are our own! We don't have the power to employ people, but we do have the power to influence others to hire our applicants. Job placement is our purpose, but our focus should be the process to affect this purpose.

While we do not have the benefit of seeing the tangible evidence of our efforts as a woodcutter does, we can feel satisfaction at the end of the day when we complete what we set out to accomplish — for example, ten telephone calls, three employment proposals and one scheduled appointment. Viewed this way, your work is satisfactorily completed at the end of the day. If your goal is placement, and it takes an entire week to generate one placement, you spend six days without the satisfaction you need and deserve.

★ BE WILLING TO PLAY THE NUMBERS GAME.

We've devoted a great deal of time to multitudes of ways to begin a working relationship with an employer and the inherent benefits derived from every contact. We have yet to consider the process of attaining your long-term objectives with employers (as opposed to short-term objectives negotiated in the course of cultivating the relationship). To be successful, you have to persist, and continue your efforts until you get what you want. This may mean that if one in ten employers agrees to schedule a time to meet with you in person, and you want to schedule three appointments in a given week, you must resolve to making thirty phone calls to obtain three appointments.

Remember, if at first you don't succeed, you're probably running about average! While there are few basic truths in the universe, the inevitability of the proverbial numbers game in marketing is one of these truths. The only way to increase the number of people who want to work with you is to increase the number of people who turn you down. As Tom Watson, the former president of IBM, put it, *"The way to double your success rate is to double your failure rate."*

"Grain by grain, a loaf — stone by stone, a castle."

Yugoslavian saying

★ DON'T BE AFRAID TO TAKE RISKS.

"Turtles travel only when they stick their necks out."

Korean phrase

Job developers only grow and prosper when they stick their necks out. Going for the sure thing may appear to be the safest route, but this course places you in danger of missing opportunities, and ultimately limits your success. Why not go out on the limb? Remember, when out on a limb, the world is at your feet. Besides, that's where you'll find the plumpest, ripest fruit!

APPLICATION: EXPANDING THE COLORS ON YOUR PALETTE

(1) Circle each of the following methods that you would like to incorporate into your job development repertoire:

TELEPHONE CONTACT

Approaches:

Employment Proposal
Before/After Mailing
Referral
Special Occasion
Applicant Interest
New Idea
Reference Check
Information Call
Thank You

IN-PERSON CONTACT

Approaches:

Employment Proposal
Information Call
Applicant Listing
On-the-Spot Interview
Geographic Scan
Industry-Specific Call

EVENTS AND PRESENTATIONS

Types:

Graduations
Interviewing Day
Employer Guest Day
Employer Appreciation/Awards Event
Training/Educational Event
Advisory Board or Committee Meeting
Observation Day
Fundraisers
Welcome to New Businesses
Holiday Celebrations/Potlucks
Organization/Project Anniversaries
Presentation to Community Groups
Attending State and Local Meetings
Joining the Local Chapter of State or
    National Associations

MAIL/FAX

Types:

Brochures
Flyers
Invitations
Applicant Listing
Articles, Newspaper
Newsletter
Information Packet
Letters
Employer Surveys
Industry Surveys
Announcements
Employment Proposals

(2) For each method you circled above, consider what you have to do to prepare and plan to use this method.

(3) Rate yourself on a scale from 1 to 5 (1 = low and 5 = high) according to the degree in which you already follow the recommendations characterized in this chapter as A Dozen Terribly Important Telephone Tips:

____ (a)   I pay attention to how I am using my voice to communicate my message to employers.

____ (b)   I know my own value as a provider of employer services.

____ (c)   I use assertive language.

____ (d)   I keep my telephone presentations brief and to the point.

____ (e)   I anticipate success before making a call.

____ (f)   I am willing to dig below the surface of an employer's first response, not taking an employer's initial disinterest at face value.

____ (g)   I am prepared with an "option plan" of requests or suggestions.

____ (h)   Once I pick up the receiver, I do not put it down until I have called every employer on my list.

____ (i)   I pay attention to my moods and take advantage of the high points in my day to initiate contact with employers.

____ (j)   I achieve something with every employer I make contact with and reward myself for every call I place.

____ (k)   I know when to persist and when to quit.

____ (l)   I do what needs to be done first; not creating unnecessary stress by postponing calls.

For any item where you gave yourself less than a three, consider how you can help yourself to improve your rating in that category.

(4) Rate yourself on a scale from 1 to 5 (1 = low and 5 = high) according to the degree in which you already follow the recommendations characterized in this chapter as Ten Tremendous Tips for Street Smarts.

_____ (a) I have a well-laid plan with specific objectives and timelines.

_____ (b) I am prepared with options for ways of working with employers while remaining flexible enough to address their immediate needs.

_____ (c) I am conscious of my attire and what I am communicating with how I dress.

_____ (d) I use my position and leverage as a customer whenever possible by seeking creative ways to assist the employer in increasing the prosperity of their business.

_____ (e) I communicate that I am an eager and enthusiastic learner when approaching new employers.

_____ (f) I follow up in-person visits in a timely and productive manner.

_____ (g) I reap the benefit of each in-person visit, regardless of its outcome.

_____ (h) I set goals and objectives which I have direct influence in attaining, rather than setting my sights on a plan which is not in my control to accomplish.

_____ (i) I am willing to play the numbers game and do not become easily discouraged.

_____ (j) I am not afraid to take risks.

For any item where you gave yourself less than a three, consider how you can help yourself to improve your rating in that category.

CHAPTER 8:
UNDERSTANDING EMPLOYER NEEDS

There are two important questions every job developer must ask when considering work with a new employer:

★ What resources, skills and opportunities do I have to offer which will motivate this employer to develop a working relationship with me?

★ What resources and opportunities does this business have to offer our program which motivates me to enter into a working relationship with them?

The employer's decision about working with a job developer is based on a myriad of possible factors, including the employer's current needs, goals and values. The answers to these two questions will be different for each employer we contact. Gathering information to gain insight into employer needs, goals and values is the purpose of conducting an employer assessment.

We have looked at the goal of developing partnerships and a variety of ways to target and initiate contact with employers. In this section we will outline questions to pose during a presentation to fully assess employer needs, goals and values. We will also examine the many considerations and motives which may influence an employer's decision to work with us.

"We do not learn to know a person through their coming to us. To find out what sort of persons they are, we must go to them."

Johann Wolfgang von Goethe, poet

EMPLOYER CONSIDERATIONS

A myriad of factors influences an employer's decision about whether or not to work with a job developer. Here is a list of some of the questions an employer might pose during the decision-making process. As you read through the list, identify which of these questions you ordinarily address in your presentation to employers and which ones you don't.

❖ How much is this going to cost in terms of time, effort and resources? What are the hidden costs?

❖ How profitable will this exchange of resources be for the business? For the department involved? For human resources in the short term? In the long term?

"My greatest strength as a consultant is to be ignorant and ask a few questions."

Peter Drucker, American business philosopher and author

❖ How will this employment proposal make or save us money? What are the start-up costs?

❖ Can we afford the investment in the short run even if it yields long-term gain?

❖ Will working with this program alter, augment or substitute for what we're doing right now?

❖ How will it improve our efficiency? Will it simplify what we're doing?

❖ What options are available from this program?

❖ Which option(s) presents the least amount of risk coupled with the greatest benefits?

❖ How will our organization benefit by hiring from the target population presented?

❖ How will the present staff, clients or customers feel about working with people from the target population?

❖ What are the risks of working with people from this population? Why do they need a special program to represent them? What isn't this person telling me?

❖ What might this program offer our workforce in terms of education, training, information or resources that we are not offering right now?

❖ What opportunities for community recognition can be gained from our association with this program?

❖ How would association with this program or this target population change or enhance our image with the larger community?

❖ Does working with this program fit or expand our corporate or organization mission statement?

❖ How credible is this agency or program? Whom have they worked with before? What are their placement and retention rates? How has the program been successful in other businesses like ours?

❖ How reliable is this job developer? How much experience does he or she have rendering services comparable to those we need?

❖ What do I have to lose from giving this person a chance to show me what he or she does? What might I gain?

Not every employer will be considering all of these questions. And yet, we know how important it is to speak to the individual needs of the employer.

In general, it is easier to fan an existing desire, or capitalize on an urgent need, than to create a new one. As we have seen, employers' answers to specific questions, along with a variety of organizational, emotional and political concerns, determine whether they will opt to work with you.

Until we know more about the individual employer, we cannot begin to respond to his or her needs, goals and values. We can only guess each employer's questions, speculate about his or her needs and the services relevant to each business. Trying to answer those questions before an employer assessment is like a doctor prescribing medical treatment before examining or diagnosing the problem.

Telling an employer you have exactly what he or she needs in terms of good employees before doing an assessment of the business is not too different from the doctor who prescribes medical treatment without diagnosing the illness. The inevitable question is, "How could this job developer possibly presume to know what I want or what this business needs?"

A classic mistake in business is taking a shoot from the hip approach — "let's do what we do best and someone will want it." It's the type of thinking that spawned the adage, "Build a better mousetrap and people will beat a path to your door." But what if your customers don't have mice, or don't care about getting rid of them?

Value is determined by the employer's perception of what you have to offer, not by what you do well. We need to identify the wants and needs of potential employers, then take inventory of our programs to see how we can meet those needs. Marketing experts refer to this process as "nichemanship" — carving a niche where your talents and strengths meet the needs and wants of the business.

Admitting ignorance about a business and simultaneously communicating a desire to learn about it, builds employer confidence in your integrity and credibility. Have you ever noticed that the person who pretends to "know it all" does not inspire your trust, but rather your suspicions?

> "*The four most important words in the English language: What is your opinion?*"
>
> *Anonymous*

> "*To know that you do not know is the best. To pretend to know when you do not know is disease.*"
>
> *Lao Tzu, Chinese philosopher and founder of Taoism.*

EMPLOYER ASSESSMENT

Encouraging employers to talk, in turn encourages them to listen.

The good news is we have the power to learn everything we need to know from the employer with the simple art of asking questions. With sincere efforts to hear the spirit as well as content of the answers, we can learn to address the goals, values and needs of individuals and their businesses. This is the goal of employer assessment, the first and most important part of a meeting with an employer.

The purpose of an employer assessment is to gain as much insight as possible into the goals, values and needs of the industry, the business, and the person you are talking to in order to have a clearer understanding of the following:

★ What you have to offer the employer which is or may be of value to them;

★ How you can tailor the presentation of your program and services to address their needs and issues; and,

★ The specific resources and opportunities this employer has to offer your program.

Before discussing the areas to cover and questions to ask during an employer assessment, here are some general recommendations for preparing the employer for your assessment:

➽ **Ask for permission from the employer to ask questions.** Explain that you would like to gain more than a cursory understanding of their employment needs, and you would like a firm grasp of how the business operates. Make plain the reason — the more you learn about the business, the better equipped you will be to tailor your services for the organization.

➽ **Ask the employer if you may take notes.** This will help you retain the information you are gathering, and it also communicates to the employer that what he or she has to say is important.

➽ **Have a questioning plan.** Be prepared to ask questions and know the direction you are heading with your questions. Be flexible — ready and willing to adjust your assessment to accommodate each employer's needs and preferences. The employer will usually lead the discussion in the direction he or she thinks is important. Asking additional questions about other areas is a good way to show your interest and enthusiasm for learning about both the individual and the business.

Following is a list of sample questions to ask in an employer assessment. The left-hand column of the chart lists the kinds of things we want to know about an employer. The right-hand column presents questions to elicit specific information and insight.

QUESTIONS FOR AN EMPLOYER ASSESSMENT

What you want to know:	**What you might ask:**
What are the employer's goals, concerns, values, and needs?	*"Tell me about your business."*
What do they think is important for you to know?	*"How is business?"* *"What is happening in your industry?"*
What is the nature of their product or service?	*"How do you do what you do? May I have a tour?"*
What is the technical language used in the business?	*"What exactly do you offer your clients or customers?"*
How does their business fit into the larger industry picture?	*"What is the history of this industry locally and how was this business started?"*
What are the outside circumstances most affecting their business right now?	*"What are the most significant factors affecting your business today?"*
How are those factors affecting their present hiring needs?	*"How have changes in technology most affected your business?"* *"How has your business/industry been affected by the recession?"*
How has the direction of the company affected its hiring needs?	*"How has your company grown or changed in the last couple of years?"*
Have these changes increased or decreased the need for staff?	*"What future direction do you see the company taking?"*
Where are the greatest possibilities for employment in this business? How would employment in these areas add to the growth and prosperity of the company?	*"Where is the greatest demand for your services or product?"* *"Where is most of the pressure from increased business felt in this company?" Which department feels it the most?"*

What does this business pride itself on? What feature or characteristic seems to keep it in business?

"How do you differ from your competitors?"

What are some of the "bottom lines" of this company given their image and key selling factors?

What does this company need from its employees and how can I speak to those needs before they show up as minimum qualifications?

"Describe your star employee. What are the qualities of people who perform best in this business?"

What kind of environment has this company created for its employees? What does it want to be known for as an employer? How much invested is the company in creating a dedicated, happy workforce?

"How do you think most of the employees would describe this as a workplace?"

"If this company were known for three things as a workplace, what do you think those three things would be?"

How do they feel about programs like ours?

"Have you ever worked a program like ours?

"What experience have you had with programs like ours?"

How do they feel about the target population?

"What has been your experience with (the target population)?"

How much risk do they feel?

"What are your present methods?"

Are they looking for an alternative hiring method?

"If you could improve your present hiring method in any way, what would that be?

Do they feel loyalty to another program?

What do they see as the possible benefits of working with us?

"How do you think I might be able to augment what you are already doing?"

What part does this person play in the hiring process? (Assume the person is responsible for each decision and comment on it, this person will usually correct you if you are wrong.)	*"Do you do the hiring for every department in the company?"* *"How do you select between two equally qualified applicants?"* *"How do you decide when to hire?"*
What are the person's most pressing needs?	*"I would like to tell you about our program and how I think we can address many of the goals you have spoken of in the next few minutes. Before I do that, is there anything you would like me to address upfront?"*
What is the company's perception of the kind of workplace it represents?	*"How would you describe your company culture?"*
How will the company's planned growth affect their hiring needs?	*"What trends do you see over the next five years that will affect your organization and your industry? What do you think your company will look like five years from now?"*
What referrals can this employer offer you?	*"Could you recommend other businesses that your establishment does business with who might benefit from our services?"* (E.g., printers, travel agent, caterers, custodial services, building manager, etc.)

Given everything the employer has said, what are the possibilities of job creation with this employer? Are there any obvious opportunites for your applicants to:

- ✓ Help the business save or make money?
- ✓ Expand the business?
- ✓ Increase their customer base?
- ✓ Solve a problem?
- ✓ Make the boss look good?
- ✓ Use old things in a new way?
- ✓ Improve the way things are being done now?
- ✓ Respond to a problem in the community?
- ✓ Capitalize on or respond to a trend?

LISTENING TO EMPLOYER RESPONSES: "THE SEARCH FOR MEANING"

"No man would listen to you talk if he didn't know it was his turn next."

Ed Howe, journalist

People like to talk about what they know. People love to be heard, paid attention to, and respected. Unfortunately, most people do not listen with the intent to understand; they listen with the intent to reply. While people speak to us, we are typically thinking about and formulating our responses.

"Nothing is quite so annoying as to have someone go right on talking when you're busy interrupting!"

Attitude of the typical listener

There is a wealth of literature in the fields of communications and counseling about the importance of practicing empathy and employing active listening skills. I believe these two concepts arise from genuine concern for enhanced communications and improved understanding. Yet I also am concerned that they can sabotage us, actually working to weaken communication and understanding.

The term "active listening" has been used to describe a skill-focused technique in which behaviors such as leaning forward, nodding the head, and making noises like "uh-huh" are intended to convince the speaker that they are being heard. Like most behavior-based techniques, they are truncated from the ethics, principles and human values that would make them effective.

Active listening is and should be defined as listening with the purpose and intent to truly understand what is being said. When one is truly listening, no contrived, artificial behaviors are necessary because the speaker can feel it. We know when we are being heard. We also know when someone is listening simply to reply. In the latter situation no amount of head nodding or leaning forward is going to make us feel better about the listener's intentions.

People don't care how much you know until they know how much you care.

"Seek first to understand, then to be understood."

Stephen Covey, author

My favorite definition of listening is "to search for understanding" because it acknowledges the listener as an active seeker. The listener does not assume meaning or impose his or her own meaning on what is said. This kind of listening is more like finding your way in the dark than frolicking along a familiar and well-lit path. Since I believe we are more often than not in the dark about what other people need, want and value, this definition of listening seems appropriate.

Stephen Covey refers to the most common forms of listening as "autobiographical" in nature. For example, we listen to evaluate — we agree or disagree based on our own values and beliefs. We probe — posing questions from our own frame of reference. We advise — offering counsel based on our own experience; and we interpret — attempting to figure people out and explain their motives and behavior — based on our own motives and behavior.

I believe our work demands all of the listening skills defined by Covey. As counselors and job developers we are in the business of evaluating, probing, advising and interpreting the language, motives and interests of our applicants and of employers. But these skills can only serve our purposes after we understand and appreciate the other person's point of view. These skills are secondary to the purpose of simply understanding.

After reading about autobiographical listening I became more conscious of how I listen. I was both surprised and disappointed to find that it is only with tremendous, deliberate effort that I am able to truly listen to others without filtering their every word through my personal screen. Since my screen is not theirs, when I listen autobiographically, I am really only discovering my meaning, not theirs. If listening is a search for the other person's meaning, we need to get out of our own way. I believe that is what Stephen Covey means when he says, "seek first to understand, then to be understood." We hear with our ears, but we listen with our hearts and our minds.

Earlier in the chapter we discussed assessment questions and what to be listening for in the employer's responses. In addition, there is another more general area of concern that we need to key into as we assess employers: the employer's key goals and values that are shaping his or her choice about working with you, and what the employer is viewing as his or her "bottom line."

> *"I learned a long time ago that employers do not have to hire people for my reasons; it's enough that they hire them for their own reasons..."*
>
> Richard Pimentel, *job development trainer*

EMPLOYER DECISIONS

No one wants to be sold, only helped to solve problems.

The goals and values *we* hold as professionals in the field are not central to an employer's decision about whether or not to work with us. The employer's *own* goals, values and motivation shape his or her decision. We can make all the sense in the world to ourselves, but if we're not singing the same song or in the same key as the employer, how can we expect to achieve harmony?

Peter Vaill, the author of *New Ideas For a World of Chaotic Change*, makes an interesting comment on the importance of understanding others' goals and values when negotiating:

"It is not the logical but the psychological we are dealing with when we are trying to understand why people make the decisions they do. I would suggest that resistance to agree to something can frequently mean simply that the person doesn't understand or agree with the values that he or she is being asked to act on.... What is important is what we decide is important. Values are nonlogical, translogical, supralogical which is different from being illogical. When we can't understand a person's behavior, it is often because we don't understand what goal that person thinks is important!" (my emphasis).

This last point reinforces the need to take the time to truly understand each employer's situation enough to be able to effectively address their needs, goals and values.

In a study conducted by Vaill's research team in 1990, several groups of senior corporate executives were asked how they arrived at decisions in a variety of business situations. The study concluded that the grounds for a decision are really the values used to make the decision. This list summarizes the competing values and considerations used as the "bottom line" in the decision-making process:

+ The law required it
+ "So and so" personally ordered us to do it
+ Another organization does it this way
+ This approach won out in competition with others
+ This makes the best use of our resources
+ It was the scientific thing to do
+ It was the surest way to reach the objective
+ It was the easiest, most expedient thing to do
+ We just knew it was right, on a gut level
+ Doing something was better than doing nothing
+ We had to compromise and this was the result
+ Basic divine revelation
+ Result of careful sustained dialogue
+ Our survival was at stake
+ Our specific ideology and beliefs dictated it
+ Pressure from the outside
+ It was politically correct
+ We threw it to the winds of chance, and here is where it landed

In his attitudinal training workshops with employers, Richard Pimentel asks participants to raise their hands if they have ever flipped a coin or played "one potato, two potato" to make a hiring decision. Typically, the majority of participants raise their hands. Job developers are usually appalled to hear this, given the amount of conscious effort they apply to make clear, logical and rational presentations to employers. Surely we have to wonder, how often are decisions really made on purely rational grounds?

I appreciate Vaill's list because it confirms that decisions are based on each individual's thoughts and responses to the world. Why would we assume anything different?

So here's the problem. People make decisions based on both their values and goals. That's fine, we can accept that. What is harder to accept is the fact that these goals and values vary in each situation and are as unpredictable and mutable as the human beings who hold them. At times they appear inconsistent and changing as our moods, thoughts and emotions. Let me give you an example.

This morning I allowed my six year old daughter to have a bowl of colorful, sugar-coated cereal (we received a sample in the mail) guaranteed to rot her precious teeth. Normally, she would know better than to even make such a request, but seeing me totally absorbed in my writing, she knew that my goal of getting work done and my immediate need for peace, quiet and harmony, would result in a "Leave me alone and be happy" response — a surefire "yes." In the grocery store my goals and values for health and nutrition reign supreme. I suspect, however, that toymakers and manufacturers of sugary foods bank (literally) on the fact that parents' goals and values are not impermeable or immutable and may be weakened by children's heartfelt pleas.

This holds true for other situations as well. Typically, we have layers of goals and values in any situation. This idea is contrary to the popular belief that everyone is holding to some almighty bottom line.

THE EMPLOYER'S "BOTTOM LINE(S)"

The existing paradigm in marketing and sales is that the bottom line in business is net profit. No one would argue that profit is a primary motivator in business and, in fact, what keeps a business afloat. Still, people in business will agree that profit is not the only bottom line. There are actually many bottom lines.

Believing net profit is the only motive of a business is like believing that staying alive is the only motivation of the human being. It is crucial, but the quality and character each human life takes on have much more to do with other issues — "bottom lines"— than simply basic survival. Values, interests, emotional needs and desires all contribute to human motivation.

A business also has values, interests, needs and desires, shared by members and stakeholders. Businesses also must respond to the pressures and forces of the marketplace and often, to the needs of community members. While net profit is critical, it is not the only basis for decision-making.

Peter Vaill categorizes the key concerns of any business in the following five areas:

➤ **The Bottom Line of Economics**

Every accountant knows the term "bottom line" is maddeningly imprecise. There are multiple bottom lines between revenue and retained earnings. There are multiple opportunities to decide whether one is going to spend, distribute or hang on to funds. Buying office furniture, planning a Christmas party, putting in a new telephone system, investing in new equipment, upgrading the skills of employees, hiring new employees or laying off present staff are examples of the range of circumstances and decisions that influence the economic bottom line and are not directly related to selling a product or service.

➤ **The Bottom Line of Procedures and Process**

This question is not about money, it is about efficiency. The organization of the 1990s must determine how it is going to do what it does,

> *"The use of money is all the advantage there is in having money."*
>
> *Benjaman Franklin, statesman and philosopher*

> *"If a person goes into business with only the idea of making money, the chances are they won't."*
>
> *Joyce Clyde Hall, Founder, Hallmark Cards*

choose its methods, and decide how close to the state of the art it can and will operate.

➤ The Bottom Line of the Workplace Community

A business is as complex and multi-layered as the people who comprise it.

A business also has to determine how it is going to relate to its employees, customers or clients. These issues involve how the employer wants its audiences — employees, customers and the community-at-large — to feel as a result of their association; policies and procedures related to employee rewards, promotions and hiring criteria and the kind of environment it will create for employees. Related concerns include the degree to which the employer is committed to staff diversity and the types of social programs and activities it will promote and support.

➤ The Bottom Line of Society

In addition to delivering products and services to stakeholders and adhering to the law, a business must establish a sociopolitical bottom line. The business must also respond to issues related to its role and image in society. What are the roles and responsibilities of the business in the community? What is its image? Is it the desired image, or should it change?

➤ The Bottom Line of Purpose and Meaning

"Money talks because it is a metaphor, a transfer, and a bridge in a community of strangers."

Marshall McLuhan, Canadian educator and writer

A business is known by what it is and does, as well as its policies and procedures. In addition to these operational issues, each organization must make fundamental decisions about its meaning for the people it employs and the people it serves.

At some point every business seeks heightened awareness of its other organizational characteristics. It may seek to identify outputs — secondary products, services or byproducts — yielded by the processes that create its primary product or service. Employees and stakeholders may ask, "What is our mission? How do we see ourselves in the future? What are our purposes beyond basic survival and beyond profitability?" While these considerations may seem like luxuries to new businesses, they are an accepted part of the "right of passage," if you will, to becoming an established player in the marketplace.

(How many of you old Psychology majors recognized the similarities between this list and Maslow's "hierarchy of human needs," as applied to the organization?)

SUMMARY OF KEY IDEAS ABOUT UNDERSTANDING EMPLOYER NEEDS

★ Job developers can't expect to understand the nature of every business. One means of establishing credibility with an employer is to ask good questions. Posing intelligent questions demonstrates both enthusiasm for and interest in employer goals, needs and issues.

★ Employer assessment serves a variety of purposes, including but not limited to:

- Making the employer the center of attention;
- Guiding the direction of the meeting;
- Gaining a better grasp of the employer needs;
- Increasing the employer's confidence that they have been understood;
- Initiating a two-way dialogue;
- Pinpointing areas where you may be able to help; and,
- Identifying possible employer concerns and attitudes.

★ Seek first to understand, then to be understood. This means to listen as a way of seeking the speaker's meaning, rather than listening simply to develop a reply. Don't listen autobiographically.

★ While we should always attempt to make good business sense when we present ideas, we also should be attentive to other factors that influence employer decisions.

★ Employers want us to address the bottom line. Contrary to popular belief, the majority of employers have more than one "bottom line."

★ For every issue or concern (bottom line) expressed by an employer, there is a number of questions which must be answered to inspire employer confidence about working with a job developer.

★ There are many reasons and motives an employer might want to enter a working relationship with a job developer. It would be foolish to assume knowledge of the employer's motive before doing an assessment of their business.

★ If employers resist your line of questioning during an assessment, respect their boundaries and follow their leads. Remember, there are many ways to learn about a business and there is no such thing as the "last chance meeting." Additional ways to get information about a business include:

- Reading annual reports, marketing materials, and other published information.

- Speaking with representatives of the business or industry at job fairs, association, or trade meetings and conferences.

- Talking to anyone and everyone associated with the business, from receptionists and marketing representatives to security guards and janitors.

- Contacting similar businesses and neighboring organizations.

★ Be sure to reflect the insight and information the employer has given you during the presentation of your program and services. Writer and educator, Elwood Murray, says, *"The fusion of knowledge is the most creative act of the human mind."* In the next chapter we will look at how to use what you have learned from the employer to effectively communicate the value and benefit of working with you and your program.

★ Bear in mind, our job isn't to go out and impress anyone. Our job is to go out and be impressed by everyone we meet!

"We are pioneers trying to find a new path through the maze of tradition, convention and dogma. Our efforts are part of a struggle to mature the conception of partnerships — in fact all relationships. In such light, every advance in understanding has value. Every step, even a tentative one, counts."

Anne Morrow Lindbergh.
writer

APPLICATION: CREATING AN EMPLOYER ASSESSMENT

Consider the following before drafting questions for an employer assessment:

◆ Typically, what questions do you ask an employer?

◆ What additional questions might you ask to gain further insight?

◆ Compare your notes from a variety of employer assessments with other job developers to determine which questions elicit the most valuable information.

Questions to ask an employer: Notes:

"Few people look upon the language they speak as an art.
Yet it is, or ought to be, the noblest of all the arts,
looked upon with respect, even with reverence,
and used always with care, courtesy,
and the deepest respect."

Mary Ellen Chase,
Educator and Writer

CHAPTER 9:
COMMUNICATING WITH EMPLOYERS:
LANGUAGE AS ART

"Genuine communication is a creative art by which you become part of me and I become part of you; it is the process by which you activate something in me and vice versa."

Pierre Casse

While we are guaranteed to have interaction with employers through our work, we are not guaranteed genuine communication as defined by Pierre Casse above. Presenting your program to an attentive, interested employer is one of the most satisfying and enjoyable parts of job development. It is also a critical stage in the development of a relationship with an employer. With the words we speak we must inform, educate, inspire, communicate value, express enthusiasm and demonstrate good judgment. We need to become true wordsmiths, using language with as much precision as any other tool.

Everyone has their own way of communicating ideas and expressing themselves. I have seen boisterous, exuberant job developers explode with enthusiasm as they present ideas and I have seen equally effective job developers with calm, unassuming, straightforward presentation styles. I encourage you to embrace and benefit from your own personal style since *who you are* will probably have a greater effect on the employer than anything you do or say. No one can offer you communication techniques more inherently motivating than the spirit, conviction and enthusiasm you honestly and openly bring to your work.

The purpose of this section is not to tell you what to say or how to say it. Instead, it offers guidelines and ideas for fine-tuning your presentation and increasing your confidence and ability to effectively communicate with a wide range of both employer needs and communication styles.

Here are eighteen guidelines to consider when presenting your ideas to employers. Read them and then respond to the questions at the end of the chapter to examine how you might incorporate these ideas in your personal communication style.

"God wove a web of loveliness, of clouds and stars and birds, but made not anything at all so beautiful as words."

Anna Hempstead Branch,
American poet and social worker

"Words are, of course, the most powerful drug used by mankind."

Rudyard Kipling,
English author

EIGHTEEN IDEAS FOR
FINE-TUNING YOUR PRESENTATION

(1) KNOW YOUR STUFF.

As job developers we are advocates for the people we serve and spokespersons on issues relating to them. When I served as a job developer for refugees I was often in the position of defending their right to seek political asylum in this country. As an advocate for people with disabilities, one can expect to be questioned about the ADA. If you work with people from minority groups in Canada, concerns and questions about Employment Equity will be posed. We must be prepared to speak intelligently about the issues related to the people we serve.

"Information is power."

W. Edwards Deming, business management theorist

We are also representatives of our agency or organization and programs. Employers expect us to know our stuff. While much of the information listed below seems superfluous to what we typically discuss with employers, we should be prepared to answer questions in all of these areas. Remember, *information is power and it is our primary currency of exchange with employers.*

What you should know about your organization:

History of the organization locally
History of the organization nationally
Goals of the organization
Other programs offered by the organization
Who serves on the Board of Directors of your program
Outstanding attributes of the organization

What you should know about your program:

Goals and objectives of the program
Funding source(s)
Goals and objectives of the funding source
Legislation pertaining to funding source(s)
Other programs in the area working with similar funding and/or
    goals and objectives
Differences and similarities of other programs
History of the program
Biggest challenges of the program
Performance record of the program in the community
Outstanding attributes of the program
Statistics relating to the success of the program

What you should know about the services you offer:

What is offered to clients
What is offered to the employer community
What are the processes and procedures involved in delivering

these services

Who is involved in the delivery of services

What you should know about the target population:

Eligibility requirements for program services

Legal definitions pertaining to target population

Detailed description of any public assistance programs available to program participants

Referral sources of participants

Mandatory requirements for participant involvement

Other support services provided for participants by your agency and other programs

Other systems or programs which refer and/or involve participants

The range of differences among the individuals who compose the target population

(2) HAVE RELEVANT MATERIALS OR DOCUMENTATION AVAILABLE FOR THE EMPLOYER.

While some employers do not want to be bothered with any kind of paperwork, others like to see written materials about the program, services and/or the applicants. Here are examples of the kinds of materials to make available for employers:

✦ Program marketing or promotional materials;

✦ Course outlines, curricula of relevant training or descriptions of work shops offered to clients;

✦ Assessment forms or evaluation instruments used to assess applicants' skills and abilities;

✦ Eligibility forms used to screen applicants for services;

✦ Sample employment proposals or resumes;

✦ A list of "happy customers" — employers who currently utilize your services who will serve as references for your program;

✦ A list of common questions and answers about the target population; and

✦ A summary of relevant statistics and facts related to employment of the target population (e.g., placement rates, retention rates, average cost of accommodation).

(3) TELL THE EMPLOYER WHAT YOU'RE GOING TO COVER, COVER THE BASICS, THEN LET THE EMPLOYER DIRECT YOU TO HIS OR HER AREA OF INTEREST.

For example,

"This is what I would like to accomplish in the next 10 minutes: to tell you who we are, what we do, how we do it, and why I think it would be to your benefit to work with our program."

Once you have covered those four basic areas, allow the employer's questions to lead you to his or her specific interests. Notice how each of the following typical questions will lead you down a different path.

⇒   *"How can you save me time and money?"*
⇒   *"How do you decide which applicant to send to apply for a particular job?"*
⇒   *"How did this program get started?"*
⇒   *"Why is the taxpayers' money invested to serve people with these kinds of barriers when there are so many people out of work?"*
⇒   *"Can you tell me about an employer who has implemented a proposal like this one?"*

Address the individual concerns of employers and allow their questions to guide and direct the course of the discussion.

(4)   STATE YOUR INTERESTS UP FRONT.

"Right up front, tell people what you're trying to accomplish and what you're willing to sacrifice to do it."

Lee Iacocca,
Chairman,
Chrysler
Corporation

Have you ever been approached by someone you knew wanted to sell you something, but wasn't telling you what it was he or she was selling? This "save the punch line until the last minute" kind of selling can drive even the most patient customer absolutely crazy!

Begin your meeting by stating your intentions at the onset of the discussion. Tell the employer what you would like to accomplish in the meeting and he or she won't have to second-guess your motives throughout the meeting. Consider these three examples:

"Good morning. I appreciate your taking the time to meet with me. I am here in the hope that you will be interested in hiring people from our program. I'd like to spend the next twenty minutes learning more about your company and giving you an opportunity to learn more about what we do. We can then decide whether the services I have to offer are pertinent to you at this time."

"Hello. My name is Roy Miller. I work for the Toronto Community College Women's Re-entry Program. I am the job developer for the Bank Teller's course. I am here to find out if we're on the right track in terms of equipping people with the kind of skills and abilities you look for in your candidates. I suspect we are. If so, I would like to offer you the opportunity to interview some of our trainees before the end of the term. We expect 85% of the class to secure employment within four weeks of finishing this course."

"It is very nice to meet you. Having taken a quick tour through your facility, I would be thrilled if any of the graduates of our program could be part of such a dynamic and unique work environment. Let's get down to business so you can see what's in it for you."

The existing sales paradigm (described in Chapter 5) stresses closing technique as the key to success. The emphasis on "closing" is based on the belief that you cannot expect to get what you want unless you ask for it. Here I am recommending a dramatically different approach — to *open* the discussion by stating what we want rather than closing with a request for the sale.

(5) THINK BIG AND ASK FOR WHAT YOU REALLY WANT.

"The eagle does not catch flies."

Native American saying

Many people adopt modest goals in an attempt to avoid disappointment. Unfortunately, low aspirations tend to be self-fulfilling. What you don't ask for, others are highly unlikely to offer. Not surprisingly, people willing to work toward higher goals usually manifest more of their desires and attain more of their aspirations than those who ask for less than what they really want.

Don't short-change yourself or your applicants; state exactly what you want and expect from employers. You have nothing to lose. If the employer disagrees, the employer will let you know what he or she is willing to give.

"The meek shall inherit the earth, but they'll never increase market share."

William G. McGowan, communications executive

Consider the differences in these two dialogues:

Asking for what you think you can get:	**Asking for what you really want:**
"I wonder if you would please look over these applications and call me if an opportunity comes up."	*"My hope is that you will find it worth your while to interview these three people and have them ready for hire when you secure your next big contract."*
In this case even if the employer agrees, the job developer has only won partial commitment from the employer. Rarely will employers themselves suggest a plan of greater commitment than the one requested.	In this case, if the employer agrees, the job developer is well on her way to job placement. If the employer does not agree to the interviews, he or she may suggest keeping the applications on file.

"There are two fools in every market; one asks too little, one asks too much."

Russian proverb

Obviously, it is very important to know what you want before going into a meeting with an employer, and to remain open and receptive to new or different opportunities. In many instances you may leave meetings with new ideas and conclusions about your interest in the employer.

Just in case you should decide to follow this guideline, it is only fair to remind you of the adage, "Be careful what you ask for, you just might get it!"

(6) FIND COMMON GROUND.

Through an understanding of our shared goals and interests we develop common ground with employers. It is here that we can explore and negotiate our differences. This is true in all relationships.

Listen for your shared goals and interests as the employer answers your questions and discusses the needs of the business. Notice in the following examples that some shared goals may not have the same underlying motivation, but provide common ground just the same:

"Under-standing does not consist in gazing at one another, but in looking outward together in the same direction."

Antoine de Saint Exupery, writer

* To not waste time and energy with applicants who are not genuinely interested in the position;

* The productivity and success of employees hired from the program;

* Growth and prosperity for both the economic community and the particular business;

* Effective allocation of funds for training opportunities and wage subsidies;

* For the business to have full access to and information about a qualified resource pool of applicants;

* Full realization of employees' talents for maximum profitability.

Identifying areas of common ground is a natural outcome of genuine, effective communication. Discovering and commenting on common goals is as important to developing the relationship with an employer as negotiating differences. When common interests and goals are shared, the distance between you as a result of differences does not seem as great.

(7) BUILD ON THE EMPLOYER'S IDEAS.

During the assessment stage of the meeting you elicit the employer's ideas. Now build on them. Use information the employer has provided as a springboard for your ideas and plans. Tell the employer how your proposal or idea is responsive to his or her (or the organization's) position. For example, you can begin a proposal with one of the following statements:

✦ *"Building on your idea, what if we..."*

✦ *"I got this idea from something you said earlier..."*

✦ *"As a follow-up to our previous discussion, it occurred to me that..."*

✦ *"Listening to all that you have said, has me thinking in a totally new direction. What would you think if..."*

Building on another person's ideas is a way of building a bridge from their thinking to yours.

(8) SPEAK THE EMPLOYER'S LANGUAGE.

A woman in one of my workshops shared this delightful story from her job development experience:

> *"One day I went into a factory and introduced myself to the person behind the desk, "Hi, I'm a job developer for U.S.C.C., a C.B.O. working under a J.T.P.A. contract in this S.D.A. under the P.I.C.. I'm here to see if I can develop an O.J.T. and offer you a T.J.T.C. just A.S.A.P."*
>
> *The receptionist leaned over her desk and replied, "Well, L-M-N-O-P!"*

> *"Incomprehensible jargon is the hallmark of a profession."*
>
> *Kingman Brewster Jr., President, Yale University*

Readers unfamiliar with the lingo associated with the Job Training Partnership Act are probably just as confused as the receptionist in the story. Confusion does not breed acceptance or rapport, it tends to have the opposite effect. We alienate people when we speak an unfamiliar language. Using a common language creates a sense of unity and promotes understanding.

At times we take for granted that everyone understands the language and jargon that has become second nature to us. The terms "referral," "placement," assessment," "wage subsidies," "OJT contracts," mean one thing to us, but may mean something completely different to persons outside our field. Worse yet, they may mean nothing at all.

I recommend we use simple, everyday language to explain who are and what we do. Consider the following examples:

Social service lingo: *"We provide follow-up services."*

Employer language: *"If you hire Ben I will be in touch with you or his supervisor every day the first week to see that all is going well. In fact, I will be in touch with you every week thereafter until I've heard you say that you don't need to hear from me any more."*

Social service lingo: *"We do a language assessment of each applicant."*

Employer language: *"I will find out from the supervisor exactly what language skills are needed in the position. I will* *draft a list of the words the employee needs to understand, read and write. This list will become the test a person must pass before they walk through your door to apply."*

Social service lingo: *"I offer support services for you as well as the applicants."*

Employer language: *"Employers ask me if there's much paperwork involved. Yes, there is. Fortunately for you, I'm the one that does it!"*

Social service lingo: *"We're a non-profit organization."*

Employer language: *"While the services I am offering to you are very valuable, I am happy to tell you that we can offer you quality services without having to send you a bill!"*

It may have occurred to you as you read that I am using the word "employer" to represent a tremendously diverse population. How then can I refer to an "employer's language"? What I am recommending is "everyday talk" — language shared by people across nearly all professions and social classes. At times you may tailor your language to accommodate the style of a particular person or the distinct culture of a business. Consider the various ways to ask for a personal meeting with an employer:

✦ *"I'd like to drop in some time this week."*

✦ *"I'm calling to schedule a meeting with Mr. Franks at his earliest possible convenience."*

✦ *"I'd love to meet and talk with you in person!"*

> *"Language is not merely the mirror of society; it is the major force in constructing what we perceive as reality."*
>
> *Edward Sapir and Benjamin Whorf, Linguists*

(9) USE VALUING LANGUAGE WHEN DESCRIBING THE PEOPLE YOU SERVE.

Consider the differences in images conjured up by the words used to describe individuals or situations in the columns below.

Remedial education	Additional preparation
A high school dropout	Someone in the process of completing his/her education
The disabled	Persons with disabilities
A dislocated worker	A worker in transition
A welfare recipient	A person who is receiving public assistance

A drug addict	A person with a substance abuse problem
Ex-offender, ex-convict	A person who has come through the judicial system
High-risk youth	Students facing a variety of difficult life situations
A street person, vagrant, homeless person, victim of...	A person in need of temporary shelter Survivor of... Person living with... A person who has...

It has been said, "If you change language, you change everything." As advocates for the people we serve, we need to gently re-educate society about how to describe situations without devaluing the people who experience these situations. Here are a couple of tips for using language which is respectful of people.

★ Use words which describe rather than define the person.

For example, the term "welfare recipient" defines the person by their economic situation rather than simply stating that the person is receiving public assistance. The term "person with a disability" does not define the person by their physical or mental condition whereas "the disabled" does.

★ Avoid terms which convey a negative judgment about the person's situation.

For example, the terms "dropout" and "vagrant" carry attitudinal connotations about the person that go beyond that of someone not completing a course of study or needing shelter. "AIDS victim" conjures up feelings of pity and sympathy while the term "a person who is living with AIDS" affords the person dignity and respect in the face of his or her illness.

Currently, there is a strong movement in our society to use "politically correct" language and terminology. I fear, as is the case with many political movements, that the concern is more about "not crossing the bounds of correctness" than "being sensitive or appropriately inclusive." Consider some of these tongue-in-cheek terms I found in *The Officially Politically Correct Dictionary and Handbook* written by Henry Beard and Christopher Cerf:

Cat	Feline American
Wife	Domestic incarceration survivor
Stoned	Chemically inconvenienced
Boring	Differently interested
Lazy	Motivationally deficient
Disorganized	Nontraditionally ordered

Girl-watching	Street harassment
Chronically late	Temporally challenged
Clumsy	Uniquely coordinated
Incompetent	Differently qualified
Anti-social	Interesting to serve
Dishonest	Ethically disoriented
Shoplifter	Nontraditional shopper

While I found these terms humorous, I also recognize that this humor is rooted in the very principles that we are asking society to take seriously. (It is said that humor reflects societal issues that are just below the surface, on the verge of consideration, and/or creating uncomfortable change.) So the question is:

> How do we bring about changes in language (and attitude) without creating more distance between the community-at-large and the target group?

I believe we do it by example. We simply walk the talk. I emphasize what I call *gentle re-education* because more forceful or assertive approaches often trigger defensive reactions rather than genuine, understanding responses.

I once worked with a man who ran a gas station. He continually referred to the individuals I served as "the hard up." I didn't object to the term, I simply spoke consistently and confidently about "the mechanics," "the attendants," and "the maintenance helpers" whom I thought he should meet. After about half an hour into our discussion, a co-worker entered the room and I was introduced as "a person working with gas station folk." I loved the transformation in his thinking that occurred in response to the images he conjured up from the words I used. From that day forward, I have referred to applicants using the name of the position for which they are applying. That is what I mean by *gentle re-education*.

(10) PRESENT THE ATTRIBUTES OF INDIVIDUALS RATHER THAN POSITIVE STEREOTYPES OF THE GROUP.

Have you ever heard statements like:

✦ *"You should consider hiring older workers; they are very industrious!"*
✦ *"People with disabilities make very loyal employees."*
✦ *"Hiring from our program is a good idea because young people are energetic and enthusiastic learners!"*
✦ *"Dislocated workers are seasoned workers anxious for a second chance."*

The truth, of course, is that we work with individuals who have some of these qualities, but not necessarily because they have a disability, are more than fifty-five years of age, or have experienced a company lay-off!

Each person we work with brings his or her own unique set of character traits and qualities, positive and negative. Rarely are similarities between the individuals you work with attributable to the shared characteristic which qualifies them for your services.

There are several reasons we should resist reinforcing the positive stereotypes of the people we serve. They are:

✓ Nothing we can say about an entire group of people will hold true for every individual in the group.

✓ Employers might believe the stereotypes, hire people because of them, and then expect the individuals to meet those expectations. This is an unfair burden for any employee to carry.

✓ When an individual does not live up to the employer's expectations, he or she may decide not to hire from the target group again. Unmet or unrealistic expectations may produce the comment, "I tried working with people like that before and it just didn't work out." Although it seems ludicrous to think a single experience with one member of a group could affect an employer's view of everyone in the group, it happens more frequently than we may care to admit. Selling positive stereotypes only perpetuates this kind of over-generalizing.

Positive stereotypes are every bit as harmful and patronizing as negative stereotypes. We need to work to neutralize attitudes toward groups of people so each individual has the opportunity to benefit from genuine, unbiased responses.

For example, rather than saying, *"Injured workers are anxious to get back to work,"* you might say, *"Let me tell you about Joe. He is so eager to get behind the wheel of a truck again that he recently moved his brother's family to the East Coast in a 40 foot U-Haul."*

Or, rather than saying, *"People with mental disabilities are content to perform one function for long periods of time,"* you might say, *"Some of the people I work with enjoy varied tasks and responsibilities. Others prefer single task work."*

(11) EMPHASIZE THE PRACTICALITY OF YOUR IDEAS.

Many employers appreciate a straightforward, logical, systematic explanation of how your services can benefit them. This may mean taking out a pen and paper and showing them actual calculations or handing them materials showing how your services have benefitted other companies. The following statements help to emphasize the practicality of your ideas:

☆ *"Let me explain what I have to offer and why it's a no-lose proposition for your company..."*

☆ *"Most employers estimate that recruiting people from our agency saves them approximately six hours of interviewing and pre-screening per person hired. That is because I will already have invested those six hours referencing and screening the applicants myself, before sending them to you."*

"Explain it to me as if I were two."

Denzel Washington, actor, from the film "Philadelphia"

☆ *"Let me explain how I go about my job and the four ways in which it is designed to make your job easier."*

☆ *"I operate on the universal hiring rule which states that unless I can make a convincing case that this person can bring your business more profit than it costs to employ her, we are going to agree that this proposal is not right for your operation!"*

(12) KEEP YOUR EXPLANATIONS AND DESCRIPTIONS SIMPLE.

"The Declaration of Independence has only 1,322 words, Lincoln's Gettysburg Address has 268 and the Lord's Prayer has 56 words. The leader who understands the art and genius of simplicity has a rare gift."

Sheila Murray Bethel, writer

"It is a luxury to be understood."

Ralph Waldo Emerson, poet

Words are our greatest tools for communication, and yet too many words get in the way — they soar above listeners' heads, or confuse and complicate seemingly simple issues. Most people are not willing to admit when they do not understand what is said. They are either embarrassed at failing to grasp the speaker's meaning, or afraid of embarrassing the speaker by asking for clarification. To increase the likelihood of being understood, seek and use the clearest, simplest approach to present your ideas. Make every effort to:

◆ Speak and explain ideas in an organized, uncluttered fashion.

◆ Distill thoughts, requests or proposals to their fundamental elements.

◆ Identify and communicate the core of the material before describing details of specific programs and services.

(13) ASSIST EMPLOYERS TO DISTILL COMMUNICATIONS TO THE ESSENTIAL POINTS.

While it is important to leave a meeting with a clear idea of what is most important to the employer, not every employer speaks in a straightforward and direct manner. We can assist them to distill and refine their ideas and plans by asking focused questions. Consider the following examples:

"I didn't say that I didn't say it. I said that I didn't say that I said it. I want to make that perfectly clear."

George Romney, Governor of Michigan

✦ *"What would you say are the three most important qualities of the people who work out well in this work environment?"*

✦ *"What do you think is the single most important way in which I may be able to assist you now in reaching the goals you just laid out?"*

✦ *"What is the most expedient way for me to get the information I need from your supervisors before sending an applicant to apply for a position?"*

(14) STRESS THE LOW-RISK NATURE OF YOUR PROPOSAL.

As we discussed in Chapter 2, business people are swimming in waters of risks and rewards (and occasionally sharks)! It is our responsibility to increase employer confidence that using our services does not increase, but actually decreases their hiring risk. We must also reassure them that we are not going to disrupt their present way of doing business. The statements listed below should help to stress the low-risk nature of your proposal:

➼ *"We hope to augment your current hiring process by presenting you with more options, not by replacing what you are already doing."*

➼ *"You apply the same hiring criteria as you would with any other applicant. The advantage of hiring through our program is that you have the seal of approval from a team of employment professionals who have spent time assessing and doing pre-vocational work with the person you're interviewing. Once the person is in your office, however, it is business as usual."*

➼ *"The individuals we work with expect to be held to the same standards as any other employee."*

➼ *"I would be happy to learn how you do things here so my involvement with you will be 'in sync' with your current way of doing business."*

(15) STRESS THE UNIQUENESS OR NOVELTY OF THE PROGRAM, PROPOSAL OR IDEA YOU ARE PRESENTING.

Employers are approached by many people from programs like ours in the course of a year, so it is crucial to tell the employer what will be different about working with you. Here are some examples:

✳ *"With the passing of the American with Disabilities Act, companies are looking for ways to prepare their workforce to integrate persons with disabilities into the workplace. Our program is a perfect first step in that direction, while simultaneously addressing your employment needs."*

✳ *"During difficult economic times nearly all organizations and businesses in our community seek ways to attract additional customers and increase profit-making activities. This employment proposal suggests a way to do both. By hiring someone to deliver your customer's dry cleaning for a fee, you will make money while attracting new business from people who presently use a dry cleaner that doesn't offer such a service."*

(16)   PROJECT THEM INTO THE FUTURE AND CREDIT THE EMPLOYER FOR ACCOMPLISHMENTS ACHIEVED AS A RESULT OF WORKING WITH YOU.

We are more likely to agree to a course of action if we have a clear picture or impression of its benefits. One way to motivate employers to work with you is to project them into the future and credit them for what will be accomplished. Offer an image or a picture of the possibilities and opportunities. Consider the following examples:

➠   *"Once an on-the-job-training contract is developed for this position, you will have created a blueprint for the position for all future trainees."*

➠   *"By hiring older workers you are going to change the community's perception of who a child care worker is and what a day care center has to offer to children. That is no small accomplishment."*

➠   *"Martha is going to make a great receptionist and you are going to be a great teacher and mentor for her. My job is much more gratifying when I know that people with your kind of vision are opening doors for people who are looking for that second chance in life."*

➠   *"By bringing Ron into the department you will successfully transform the perceptions of your staff about the abilities of a person with a mental disability."*

"Kodak sells film, but they don't advertise film. They advertise memories."

Theodore Levitt, American educator

(17)   FOCUS ON THE BENEFITS RATHER THAN THE FEATURES OF YOUR PROGRAM AND SERVICES.

There is a common theme in sales and marketing literature: People do not buy features, they buy benefits.

Think about advertising techniques used on television commercials, magazines and billboards. The advertisers don't tell us what a product is made of, its price value, or how it works. They tell us how we're going to feel about having it. Sexual appeal, glamour, and instant popularity are among the most popular and enduring themes of advertisers today.

For example, when we go to a department store, we don't want to buy clothes; we want to buy a sharp appearance, style and attractiveness. When we buy insurance, we have little concern about the policy, we want peace of mind and security for our families. When we buy a book, we're really buying knowledge, a pleasant way to pass a bus trip or ideas about what to make for dinner. We buy toys to keep our children happy and occupied. We don't buy aspirin, we buy pain relief. We don't buy resume-services to receive a professionally written, attractive resume, we buy an image to convey to prospective employers. We don't want things; we want ideas, feelings, security, pleasure, self-respect, family life and happiness!

Every time you tell an employer about a service you offer, picture the

178

employer asking, "So what? What's in it for me?" Train yourself to speak in terms of employer benefits which include:

☆ Convenience and ease in recruiting candidates pre-screened for their business;

☆ Saving time and money in advertising, interviewing and hiring;

☆ Expanding their resource pool of qualified applicants;

☆ Taking advantage of financial incentives and or on-the-job training funds;

☆ Decreasing the risks of hiring walk-in applicants, thus increasing employee retention;

☆ Taking advantage of a unique employment proposal;

☆ Cutting down on the lag time of having a position unfilled;

☆ Increasing the diversity of present staff while simultaneously taking advantage of support services;

☆ Meeting Affirmative Action or Employment Equity plans;

☆ Building relationships with community programs, thus improving reputation as a community player;

☆ Keeping with the company's mission statement;

☆ Enjoying personal, emotional reward of giving someone a chance;

☆ Affirming personal affiliation with the target population; or,

☆ Increasing hiring options.

"People don't buy goods, they buy solutions to problems. They don't buy quarter-inch bits, they buy quarter-inch holes."

A popular marketing axiom

(18) COMMUNICATE YOUR IDEAS IN A WAY THAT SUITS THE STYLE OF THE EMPLOYER.

Have you observed these differences among employers?

⇒ Some are willing to talk to you all day, while others barely give you five minutes to state your case;

⇒ Some want to get right down to business, while others are insulted if you don't make the effort to establish rapport;

⇒ Some want to understand every aspect of what you do, while others want you to cut to the chase and paint the big picture; and,

⇒ Some want to hear the true personal accounts of individuals you've served, while others would have you escorted off the premises if you wasted their time with "fairy tales."

If these differences ring true from your experience with employers, welcome to the world of style differences!

Much has been written about the four basic "styles" of human interaction. The perspective I am going to share with you in this section is based on work initiated by Carl Jung in 1923 and amplified by psychologists and sociologists since that time (including Myers and Briggs). I doubt that the four styles will be new to you, since they have had many incarnations, in our field alone. You may be familiar with the terms value orientations, personality types, communication modes or management styles. The applications and the translations of these four styles are virtually endless.

It is wise to pay attention to differences in communication style because these differences affect both the process and content of our interactions with other people. Miscommunication can easily occur if two people are interacting in different styles. We benefit as job developers when we adapt our presentations to the style of each employer. This adaptation increases understanding and facilitates genuine communication.

Each of the four styles is summarized below and accompanied by recommendations for communicating with employers who use each style. You may recognize many of the recommendations from the guidelines presented earlier in this chapter. Observe that for certain styles I have intentionally omitted some of the guidelines. That is so because not all methods of communication are effectively applied to the different communication styles. As you read this, see if you recognize your style and the styles of others you know.

RESPONDING TO FOUR EMPLOYER STYLES

THE ACTION-ORIENTED EMPLOYER

The primary concerns of action-oriented employers are goals and objectives, results, effectiveness and productivity. Their main question is "What is happening at this moment?" Action-oriented employers believe facts speak for themselves and they look for evidence and proof from the past to predict the present and immediate future. They are perceived as driven, energetic, hard-working, down-to-earth, and decisive.

Recommendations for communicating your ideas to an action-oriented individual include:

◆ State your conclusion at the onset.

◆ Be brief, to the point and well organized.

◆ State your best recommendation. (These are not the people who want to hear all the alternatives!)

◆ Emphasize the practicality of your ideas.

◆ Focus on "the bottom line(s)!"

◆ Be prepared to use statistics, data and other facts to support your proposal. (Know your stuff!)

◆ Stick to the facts and don't get philosophical unless you're invited to.

◆ Be results-oriented. Once mutual benefit and interest have been established, ask for a commitment with set timelines. These individuals respect and appreciate your need to clarify how goals and objectives set forth in the meeting will be accomplished.

THE PROCESS-ORIENTED EMPLOYER

The primary concerns of the process-oriented employer are policies and procedures, systems, planning, controlling and testing, research, scientific observations and quantitative analysis. Process-oriented employers value consistency and efficiency. Their main question is, "How are we doing what we're doing?" They believe logic leads to the right conclusion(s). They are perceived as organized, analytic, cautious, unemotional and systematic in their work.

Recommendations for communicating your ideas to a process-oriented manager include:

◆ Be willing to take your time to be thorough and detailed in your description of the program and services.

◆ Talk not only about what you do, but how you do it.

◆ Have relevant documentation available (e.g., resumes or applications of applicants, program descriptions, course curricula).

◆ Organize your presentation logically. One example of the order you might follow is:

> Background of the program
> Objectives of the program
> The reason(s) you contacted the employer
> Options for working together
> Decision on how to proceed

◆ Be logical and systematic when presenting the benefits of the program.

◆ Stress the low-risk nature of your proposal.

◆ For each alternative, offer facts as proof (cause and effect) and rationale.

◆ Allow time for these employers to think things through; don't try to rush a decision. They will appreciate your respect for their need to proceed slowly.

THE PEOPLE-ORIENTED EMPLOYER

The primary concerns of the people-oriented employer are communication, cooperation, feelings, values, beliefs and teamwork as well as harmony, awareness and sensitivity to other people's needs. People-oriented employers focus on "How do we feel about what is going on here?" They believe anything can be negotiated with compromise and understanding. They are perceived as empathetic, warm, perceptive, sensitive, spontaneous and emotionally invested in their work.

Recommendations for communicating your ideas to someone who is people-oriented include:

◆ Establish rapport by taking the time to relate to the person in a friendly manner before "getting down to business." Allow for small talk. (Not hard for most job developers to do!)

◆ Show interest in what the employer is saying and appeal to his or her feelings and beliefs.

◆ Identify the individual's values and adjust to them accordingly.

◆ Stress the relationship of your proposal to the people involved. (Do not assume that a people-oriented person is automatically going to be open to your program. This orientation is frequently associated with a highly protective attitude toward staff, customers, clients, patients, or other stakeholders. They may be less willing to hire people from "high-risk populations.")

◆ Be ready to describe success stories about individuals who have gone through your program. Give examples of people from your program who were a "good fit" and exceeded employer expectations in performance and productivity.

◆ Often, people-oriented managers observe and express, "You must find your job very rewarding." Invite them to share this feeling of satisfaction by working with and contributing to the success of your program.

THE IDEA-ORIENTED EMPLOYER

Idea-oriented employers are enthusiastic about innovation, change, and new possibilities. Interested in concepts, issues and principles, they like to examine a variety of options and alternatives before arriving at a decision. They ask, "How can we improve what we're already doing?." They believe imagination and flexibility can solve any problem. (A concept after my own heart!) Perceived as very creative, imaginative, charismatic, enthusiastic and provocative, they are risk-takers.

Communicating with an idea-oriented employer is easier when you:

◆ Present the "big picture" and focus on the situation as a whole. Don't get bogged down in too many details or facts. Tell them "why" the program exists.

◆ Stress the uniqueness or novelty of the program, proposal or idea you are presenting.

◆ Project them into the future and give them credit for what will be accomplished by working with you.

◆ Take your cues from these employers. Observe and build upon their reactions. Use their responses to decide which benefits to highlight.

◆ Tap into the imagination and creativity of idea-oriented people. For example:

"I would love your ideas about how we could further tailor our pre-employment workshops to prepare the trainees for the needs of your particular business."

"We are free to structure this partnership any way we want. Let's brainstorm possible options for working together."

IMPORTANT THINGS TO REMEMBER ABOUT RESPONDING TO DIFFERENT COMMUNICATION STYLES:

★ These ideas about effective modes of communication are based on generalizations. We must remain open to the endless variations in styles among employers. It is a safe bet that each person you meet will present an absolutely unique variation of his or her dominant style!

★ Most of the people in our field are people-oriented, which partially explains how we ended up in this field. People-oriented presentations are appropriate for a very limited employer audience. The extent to which you can be flexible when you present ideas, increases the likelihood you will successfully communicate with employers of all types.

★ The purpose of paying attention to communication styles is simply to increase your ability to effectively communicate your ideas in a variety of ways in order to respond to style differences.

★ While we all use all four styles, nearly everyone has a dominant orientation or style which is most comfortable.

★ No one style is better than any other, although the use of one style may be more effective than another depending on the situation.

★ We all have the capacity to switch from one style to another.

★ Knowledge of an individual's general "style" doesn't always explain or offer insight into behavior, values and/or motives.

★ If, during a meeting, a person's style is not evident from their words and actions, listen to their questions and concerns to gain insight into their interests.

★ For additional insight about employers' interests, concerns and styles, pose the questions, "Tell me about your business?" and "How do you differ from your competitors?" Listen closely to the responses.

★ When you meet with more than one person, each may have a different style. In this case simply address the main concerns of all four styles in your opening statements and then allow questions and reactions to direct the discussion.

APPLICATION: FINE-TUNING YOUR PRESENTATION

Consider your typical presentation to employers and how you might incorporate the following guidelines in your style:

(1) KNOW YOUR STUFF.

What additional information do you need to speak intelligently and confidently about the program, services and people you represent?

(2) OFFER THE EMPLOYER RELEVANT MATERIALS AND DOCUMENTATION.

What additional materials or documentation could you make available or distribute to support and reinforce your presentation to employers?

(3) TELL EMPLOYERS WHAT YOU ARE GOING TO TALK ABOUT IN THE MEETING. ADDRESS THE BASICS, THEN LET EMPLOYER QUESTIONS AND RESPONSES GUIDE YOUR PRESENTATION.

Give a one or two sentence synopsis of what you cover in presentations to employers.

(4) STATE YOUR INTERESTS UP FRONT.

Come up with at least four opening statements to describe what you want to accomplish from your meeting with the employer.

(5) AIM HIGH, THINK BIG AND ASK FOR WHAT YOU WANT.

Draft a list of agreements you would like to arrive at with employers. Review your list and circle those which best express what you want to achieve with employers.

(6) FIND COMMON GROUND.

Think about the last four relationships you developed with employers. Identify the common ground you had with each.

(7) BUILD ON EMPLOYERS' IDEAS.

When have you used an employer's ideas as a springboard for your own?

(8) SPEAK THE EMPLOYER'S LANGUAGE.

Draft a list of the words, terms and concepts commonly used in your office. Identify which may be unfamiliar or confusing to a person with little or no exposure to comparable programs. Try to replace jargon or technical terms with simple, commonly used language. Be prepared to define terms and explain acronyms.

(9) USE VALUING LANGUAGE TO DESCRIBE THE PEOPLE YOU SERVE.

Draft a list of the words you commonly use to refer to the people you serve or with whom you have regular contact and consider if you are using terms that respect and value those individuals.

(10) PRESENT THE ATTRIBUTES OF INDIVIDUALS RATHER THAN POSITIVE STEREOTYPES OF THE GROUP.

Look over your marketing materials and consider how you usually describe your applicants. If you find positive stereotypes in written materials or oral presentations, consider how to attribute the same positive characteristics to an individual, rather than the group.

(11) EMPHASIZE THE PRACTICALITY OF YOUR IDEAS.

For each service you offer employers, come up with a logical and systematic way of describing its practical benefits.

(12) KEEP YOUR EXPLANATIONS AND DESCRIPTIONS SIMPLE.

Imagine you only have six minutes to communicate your message to employers. What would you say?

Given two and a half minutes to communicate your message, what would you say?

With just one minute to communicate your message to employers, what would you say?

(13) HELP EMPLOYERS TO DISTILL THEIR COMMUNICATIONS TO INCLUDE ONLY THE ESSENTIAL ISSUES AND CONSIDERATIONS.

Write five questions to ask employers to assist them to identify their most basic needs.

(14) STRESS THE LOW-RISK NATURE OF YOUR PROPOSAL.

Write four statements which clearly communicate the low-risk nature of your services.

(15) STRESS THE UNIQUENESS OR NOVELTY OF THE PROGRAM, PROPOSAL OR IDEA YOU ARE PRESENTING.

Identify at least three novel aspects of working with you, your program or your applicants which benefit employers.

(16) PROJECT EMPLOYERS INTO THE FUTURE AND CREDIT THEM WITH WHAT WILL BE ACCOMPLISHED BY WORKING WITH YOUR PROGRAM.

Come up with four relevant examples of employers who have been praised and rewarded for the achievements of your program and applicants.

(17) FOCUS ON THE BENEFITS, NOT THE FEATURES, OF WORKING WITH YOUR PROGRAM AND OFFERED SERVICES.

List all the features of your program. For each, identify at least three employer benefits.

(18) COMMUNICATE YOUR IDEAS IN A WAY THAT SUITS THE STYLE OF THE EMPLOYER.

Practice speaking to employers with varying communication styles. Review the guidelines for each style.

CHAPTER 10:
RESOLVING EMPLOYER CONCERNS

E tched in the door of a public bathroom, I recently read, "People are lonely because they build walls instead of bridges." Those very walls may account for much of the loneliness and isolation preventing entire groups of people from participating in their communities. In our field we are fortunate to be in positions which enable us, piece by piece, to take down walls built of fear, apathy, and ignorance. We can build bridges of understanding and acceptance. Resolving employer concerns affords us an opportunity to realize this important purpose.

Richard Pimentel once described the role of the job developer as "the bridge between people who are ready, willing and able to work and employers who don't believe it." Nowhere is his description more fitting than in the discussion of resolving employer concerns. Before examining the purpose and substance of the bridge, let's look at the nature of the gulf separating our applicants from potential employers.

On one side of the bridge we have individuals seeking employment, many of whom are anxious about and eager to work. Their capabilities and potential have been assessed and targeted. Most of these individuals are also characterized by past or present situations or conditions which may color others' ideas about who they are and what they should or shouldn't do for a living. Unfortunately, too few of these people have the ability to communicate their strengths and proactively resolve employer concerns about their limitations and/or circumstances.

On the other side of the bridge are employers with many questions about the value and the risk of hiring from the job applicant side of the bridge. Many are hesitant to voice their concerns. Some worry about the legal liability of what they may and may not ask, others do not want to risk appearing ignorant or prejudiced. Some employer concerns are substantiated in reality while others are based on misconceptions or stereotypes about the target group. Regardless of the roots of the concern, every unresolved question in an employer's mind has the power to prevent the drawbridge of opportunity from lowering to permit passage to the other side.

What do we as employment specialists use to craft this bridge? How do we encourage and motivate individuals on both sides to walk across it and meet on common ground? How do we help people to realize that much of what separates them from others can be easily overcome with simple understanding and insight?

This chapter contains suggestions for dealing with these pressing questions. It is about using discernment, understanding, patience, gentle reeducation, information, insight, experience, and perspective as tools to address and resolve employer concerns. We will look at general guidelines for resolving employer concerns, specific strategies for dealing with stereotypes, ways to facilitate attitudinal change and responses to twenty-five of the most common employer concerns about hiring people from our programs.

"We are not troubled by people or things, but by the opinions which we hold of them."

Epictetus

191

BUILDING THE BRIDGE: SEVEN GROUNDRULES

(1) RESPOND PROFESSIONALLY RATHER THAN REACTING PERSONALLY.

Have you ever felt angry, frustrated, hurt, misunderstood or even exasperated when an employer voiced objections to using your services or hiring your applicants? If so, you may have been tempted to react personally to an employer's concern, and you are certainly not alone.

In physics class we learned that "for every action, there is an equal and opposite reaction." Newton's law, however, applies to objects, not people. Objects react. People can choose not to react. We know that reacting personally to an employer's concern, even if we win the battle at hand, doesn't bring us any closer to winning the war. When we deal with employer concerns our objective is not to win, but to agree.

Responding professionally rather than personally is easier said than done. The recommendations below will assist you to respond professionally.

(2) LISTEN FOR THE UNDERLYING ISSUES AND CONCERNS VOICED IN THE OBJECTION.

Employer objections are rarely intended to offend you, your program or applicant group. Most employers expressing concerns are not really objecting to anything. They are requesting information, and their questions are disguised in a response that sounds like an objection.

Reframe the stated objection into a question for problem-solving. While every message is subject to interpretation, you have the power of positive perception — the ability to put a problem-solving frame around employer responses, concerns and objections. The first rule of thumb is:

Listen for the question hidden in the objection.

For example, when an employer says, "I don't want drug addicts working for me!" you can take this statement to mean the employer believes everyone receiving your services is addicted to drugs, or you can interpret it as the question, "Do the people you serve have problems with drugs?" The first interpretation might be an insult, the other is simply a question.

As another example, one possible interpretation of the statement, "I'm not interested in working with people who have mental disabilities because I can't afford to baby-sit my employees" is that people with mental disabilities need to be treated like children. Another interpretation of this statement is the employer inquiring, "Can people with developmental disabilities work independently?"

(3) SEPARATE THE EMPLOYER'S CONCERN FROM HIS OR HER BELIEF.

Employer objections are responses to both their concerns and their beliefs. Employer concerns must always be treated seriously and respectfully, they are a valid reflection of the risk inherent in the hiring process. Beliefs, on the other hand, may be based on stereotypes or may indicate the employer's need for additional information or insight. The second rule of thumb is:

Speak to the employer's concern before attempting to change the belief.

In order to address an employer's concern, you must be able to identify it. Take the following examples:

Employer: *"I don't care to work with migrant farmworkers because we look for permanent employees in our business."*

Concern:	**Belief:**
Employee longevity, return on the investment of training new employees	People with a history of migrant farmwork are only interested in seasonal work

Employer: *"We would hire from your training program except that we would rather train our employees our own way."*

Concern:	**Belief:**
Trainees will not learn as well as people who have not received training. Productivity will suffer and more training and supervision will be required.	People with vocational training are less flexible in how they work and how they can be trained in a specific work environment.

"The greatest challenge of the day is to bring a revolution of the heart which has to start with a revolution of our beliefs."

Margaret Mead, anthropologist

"Live the revolution now."

Credo of Quaker Movement for a New Society

(4) ACKNOWLEDGE THE EMPLOYER'S CONCERN AND BUILD A BRIDGE CONNECTING THEIR CONCERNS WITH WHAT YOU HAVE TO OFFER.

Remember, the feeling of being right is not as important as making the other person feel that they are understood.

Earlier in this chapter, I stated that the goal of dealing with employer objections is not to win, but to agree. It is critically important to let employers know you share both their goals and concerns. You are not there to compromise what they want; you are there to support their goals and interests. When an employer expresses a concern, we must immediately acknowledge that we have heard it and are willing to address it.

To acknowledge employer concerns, we simply step to their side. Identify the concern you hear in the employer's statement, comment on it, and validate its importance. What you are doing, in effect, is communicating to the employer that you are a partner in dealing with this concern.

Take the following examples:

Employer: *"I don't want to deal with people who are used to living off the system and don't really want to work."*

Job Developer: *"I am with you. You need employees who want to make a real commitment to your workplace. I look for the same thing in my applicants that you look for in your employees."*

– or –

Employer: *"Times are tough enough as it is without having to take on a disabled employee who presents all kinds of special needs."*

Job Developer: *"Thank you for raising this important issue. Many people are under the impression that people with disabilities cost businesses more than they produce. Your profitability as a business is the key issue here. If what an applicant has to offer does not add to your profitability, but instead detracts from it, we will agree that hiring the person is not a good idea."*

"You may be surprised, however, by how little an employee's disability affects his or her work. As with all employees, people with disabilities choose their vocations based on their capabilities and interest in doing the job. They base career decisions on their strengths, not their limitations. If I present you with someone who is not capable of performing the job to your standards, with or without a reasonable accommodation, I have not done my job properly."

"The world of tomorrow can be tamed either through outside force or by the communion of shared values and recognition of common ground."

Ali Mazrui, African researcher of world order

As practitioners of Japanese martial arts have long recognized, it is hard to attack someone who is suddenly on your side. It is impossible to argue with someone who has just told you that he or she is a partner who wishes to help resolve your concern. The employer quickly understands that there is no one with whom to argue. You lessen the employer's feelings of risk by doing exactly the opposite of what is expected. Employers expect you to resist, disagree or argue, or at least to apply pressure. Instead, you end up side by side — just where you want to be in order to engage in problem-solving.

Notice that acknowledging employers' concerns does not mean you agree with their underlying beliefs. In the preceding example, the acknowledgment that the desire to work is an important quality in an employee did not mean the job developer agreed that people who have received public assistance do not have a desire to work. Before you can address employers' underlying beliefs, they need to know their issues and concerns have been heard.

It is also important to note that by acknowledging the validity of what the employer has to say, his or her objection begins to lose its emotional charge. You create psychological room for the employer to accept that there may be another side to the story or another point of view. It is at this point that you can begin to deal with deep-seated beliefs and concerns.

(5) ENCOURAGE THE EMPLOYER TO RECONSIDER HIS OR HER BELIEFS BY PRESENTING NEW INFORMATION OR INSIGHT.

After identifying and acknowledging the employer's concern, we can work to change the thinking that created the belief. This does not mean imposing your view. It is an opportunity to present ideas in a way that employers can readily approach, it encourages them to accept your view on their own terms. Rather than attempting to pound in a new idea from the outside, encourage them to reach for it from within. Rather than telling them how to think, let them figure it out for themselves using the new information or insight you bring to the situation. In other words, rather than pressuring employers to change their minds, create an environment in which they are able to view the situation from a new perspective.

"It is no use walking anywhere to preach unless our walking is our preaching."

St. Francis of Assisi

To accomplish this goal, you need to suspend your reaction when you feel like striking back, to listen when you feel like talking, to ask questions when you want to provide answers, to bridge your differences instead of pushing for your way, and to educate when you feel like attacking.

Dealing with employer stereotypes and negative beliefs about hiring from specific target groups is not simply about getting employers to agree to something they wouldn't normally agree to, it is about facilitating attitudinal change. I have found the single most powerful tool or strategy for promoting attitudinal change is exposure to real people from the target group. Meeting, speaking with, or simply observing real people from the target group is not only enlightening but also very healing.

In the face of a lack of information, people usually imagine the worst case. So if you say "ex-offender," most people will imagine a serial killer before they will imagine someone involved in tax fraud. The more information we share, and the more exposure we give employers to members of the target group we serve, the better our chances for facilitating a lasting understanding of the real issues faced by the target group.

Here are some suggestions for creating opportunities to offer employers exposure to your applicants:

◆ Ask applicants to accompany you on employer visits;

◆ Have applicants deliver their own employment proposals, resumes or applications;

◆ Arrange a company tour for your applicants;

◆ Invite employers to sit in on classes or workshops or to participate in other program events;

◆ Forward copies of relevant articles or newspaper clippings which highlight the accomplishments of people from the target group;

◆ Include photographs of applicants on marketing materials;

◆ Make a videotape of individuals from the target population working in real jobs available for employer viewing.

(6) WHEN THE EMPLOYER HOLDS AN OPPOSING VIEW WHICH IS NOT ALTERED IN LIGHT OF NEW INFORMATION, PRESENT YOUR VIEWS AS AN ADDITION TO, RATHER THAN A DIRECT CONTRADICTION OF, THE EMPLOYER'S POINT OF VIEW.

Have you ever noticed that the standard mind set about conflicting viewpoints is "an either/or paradigm": either you are right or the other person is right? The alternative mind set, and a far more effective one, is a "both/and paradigm." The other person can be right in terms of his or her experience, and you can be right in terms of yours. You can acknowledge his or her view and, without challenging it, express a contrary one.

Here are four approaches for creating an inclusive atmosphere in which differences can coexist peacefully while you find the common ground which forms the basis for working together:

➤ **Frame even a direct disagreement inclusively with a statement such as:**

✦ *"I can see why you feel strongly about this, and I respect your opinion. Let me tell you, however, how it looks from my angle."*

✦ *"I am in total agreement with what you are trying to accomplish. What you may not have considered is..."*

✦ *"I can see why you feel the way you do. It's entirely reasonable in terms of the experience you have had. My experience, however, has been different."*

➤ **Ask problem-solving questions.**

Ask problem-solving questions to focus on common interests rather than concentrating on the issue of difference. Instead of giving the employer what you consider to be the right answer, ask the right questions. Let the problem be the teacher. For example, if an employer complains that the expense of employment programs is on taxpayers' shoulders, respond with a question like:

"While the program requires an investment of taxpayers' money, how else would you suggest we lessen the burden of taxpayers who bear the costs of increased public assistance, unemployment, and disability payments? Services like these work to increase employer profits as well as stretching the taxpayers' dollar."

➤ **Turn the conversation into a brainstorming session.**

Take the employer's position and reframe it as one of several possible options. Then add,

"Let's put all the other options on the table. What haven't we considered?"

➤ **Ask employers for their advice to engage them in a discussion of options.**

Communicate not only your interest in what they have to say but also your respect for their viewpoints with statements such as:

✦ *"What would you suggest I do?"*

✦ *"I understand your dilemma. Is anyone able to grant an exception?"*

✦ *"Whom do you suggest I contact in the union?"*

✦ *"You know this industry so much better than I. How would you advise our program to overcome the barriers you have mentioned?"*

✦ *"What recommendations would you give a person wishing to enter this field?"*

Frequently, when you ask people for their advice, they end up adopting the very viewpoint you have been promoting all along.

(7) DO NOT END A CONVERSATION WITH AN EMPLOYER WITHOUT MAKING OPPORTUNITY FOR ALL OF THEIR CONCERNS TO SURFACE.

The most common way employers with unresolved concerns end meetings with job developers is to smile and say, "Well, your program sounds very interesting. If I ever need your services, I will give you a call. Thank you for coming." In general, you never hear from them again!

Just because employers do not voice any concerns, it doesn't mean they don't have them. Here are some ideas for creating an environment in which employers feel free to express their concerns:

FOUR WAYS TO UNCOVER EMPLOYER CONCERNS

➤ **Most employer concerns are predictable.** Be prepared to raise concerns which have not come up in the meeting with statements like:

✦ *"Some employers have questions regarding job accommodation, health and safety risks, and the social integration of employees with disabilities into the workplace. Do you have concerns in any of these areas?"*

✦ *"I don't know if you have had any experience working with a program serving workers in transition, but let me address a few issues that seem to be of universal concern to employers..."*

✦ *"I imagine you have a number of things going through your mind as you think about hiring people who have spent time in prison. I would like to ease your mind a bit with a few statistics that speak to some of those concerns..." (give placement, retention and recidivism rates).*

> ➤ **If the employer is not forthcoming with his or her true interests and concerns, communicate what you suspect the concerns might be, and ask him or her to correct you. For example,**

"Nothing in life is to be feared. It is only to be understood."

Marie Curie, French chemist

✦ *"I have a feeling you're not fully comfortable with the idea of having a job coach on site. Is that true?"*

✦ *"Am I correct in assuming you would just as soon not have to deal with a work experience volunteer, but would prefer to hire the person outright?"*

✦ *"Sam's past work record has you feeling a little less than enthusiastic about hiring him, doesn't it?"*

This is a great strategy because it encourages people to voice their own concerns, and few people can resist the temptation to correct a misunderstanding of their thoughts or feelings.

> ➤ **Once you have addressed concerns that have surfaced, invite the employer to voice any additional concerns by asking, "Can you think of any other reason why we should not begin working together?"**

> ➤ **Using the conditional tense, project the employer into a future where his or her concerns have been resolved and ask for agreement.**

Imagine that the employer states:

"People say they want to work but they end up coming in late every day or quitting altogether";

"I am under tremendous pressure to operate at optimum speed at all times";

"I have had bad luck with agencies like yours. When I need people, they don't follow through. When I don't need people, they won't leave me alone."

You can respond by saying:

"As I understand it, if you were to use any agency again, you would need a service that could (1) prescreen and refer only those applicants who are going to be here when the work day begins and are committed to keeping their jobs, (2) provide you with applicants who are either experienced or could learn quickly enough to be able to make you an immediate profit, and (3) respond quickly when you have employment needs and leave you alone when you do not. Am I correct in my assessment?"

Once you have agreed about their needs or concerns, you can speak to each with a separate plan of action.

In the next section we will look at eight ways to resolve employer concerns and responses to the 25 most frequent employer concerns. Naturally, everyone must develop a style well suited to his or her own personality and unique way of relating to other people. As you read these sections, I recommend you note the responses that appeal to you most, as well as those with the least appeal. Observe the common elements or patterns of the responses and strategies best suited to your style.

CROSSING THE RIVER: EIGHT STRATEGIES

✶ THE FEEL/FELT/FOUND METHOD

This is a very effective approach to resolving employer concerns because it communicates that you are attuned to the concern, have dealt with it before, and can draw on the experiences of other employers to address the concern.

For example, you may respond to an employer's concern by saying,

"I know how you feel because I have worked with many employers who have felt the same way. Let me tell you what they found once they hired from our program..."

✶ TURNING THE EMPLOYER'S STATEMENT INTO A QUESTION

If an employer says "Your people are not qualified enough to work here," you can convert the statement into the question, "Exactly what qualifications are you looking for?" A statement such as "The people you work with don't speak good enough English," can be converted into the question, "What level of English proficiency is needed enough for this position?"

By converting an objection into a question, you are focusing the attention of the conversation back to your common interests and goals — addressing the real needs of the employer. Speaking directly to these needs will help to lessen the employer's fears.

✶ THE BOOMERANG TECHNIQUE

Think of a boomerang and what it does. Once thrown, it makes a wide arc and then immediately comes back to the person who threw it. You can boomerang an employer's concern. For example,

> *"A gentle hand may lead even an elephant by a hair."*
>
> *Iranian saying*

Employer: *"With all of the applicants who have responded to our ad in the paper, I'm just too busy to work with your program right now."*

Job Developer: *"That is probably one of the biggest reasons you should be using our service. The fact that you have so many applicants for the same job means you could benefit from a program like ours to save you the time spent screening through applications, checking references, setting up interviews, interviewing and then responding to all of the people you aren't going to hire! I agree that I should not add to your long line of applicants at this time, but I recommend that we set up a system for working together so that when your next hiring need arises, you will not find yourself in this situation."*

✯ CHANGING THE EMPLOYER'S FOCUS

Take the basis upon which the employer is founding a response and change it so that he or she can see things in a different light. Sometimes employers have to be reminded of the benefits of the program as they consider its inherent risks and/or disadvantages.

Employer: *"Having to deal with an on-the-job training contract is not the most convenient way of bringing people on board."*

Job Developer: *"You're right. However, the purpose of an OJT is to finance some of your training costs involved with bringing a new employee on board. For many employers the economic benefit far outweighs the inconvenience of having to use our forms to chart the employee's performance or to invoice us for payment."*

✯ THE "HERE'S-WHY-IT'S-WORTH-IT" RESPONSE

Sometimes a concern is not based on a belief, but on a real shortcoming or inconvenience that must be acknowledged. When this is true, do not deny the disadvantage, instead help the employer to weigh the disadvantage against the benefits. For example,

Employer: *"I would have to accommodate this person."*

Job Developer: *"You're right, and the accommodation we're looking at could cost upwards of $2000. We will work to secure financial assistance for you from a community based program, but this aid will not cover the entire cost of the accommodation. Despite the initial cost, I feel confident that you will find it a very beneficial investment. Recently an employer made the analogy that her investment in an accommodation for an employee with a disability was every bit as worthwhile as the more costly expenses associated with relocating employees from one city to another in order to make more or better use of their skills."*

★ ANSWERING THE QUESTION ASKED

Employer: *"I'm sorry, but I just cannot believe it is possible to effectively teach someone to be an auto-mechanic in a classroom!"*

Employment Specialist: *"Thank you for that opening. It gives me the opportunity to explain how we effectively train people to be auto-mechanics in our environment. Here is a copy of the course curriculum...these are the qualifications of the instructor...here are the performance standards trainees must meet before they can be certified by the school..."*

★ USING THE EMPLOYER'S OBJECTION AS AN INVITATION
    TO PROMOTE AN ASPECT OF YOUR SERVICE

This is my personal favorite of all of the responses and you will recognize variations of it throughout the chapter. Basically, rather than rejecting or arguing the employer's position, you use the objection as an opportunity to talk about how you handle the problem or resolve the concern. View the objection or statement as an invitation to highlight a specific aspect of your services or program, your personal style or abilities or even the attributes of a particular applicant.

For example, if the employer expresses concern about the credibility of your training program, you may respond by saying,

"Thank you for bringing that up. I was hoping to have the opportunity to sing our praises. Let me tell you about our track record..."

★ PRESENTING THE POSITIVE ATTRIBUTES OF AN INDIVIDUAL
    IN ORDER TO BUILD CONFIDENCE IN THE TARGET GROUP

While it may be nearly impossible to change the employer's present mind set about the target group, it is possible to instill employer confidence about the skills, abilities and personal characteristics of one member of the group. This is an example of moving from the general to the specific.

For example, *"While it is a commonly held belief that a person whose work experience has been limited to migrant farm work will resist working in a highly structured environment, let me tell you about our experience with Juan. He has demonstrated such a talent for and interest in working on computers that he is putting in extra hours in the lab after classes. What is hard for me to imagine is that Juan survived for so long in such an unstructured environment!"*

RESPONSES TO TWENTY-FIVE EMPLOYER CONCERNS

In job development workshops over the past ten years I have asked participants to write down the most common objections and concerns voiced by employers. The twenty-five concerns listed here represent those mentioned most frequently. Using a combination of the strategies and techniques discussed previously, here are responses to each objection.

(1) Why should I hire people who have barriers to employment when there are so many people looking for work who do not have those barriers?

"The impetus for using our services is not to give people with barriers a break, but rather, to take advantage of a resource pool of qualified applicants who have been pre-screened for your workplace. You want employees who add to the well-being of your business, not detract from it. With that in mind, I operate on the universal hiring rule which says if I cannot show you how a person will bring you more profit than cost when you employ them, I am not going to suggest you even consider employing the person.

While it is true that many of the people I see are dealing with some very difficult life situations, I have to be convinced that these circumstances will not interfere with their ability to be valuable employees before I recommend them as potential employees."

(2) Your people are over-qualified. I would rather not hire people who have worked for a higher wage than we are offering.

"Clearly you want to hire employees who intend to stay with you and aren't sitting on the edge of their seats waiting for a higher-paying opportunity. I share this concern.

When it is obvious to me that someone is over-qualified for a given position, they need to sell me on the idea that the position holds enough opportunity for them to make a long-term commitment to the job or I will not refer them to that business. Like you, I am interested in permanent employment, not make-shift or interim employment situations.

I have found that people are motivated in different ways and by a wide range of factors other than money when it comes to making employment decisions. I've witnessed people taking a significant cut in pay in order to work in a specific environment, use a particular skill or simply be part of a cause that means a lot to them. Frankly, I think it would make me a little nervous as an employer if someone was interested in taking a job simply because of the pay. I would want to know that other characteristics of the position were important to the applicant."

(3) We would rather not work with a government agency.

"Let me explain that while we are funded in part by the government, we are not actually a government program. I work with a community college (or a community based organization). This is similar to a business which works with government monies under a defense or construction contract, but is not a government entity.

Some businesses fear that because we receive government funding there will be too much red tape or paperwork. I admit that from my end of it, we have our share of both. Fortunately for you, however, my job is to prevent the red tape from ever appearing on your end while still providing the benefits of a government funded project such as wage subsidies or pre-trained applicants."

(4) We like to hire people who have more experience and qualifications.

"I am sure you do because experience and education can be good reflections of skill and ability. In tough times like these you don't want to have to worry about hiring people who are not going to be productive from the get-go.

Past work experience, of course, is not the only predictor of productivity and potential. Other things we look at which reflect the qualities of a valuable employee are volunteer and training experience, community and family involvement, and projects at home. We're looking for the skills and qualities a business like yours requires of its employees — perseverance, people skills, and problem-solving abilities.

Once I have a good handle on the characteristics and abilities of the people who work out best in this business, these will be prerequisites for the people I send to you. I want you to rest assured that I am as concerned as you that we place people in the job who are fully capable of meeting your performance standards. The only guarantee I can make is: If I do not find the person who is qualified to meet your work standards, I promise not to send anyone at all."

Note: Employers respond extremely well to this last statement. It helps to alleviate their fear that if they offer to work with you, your primary concern will be to place someone in their business, rather than working to see whether you have the right person for their business. At this point, steer the conversation toward standards rather than qualifications.

(5) How can you expect me to hire someone who is homeless? Isn't that like putting the horse before the cart?

"I know what you mean, it would be nice if permanent housing was a reality for everyone before the need for work. Unfortunately this is not the case. It is important for you to know that anyone who is working with me has temporary shelter and is capable of maintaining a normal work life. Our applicants also have access to bathing facilities, a telephone, and are not in want of food or immediate medical services.

Securing permanent housing is a primary concern. There are many people in our community who are homeless and are not able to work given their immediate circumstances. Perhaps they need medical attention or other services before employment is even a consideration. The majority of people I work with are further down the road, and prepared to assume job responsibilities.

Do you have other concerns about this situation that I can address at this time?"

Note: Depending on the situation, you might add the following observation:

"It is amazing how few steps most of us are away from the kind of economic situation that precipitates the need for temporary shelter. Take Paula, for example. She is twenty-four and has a child. She lost her job due to a company layoff more than two years ago, and has had a difficult time making a go of it with her three year old child. She is a classic example of someone who had serious economic problems and no personal network of people to see her through them. Her situation is different now.

Paula has done a great job of making contact with agencies and programs to provide her with the resources she needs to get back on her feet. She has spent the last three months in a temporary shelter and hopes to rent a room in a house downtown. With the money she would earn on this job, she could afford the first and last month's rent within four weeks."

(6) **We're not interested in hiring people who have drug or alcohol problems.**

"I'm glad that you brought that up because it is a concern of ours as well. In fact, it's the reason our program exists. Clearly, if a person has an active substance abuse problem, this person is not considered employable until the problem is under control. Once in a while we do see people in this situation and we deal with it directly or refer the individual to agencies better able to help.

You have, indirectly, identified one of the advantages of working with a program like ours. It is virtually impossible to know the nature or extent of the problems of an applicant walking through your door. With the people who come through our program, there is the assurance that they have confronted and are actively overcoming any problems with chemical dependency. In addition, our program receives recommendations from professionals trained in addiction treatment and recovery."

(Note: The point made in the last paragraph — that your program identifies and oversees professional resolution of problems — is an important one when responding to almost any employer objection about the target population.)

(7) **I don't want to hire people who speak limited English.**

"Clearly you do not want to have problems communicating with your employees nor do you want to have to put them in positions where their

limited English presents a problem. For this reason it is vitally important that I understand the exact language and communication needs of your employees.

If I could take a few minutes with you (or the prospective supervisor), I would like to draft an inventory of the words employees in various positions need to speak, understand, read and/or write. This list will become my language test. Anyone interested in working for you would have to pass this test before they could apply to work at your business.

My experience with other businesses with similar concerns is that the communication needs of their workplaces were simpler than suspected. I must also add that most applicants who speak limited English are pursuing English classes outside work. Language acquisition is an ongoing and typically fast-paced process."

(8) People with disabilities (or industrial injuries) present too much of a health risk. Aren't my insurance rates going to go up?

"Thank you for raising this issue. One of the most common myths about hiring people with disabilities (or industrial injuries) is that they present a greater health and safety risk and take more medical leave than employees who do not have disabilities. It is such an important question that studies have been conducted to determine if there is an added risk, and the extent of the additional risk.

The most famous study was carried out by the DuPont Corporation in 1981. It compared the health and safety records of 1000 employees with disabilities with the health and safety records of employees without disabilities. Their findings showed that people with disabilities incurred one percent less of a health and safety risk than those without disabilities!

Insurance rates do not automatically increase when a business hires someone with a disability or an industrial injury. Most insurance policies are actuarial — rates go up according to the actual number of accidents incurred or health risks of employees of the particular business and are not related to the perception of potential risk."

(9) I don't want to have to worry about the reinjury of someone who has already been on Worker's Compensation.

"I appreciate your concern and can tell you that no one is more concerned about reinjury than the workers themselves. Luckily, the recovered worker has learned how to prevent such an incident and is extremely careful to avoid situations that could provoke reinjury.

I am aware of the stereotype of the injured worker who wants to remain on Workers' Compensation and is looking for further cause to return to it during subsequent jobs. I am sure there are people who fit that description. However, far more common in my experience is that people with industrial injuries are eager to get back to work.

Phillip is a good example. He's been so eager about getting back to work that he persuaded his doctor to reevaluate his condition four weeks earlier than originally scheduled. His doctor later told me that Phillip is a great example of a person who successfully used mind over matter in the recovery process and he gave the okay for him to resume work.

Believe me, I am trained to spot the person who is not truly eager to go back to work. On the rare occasions when I do identify such a program participant, it just means I have work to do. To tell you the truth, most of the people who appear to be unmotivated to work, are motivated, they just aren't sure what it is they want to do, or how to go about getting it. By the time I make a call like this one we are well beyond that point."

(10) If the people you work with are so great, why do they need services like yours in order to get a job?"

"That's a good question. If our services were the person's only avenue for pursuing employment, it would be an even better question. The truth of the matter is that most of the people we see are using every avenue available to them to expedite job search. In the same way you or I might use a head hunter or a professional search firm to land an opportunity sooner, rather than later, the people I work with are resourceful enough to take advantage of services that might give them an edge during a time when competition for jobs is so great. You would be surprised at how many of the people I am working with obtain employment before I have the chance to set them up for something myself!"

(11) Youth are undependable, irresponsible, and don't have the maturity required for this environment.

"I know what you're talking about because I share the same concerns as I go about matching young people to jobs. I am guaranteed one thing in my business: if I send you someone who quits after the first week of training, or someone who shows absolutely no potential as an employee, you are not going to continue to work with me. I have an equal investment in finding young people who have the kind of maturity and work attitudes you're seeking.

There are young people in our program I would never send on an interview and others I would hire in a minute if I were in business. That's why I am here, to screen one from the other. Tell me, how do you screen applicants for maturity? Is there a question you ask or a test you give? I'll use your question to screen people for your business."

(Note: The above-mentioned strategy of asking the employer how applicants are screened for a specific quality is an approach that works well in a variety of situations.)

(12) I don't think we have any jobs people with disabilities can do.

"This may come as a surprise to you, but I am certain there isn't a single

position in your business that could not be filled by someone who has a disability. The nature of disabilities is as diverse and distinctive as the abilities and interests of the people who have them. More importantly, the range of ability within each category of disability is so vast that there is no way we could predict the range of positions people within these categories might fill. I work with everyone from artists and mechanics to bus drivers and account clerks.

The question is not whether you have jobs people with disabilities can do, but whether I have the right person to meet the specific requirements of the job at issue."

(13) I am concerned that hiring someone with a disability is going to cause great discomfort for the rest of the staff and our customers.

"I have spoken with many employers who felt the same way. Once they actually hired a person with a disability, they were pleased to find their fears in this area were unfounded.

Typically you'll find that the first day or two on the job people focus on the new employee's disability. A few more days on the job, people start paying attention to how the new employee does the job, and they begin to relate to him or her on terms other than the disability. This really isn't so different from the way people respond to all new employees. Employers notice that within a very short period of time, the new hire becomes just another member of the team, with strengths and weaknesses just like everyone else. The disability becomes less and less a focal point once this natural integration occurs.

As for the reactions of customers, employers seem to overwhelmingly agree that if there is a response from a customer, it is a positive one. Perhaps that is true in part because disability is not a 'we versus them' kind of thing. Approximately 15 percent of the general population have some sort of disability. The odds are good that nearly everyone knows at least one person — a member of the immediate or extended family, friend, neighbor or co-worker — with a disability.

The integration of persons with disabilities into society is widely accepted and supported by the public. Have you noticed how people with disabilities are presented more and more in advertisements, magazines, television and movie productions? I recently read an article in which a representative of McDonald's corporation explained that they are including persons with disabilities in all their commercials because "it would be economically unwise to not give the body politic what they are asking for.

While I don't want you to hire people with disabilities simply to advertise a more inclusive workforce, this move certainly is not going to work against you where your customers are concerned. I am simply recommending that you consider individuals with disabilities in terms of their contributions as employees.

Would you like names and numbers of other businesses which have hired through our program and could relate their experiences to you?"

(14) I'm not interested in hiring people with mental disabilities because we need employees who are fully productive and able to take on additional tasks when the business requires it.

"You raise two very important issues, productivity and flexibility. I want to address them both and add a third issue — profitability. If it is not perfectly clear to us both that a prospective employee can bring more profit to your business than it would cost to employ her, we will agree that you should not consider her further.

My experience with other employers who have hired people with mental disabilities is that employees can generate as much profit from consistency and quality as they can from high speed productivity and maximum flexibility.

Persons with mental disabilities have a very wide range of abilities and interests. Some perform best if they are handling one aspect of a multi-task job. Many employers find it to their benefit to hire people to perform a single function, and can easily accommodate employees who excel when given one task or responsibility.

Other workplaces cannot make these kinds of accommodations. For example, if there are very few people on staff, it may be important for all employees to be able to perform a variety of duties. Then again, there are people with mental disabilities who are capable of performing a wide range of activities.

If I could find out more about the work performed here in your business, I could make some specific recommendations along these lines. I just want to assure you that the profitability of your business is of the utmost importance to me when we consider the feasibility of applicants from my program working here."

(Note: To further resolve this concern, provide a list of examples of the kinds of jobs held by your applicants in various businesses.)

(15) We can't afford the extra supervision and training (e.g., supported employment or job coaching) required to work with people with disabilities.

"I understand your concern. I am happy to tell you that most people with disabilities do not need extra supervision or training, they just need good supervision and training.

Let me assure you that any extra supervision or training that may be required will be provided by our staff. The purpose of our program is to assist people to become productive and independent members of the workforce. Sometimes people need instruction that is more in line with their way of learning than is typically offered in the workplace. When that is necessary, we offer what is called "job coaching." This is designed to support the person while they are acquiring the necessary skills to work independent-ly. In fact, that is why it is sometimes referred to as 'supported employment.'

Recently, I spent a few days on the job with an office clerk who has a men-tal impairment and does not read or write. We color-coded the files and developed a system by which she will organize the files of a busy insurance firm using this simple method.

We provided the initial training accommodation and the business may call for our assistance again if and when her job changes or she takes on new responsibilities. In the meantime, she's on her own.

Our intent is simply to provide training and to ready the work environ-ment, enhancing the abilities of the worker and decreasing his or her need for our services."

(Note: Provide a list of other specific examples of the use of a job coach or of supported employment.)

(16) I'm sorry but we don't hire from outside the union.

"I realize that, and should we develop a working relationship with one another, I will see to it that any applicants you seriously consider hiring become members of the union.

I would also be happy to talk to your union representative and present the key features of our program so union leaders and members are aware of the services we offer. Most unions are enthusiastic about the involvement of the businesses they represent in programs like ours. Many, in fact, encourage it.

All of that aside, first we have to determine that what I have to offer is going to interest you enough to pursue our involvement with the union."

Note: Many employers anticipate a negative reaction from their unions if they make an effort to hire people from special groups. Unions and orga-nized labor groups have diverse interests and practices. Certainly there are unions with no interest at all in programs like ours. Many unions have, however, been instrumental in developing programs to help people from diverse populations gain employment. The majority of unions in the United States have affirmative action goals and many unions in Canada have an Employment Equity Plan. Union goals for the businesses they rep-resent are usually consistent with the goals businesses hold for themselves.

Unions are primarily concerned about protecting their members. Contracts negotiated with employers contain provisions to protect both job security and the individual integrity of union members. It is important to present your program or proposal in a manner that ensures you are not attempting to compromise the work situations of present employees.

As job developers we must take it upon ourselves to become well informed about union representation of the businesses we contact. Specifically, you should address these questions:

✓ Which union represents workers at this company?

✓ What are the union's rules with regard to placement of new workers in company jobs?

✓ Which union leaders are responsible for negotiating with company management?

✓ What are the possible arrangements that might be made with the union to facilitate placement of applicants from your program?

Labor organizations are not a homogeneous group. They represent a diversity of individuals and have a variety of practices. They can become important allies in the promotion, hiring and advancement of people from our programs. In no instance should the presence of a union deter your efforts to initiate a working relationship with an employer.

(17) I'm afraid the people you are working with just have too many problems.

"I appreciate your concern along these lines. Obviously, it is a concern of ours as well. One of the most important aspects of my job is to identify the kinds of support services people need in order to keep their jobs.

You are right that many of the people who come through our door have more than their share of difficult circumstances. I have observed that some of the situations have only served to make them more resourceful.

For example, some of the women I work with are single parents with more than just one back-up system for childcare. When they need help with their children, they can call upon two or three alternative arrangements. Other job seekers, especially those who have never owned a vehicle, don't worry about the car breaking down. They know every possible route on the public transit system.

A primary purpose of this program is to enable people to be independent and self-sufficient. We wouldn't be doing our job if we left a single stone unturned — the applicants I would send you are able to maintain a normal work life. If they were unable to, you wouldn't be seeing them.

Are there any specific problems or situations you are concerned about?"

(18) Can you guarantee that these people are not going to quit?

"No, I cannot give you any more guarantees than those you get when you hire people who walk in your door to apply. The added assurances you do have are recommendations from other professionals, quick response to your hiring needs if and when someone does quit, and all the benefits associated with not having to advertise your hiring needs! If it helps any to know, I am just as concerned as you about finding people who will make a long-term commitment to the job. I also have the time to get to know people. I know more about the participants in our program than you can possibly learn about an applicant during the typical 10-15 minute job interview."

(19) I don't think this is the type of business for older workers.

"Perhaps your question is whether an older person would fit in to this environment or would be interested in this kind of work. Let me answer by saying that some would and some wouldn't. It would be my job to find those who would. One of the greatest lessons I have learned in this business is that it is absolutely impossible to predict what one can or cannot do, or will want or not want to do, solely on the basis of age. Who knows what either of us will have it in our hearts to do twenty (or ten) years from now!"

(Note: Cite examples of the wide range of jobs and the variety of workplaces that employ older workers.)

(20) I don't want to have to worry about having illegal workers (e.g., immigrants, refugees, migrant farmworkers) in my place of employment.

"Good, neither do I. In order to be served by our agency, people must show proper legal documentation."

(21) I can't afford to take the risk of hiring an ex-offender.

"I understand. No employer can afford the risk of hiring a person who is less than likely to be a good employee. I am happy to report that last year we successfully placed thirty participants in customer service positions of one type or another, positions not unlike the opportunities in your business. Of the thirty, twenty four are still working in the original positions and two have already been promoted! Contrary to the stereotype that once someone has been to prison they will always be in trouble, the recidivism rate of individuals going through our program has been impressively low. While I can't generalize about the value of hiring any and all ex-offenders, I can speak about the qualities and potential of the people I have worked with through our program."

(22) We've had bad luck working with agencies like yours.

"I am so sorry to hear that, and to be honest, it's not often that I do. I would really appreciate it if you would tell me about your experience. If you were to take the risk again and work with our agency, I would be responsible for ensuring that your experience was a good one. What exactly was the problem?"

(Note: Once the employer explains the problem, tell him or her exactly what steps you would take to prevent the problem from recurring.)

(23) I've had bad luck with your agency.

"I'm very sorry to hear that and I would like to know what your experience was so I can take the necessary steps to provide you with the quality of services and applicants you expected. Let me also add, you haven't worked with me before. Let me tell you how I work..."

(Note: In this case don't try to salvage the reputation of the agency, sell the employer on working with you. Even if the employer lacks confidence in the agency, they might gain enough trust in your abilities to take the risk of working with your program again. Trust in your agency will develop over time as the employer begins to reap the rewards of the services you provide.)

(24) We're laying off and we do not foresee any employment opportunities in the near future.

"As you can imagine, I hear that a lot. Your business is certainly not alone in the need to cut back and stretch every dollar. Actually, this is good timing because I am not here to sell you on hiring anyone. I am here to learn more about your business, the industry and how your company operates. In addition to recruitment, we offer a variety of services to businesses like yours and you may want to take advantage of these. We can also learn from you, which could benefit our program."

(Note: There are many avenues for exchange between an employer and a job developer other than people for jobs. On this basis alone, the approach described is worthwhile. In addition, as we observed earlier, the fact that the employer does not have job openings does not necessarily mean there are no employment opportunities. If you can show an employer how to make or save money by hiring someone to do something the business has never done before, you will find yourself with one eager listener.)

(25) We use a temporary agency.

"That's fine. I am not proposing that you replace your present hiring methods with our services. There may come a time when there is a position you want to fill with someone who is prepared to give his or her all for the job. While hiring a permanent employee requires upfront investment in items like benefits, orientation and training, most companies feel it is a smart investment in the long run, in terms of both the quality of work and the quality of the workforce.

Apart from this consideration, it would be very beneficial for our agency to get feedback from a company like yours about the kind of services our program could offer a company using recruits from a temporary agency. Would you be willing to speak to the agency advisory board during one of our monthly meetings?"

(Note: You don't want to pass up an opportunity to start a relationship with a company that recruits from a temp agency since this hiring practice is often a temporary method! Further, there may be other employer resources to benefit your program. And you can be sure that eventually, the employer will need you!)

ENHANCING EMPLOYER TRUST

Here are some of the most common reasons employers resist working with an employment and training program:

✦ They have no perceived need for your services.

✦ They lack trust or confidence in your program, applicants or ability to meet their needs.

✦ They are in no hurry to pursue an immediate exchange of resources and do not perceive any urgency about taking advantage of the services you offer.

✦ They must get approval or advice from other people.

✦ They are unclear about how, when, where, and with whom to proceed to initiate work with your program.

✦ They have not met a job developer who has earned their trust and respect.

While it is not readily apparent which, if any, of the objections or reasons listed above are true for the employer who resists working with you, by following these few simple guidelines you can build employers' trust and lessen some areas of resistance.

✸ Provide information willingly and openly about both yourself and your program.

✸ Encourage employers to talk with other employers with whom you have worked. Provide a list of employers who have agreed to serve as references for your program.

✸ Learn about and understand the organization as the employer understands it. Anticipate how an employer might react to an accommodation or feel about a particular applicant.

✸ Show your respect for the organization and its accomplishments. Study what it does well and praise success.

✸ Demonstrate respect and honor for the culture of the organization. If the business day ends at six and interviews are conducted in the evening, willingly schedule evening interviews. If the employer speaks formally, respond similarly.

✸ Be absolutely clear and specific about what you want and expect from the employer. Do not leave it up to the employer to bring the meeting to a close by coming to an agreement. There is no magic in

"Example is not the main thing in influencing others, it is the only thing."

Albert Schweitzer, philosopher and physician

"The true teacher does not preach what he practices til' he has practiced what he preaches."

Confucius

closing, there are just choices. Presenting options for working together is the natural beginning to a meeting. Deciding how to proceed is the natural and logical end to a meeting.

One of our major responsibilities to employers is to help them overcome indecision. Present the option that makes the most sense given the context of your meeting and ask the employer if he or she agrees with your assessment.

"Truth begins with respect."

*Max De Pree,
writer*

★ Point out how you are trying to help employers accomplish their ends. Make their goals your goals and remind them regularly that you value and share their goals and objectives.

★ When you see risky situations, point them out. Help employers to view you as a resource to help them through tough situations. Model, display and celebrate risk-taking. Show employers you too are willing to risk in order to meet their needs and exceed their expectations. Voice doubts and fears, as well as hopes and joys. Demonstrate that you are as fearless as they.

★ Make commitments and follow through on them. Show employers you truly want something to happen — and that what you want is consistent with what they want.

★ Seek opportunities to take actions that demonstrate your support of shared goals and objectives. Words only go so far.

★ When faced with a challenge, describe comparable situations you have successfully navigated or negotiated for other businesses. Offer considerable detail about each experience to assure the employer that you know what you are doing.

*What we can do
is merely a
consequence of
what we can be.
To engender
employer trust,
be trustworthy.*

★ Remember, a whisper from one satisfied employer to another is louder than the convictions of any single job developer. Ask employers who are happy with your services to write a letter for use as testimonial about the quality of your work. Save and photocopy these letters, and have them on hand when visiting employers.

Work with satisfied employers to generate a steady flow of testimonial letters. A simple and effective method is to call and ask what they found most valuable about working with you or your program. Make a note of the response and then ask the employer if you can put their feedback in letter form. This is an example:

"Patricia, I am so glad you were happy with our services. While listening to your comments, I noted three things you found most helpful: We were efficient, you appreciated the quality of the applicants you interviewed and were impressed by the resourcefulness of the job coach in redesigning the job. Is this assessment accurate?

"Patricia, as you know, we would like to recruit more businesses like yours and a letter from you would go a long way toward encouraging employers to try our services. Would you be willing to give us a written testimonial? If so, I'll write a brief memo of your comments and fax it to you. Look it over, edit it as you please, have it typed on your letterhead and return it to me."

✦ Include the following question on your employer feedback survey: Would you allow us to quote you about our services? Prepare a page or two of complimentary quotes.

✦ Once an employer agrees to work with you, congratulate him or her on the wisdom of the decision and offer two or three reasons you believe he or she will be pleased with the decision. This is an important step because many employers will agree to work with you because they like you and are caught up in the enthusiasm of the moment. That's great, but decisions made in the heat of the moment are not always acted on when the excitement subsides. At the close of your meeting, remind the employer that he or she has made a good, logical choice. This reminder may act to prevent or at least minimize buyer's remorse.

✦ Put the ideas set forth in the next chapter (about delivering quality services to employers) into practice.

"What you do speaks so loudly about who you are that I cannot hear your words."

Chinese saying

EMPLOYER CONCERNS:
OBSTACLES OR OPPORTUNITIES

Concerns as obstacles	Concerns as opportunities
Hears concerns as sign of disinterest	Hears concerns as sign of interest
Sees concerns as unwanted obstacles or problems	Sees concerns as opportunity for joint problem-solving or request for information
Goal is to win	Goal is to agree
Reacts personally	Responds professionally
Presents opposite viewpoint	Steps to the side, presents the same viewpoint with added information
Shows strength through the power of argument	Shows strength through acknowledgment of other person's perspective
Wants to persuade and change the person's view from the outside	Wants to help others to draw their own conclusions so that change comes from the inside
Focuses on differences	Focuses on common ground and mutual interests
Fixed on one solution, narrow thinking	Open to multiple options, generating possibilities for mutual gain
Has ready answers, wants to be the teacher	Has lots of questions, lets reality be the teacher
Hopes to avoid areas of employer concern	Looks for ways to uncover areas of employer concern

Summary Of Key Ideas:
Concerns As Opportunities, Not Obstacles

★ Since most employer concerns are predictable, bring them up early in the meeting. If you address them right away, they won't pop up later as objections.

★ Employer concerns are more often questions than problems. Listen for the question in the employer's statement.

★ Separate the employer's concern from his or her underlying beliefs. Do not try to change the belief until the concern has been acknowledged and validated.

★ Stand up for your views, defend your opinions, but do not believe they contain the whole truth or the only truth. Work to create an inclusive environment with room for even opposing views to co-exist.

★ We all have the power of positive perception. Put the best possible frame around the words and actions of every person and every situation.

★ Don't react to an unfavorable comment with the same strategies you learned in the sandbox. Be aware of your own "hot buttons" so you can exercise the extra tolerance and patience expected of someone in your role. It also helps to remember that while we frequently find ourselves within range of an employer's hostility or frustration, we are rarely the intended target.

★ It is easier to listen to someone who has listened to you first. Respect breeds respect. If you want employers to listen to you, begin by listening to them. If you want them to acknowledge your point of view, acknowledge theirs. When employers express concerns, step to their sides. This means listening, acknowledging, and finding common ground about the issue or concern. It is harder to oppose someone who hears you out and acknowledges what you say and how you feel.

★ Assist employers to define their real needs. Help them to understand the basic issue underlying their concerns. Don't just relate to the concerns, address the situation or experience that prompted these concerns. Displaying genuine interest in the employer's underlying beliefs and views helps to yield a mutually productive agreement. One of the greatest challenges for the job developer is to uncover the underlying reasons for employer resistance.

★ When confronted with a concern, resist the temptation to back off too

217

"The hardest thing to learn in life is which bridge to cross and which to burn."

David Russell, American educator

early. Hang in there. Resist the urge to walk away from a meeting when you know the employer's concerns have not been fully resolved, even when the employer has agreed to work with you.

★ Channel your efforts to areas you can influence, do not get stuck in areas where you can't affect change. You are not going to win over every employer you meet and that is okay. There are more opportunities in every community than we could ever take advantage of, so don't waste time with employers who are uninterested and/or unreceptive to change. Realize that while there are employers who truly do not need your services, there are many more who do.

★ Keep a positive attitude. Don't take yourself too seriously. Remember, he who laughs, lasts!

"The grass is not, in fact, always greener on the other side of the fence. No, not at all. Fences have nothing to do with it. The grass is greenest where it is watered. When crossing over fences, carry water with you and tend the grass wherever you may be."

Robert Fulghum, author

APPLICATION: PREPARING FOR EMPLOYER CONCERNS

(a) List the most common employer objections you hear about hiring applicants from your program.

(b) For each employer objection, distinguish between the stated concern and the employer's deeply held beliefs.

(c) Reframe concerns into questions you can answer.

(d) Given the nature of the belief, consider which approach to take to alter the employer's thinking and motivate him or her to consider another point of view (e.g., exposure to members of the target group, anecdotal reports of other employers' experiences, statistics and other relevant data, employer testimonials).

(1) OBJECTION:

CONCERN: BELIEF:

QUESTION: APPROACH:

(2) OBJECTION:

CONCERN: BELIEF:

QUESTION: APPROACH:

(3) OBJECTION:

CONCERN: BELIEF:

QUESTION: APPROACH:

(4) OBJECTION:

CONCERN: BELIEF:

QUESTION: APPROACH:

(5) OBJECTION:

CONCERN: BELIEF:

QUESTION: APPROACH:

(6) OBJECTION:

CONCERN: BELIEF:

QUESTION: APPROACH:

(7) OBJECTION:

CONCERN: BELIEF:

QUESTION: APPROACH:

(8) OBJECTION:

CONCERN: BELIEF:

QUESTION: APPROACH:

(9) OBJECTION:

CONCERN: BELIEF:

QUESTION: APPROACH:

(10) OBJECTION:

CONCERN: BELIEF:

QUESTION: APPROACH:

(11) OBJECTION:

CONCERN: BELIEF:

QUESTION: APPROACH:

CHAPTER 11:
PROVIDING QUALITY SERVICE TO EMPLOYERS

"If a man write a better book, preach a better sermon, or make a better mousetrap than his neighbor, though he build his house in the woods, the world will make a beaten path to his door."

Ralph Waldo Emerson, poet

For the job developer, placing someone in a job is like the end of a journey — it is the final destination. For the employer and the new employee it is just the beginning. Not unlike childbirth.

Nearly all new mothers report that throughout pregnancy their thoughts center on preparation for birth, as if birth was the only goal — the final destination. Ultimately, the miracle occurs, and the baby is born. Then there is a shocking realization. The new mother gazes lovingly at the infant entrusted to her and wonders, "Now what do I do?"

New mothers soon understand that birth is a beginning, rather than an end unto itself. Job placement is a similar situation. Once the person is newly employed, we cut the umbilical cord to the applicant, leaving employee and employer to work out the day-to-day details of life in the workplace.

To this point we have concentrated on the inception and birth of employment opportunities. This chapter deals with post placement issues, i.e., preventing "postpartum blues" by making good on your promise to help employers and employees meet each other's expectations.

This chapter offers inspiration for providing quality customer service to employers before, during and after placement, getting ongoing employer feedback and successfully managing problems and complaints. The purpose of this chapter is to empower you to go the extra mile with employers to strengthen partnerships between job developers, programs, agencies, employers and employees.

"The magic formula that successful businesses have discovered is to treat customers like guests and employees like people."

Tom Peters, business writer

VALUING EMPLOYERS

How would you treat an employer if you knew that:

✓ Your services were needed to contribute to the prosperity and well-being of the business?

✓ The survival of your program depended on their involvement with you?

✓ This employer may be one of the select few to consistently work with your program?

"A customer once remarked to a rude clerk, "I believe you have things backward. You are overhead. I am profit."

✓ An excellent opportunity for one of your applicants exists with this employer?

✓ Following each contact or visit, the employer will reconsider the decision to work with you or a competitor?

If we kept these questions in mind as the distinct possibilities they are, my guess is that the quality of job development services to employers would greatly improve. To treat employers as any less than a rare and valuable commodity would be foolhardy. If relationships with employers are neglected or taken for granted, they weaken. When they are cultivated and nurtured, they grow stronger. It's just that simple.

"THEY LOVE ME, THEY LOVE ME NOT"

Just as the telephone operator's manner affects the reputation of the phone company, and the waiter's service influences customer perception of the restaurant, the individual job developer's actions greatly determine employer satisfaction with the entire program!

When an employer meets you, visits a classroom, attends a function, tours your facility, interviews an applicant, reviews proposals or resumes, telephones your office, or hires someone from your program, you can be sure of one thing: he or she will have an opinion about the experience!

The decision to work with you again depends largely on the consequences of the last experience the employer had with you. The more rewarding the experience, the more likely the relationship will continue. Should an employer feel undervalued or discouraged by a less than optimal experience, the odds are that the relationship will not continue. In short, developing an ongoing relationship with an employer depends on rewarding them for being in partnership with you through the quality of service you provide!

"Every time customers come into contact with you, they come away feeling better or worse about it. It's how well you manage those numerous moments of truth every day that ultimately determines how successful you will be."

Ron Zemke, writer

QUALITY IS IN THE EYE OF THE BEHOLDER

Typically, service providers are content when they feel they have done everything they need to do to satisfy the customer's need. Quality service providers, however, are distinguished by a desire to exceed employer expectations — to go the extra mile. The definition of quality service is entirely subjective. For this reason, job developers must not only fulfill professional quality standards in their own terms, but also in the employer's terms.

I recall a restaurant co-worker who, at the end of an evening yielding few and low tips, complained that, "Customers don't recognize great service when they get it." I recall thinking, "Isn't the customer's feeling about the service received a more telling assessment of quality than the waiter's perception of the service offered?" My co-worker failed to consider his customer's satisfaction as an important measure of quality.

Quality is in the eye of the beholder. For job developers, it is the

"Quality could be defined as having a fine sense of one's obligations."

Max DePree, author

employer perception of quality that must be met or surpassed in order to create effective, enduring working relationships. The definition of quality, however, varies from person to person. In his book, *How to Win Customers,* Michael LeBoeuf offers a succinct definition, *"What people perceive as quality is the difference between what they get and what they expect."*

Each employer holds expectations about the quality of applicants and services as well as the process of working with you and your program. Should you fail to meet employer expectations, the program will be viewed as lacking quality. When reality meets or exceeds the employer's expectations, your program will be characterized as *quality.*

THE EMOTIONAL BANK ACCOUNT

Steven Covey introduces an interesting framework for viewing human relationships in his book, *The Seven Habits of Highly Effective People.* He suggests that each new relationship constitutes an emotional bank account to which we make deposits and withdrawals. By helping others to get what they want and feel better about themselves we make deposits to the account. Unfulfilled commitments, or actions that disappoint others, are considered withdrawals. Withdrawals not only increase the risk of an overdrawn account, but also the potential of losing the account completely.

This chapter presents strategies to enable you to make deposits in your emotional bank accounts with employers. It defines the "service difference" and describes how to go the extra mile, as well as ways to elicit employer feedback and manage dissatisfaction in a manner that is both responsible and responsive.

THE SERVICE DIFFERENCE

Most employers will agree that in order to qualify as quality service the job developer needs to be consistent. You must:

➤ Do what you say you are going to do.
➤ Do it when you say you're going to do it.
➤ Do it right the first time, and if not, respond quickly to better the situation.
➤ Get it done in a timely manner.
➤ Not promise things you can't deliver.

I can imagine what you are thinking as you read this list of five criteria: "Everyone knows that, there isn't a job developer in town who doesn't offer those same things to every employer he or she meets!" If that's what you're thinking, you're right.

So here's the bottom line: When there isn't much difference between what your program and other programs are offering, there had better be a big difference in the way you deal with other people. In other words, you need to be the difference!

> *"In every instance, we found that the best-run companies stay as close to their customers as humanly possible."*
>
> *Thomas Peters, business writer*

> *"IBM always acts as if it were on the verge of losing every customer."*
>
> *Jacques Maison-Rouge, IBM executive*

Going the Extra Mile

"There are no traffic jams in the extra mile."

Jim Cathcart, author

I hold to the philosophy that we should treat people the way we want them to be. For better or worse, we all tend to live up to others' expectations of us. When generous behavior is anticipated, it is difficult not to respond with generosity. We teach our children to be respectful by treating them respectfully. Similarly, if we want to maintain long-lived relationships with employers, we must treat them like lifetime partners. While we are all willing to go the extra mile for the employer who eagerly hires people from our programs, it is important that we approach every employer as someone who intends to establish an ongoing partnership.

Ron Zemke, a celebrated authority on quality customer service, proposes that service providers think of their customers (employers in our case) as members of their club. He writes, *"When someone begins working with you, they have become a member of your club. As members of your club, they deserve two things: recognition and special treatment."*

When you go the extra mile for employers, you and the services you provide will be the distinguishing features of your program. This service difference is rewarded by the continued exchange of resources and opportunities between your program and the employers with whom you enjoy these partnerships.

Ideas For Delivering Quality Service To Employers

Since programs vary, only you can determine how your program can go the extra mile. The following suggestions are intended to encourage efforts to distinguish your program in the areas of:

Ongoing Communication with Employers
Assessment and Referral
Pre and Post Job Interview Practices
Education, Training and Special Events
Job Coaching and Supported Employment
Post Placement and Follow-up
Maintaining Contact with Employers

ONGOING COMMUNICATION WITH EMPLOYERS

◆ Orient employers to your agency, the program and team of people with whom they will interact. Encourage employers to feel they are calling a friend when they phone your office. Prepare them to work with others in your program by describing each individual's role and responsibilities. Advise them about who will receive their call and whom to ask for when you are unavailable.

◆ Orient your staff to the employer. This will enable them to make employers feel warm and welcome each time they contact your program.

For example, an informed receptionist can respond knowingly to an employer call, *"Oh yes, Mr. Burns, Joanne mentioned that you would be calling. She's in a meeting but I am certain she is going to want to take your call."* Information coupled with a personal approach go a long way to communicate to callers that they are important and respected.

◆ Keep notes of key conversations, document agreements, due dates, negotiations and other significant interactions. To ensure clarity of your communications, mail or fax a copy or summary of your notes to the employer (excluding inappropriate doodles, of course)!

◆ To ensure that you are using a common vocabulary and share a common understanding of terms, send the employer a list of relevant terms and definitions. Include any acronyms you use regularly. This kind of "glossary" may only be necessary in situations where there are unfamiliar terms (e.g., medical, legal or technical language).

◆ Call the employer when you know you are going to be late, even if you are only delayed a few minutes, to show that you respect his or her time.

◆ When an employer asks a question you cannot answer immediately, offer to find the answer and respond quickly. Use employer inquiries as opportunities to demonstrate your ability to follow through on commitments.

◆ When a problem occurs or something goes wrong that will affect the employer, let him or her know immediately. Even if you feel like the proverbial bearer of bad tidings and your news provokes disappointment, keeping employers informed is vital. It builds the confidence and trust necessary for a continuing relationship. Allowing employers to discover bad news for themselves will almost inevitably worsen the situation. The employer will wonder why you didn't phone and may even suspect that you caused the difficulty. Doubt and mistrust will come between you and it will be much harder to earn the employer's confidence.

◆ When things go wrong, take responsibility and tell the employer how you are going to make things right. Don't criticize your agency or co-workers, or make excuses. Employers don't want reasons, they want results.

ASSESSMENT AND REFERRAL

☆ To fully understand the needs and wants of the employer and be better qualified to recruit employees, request to participate in employee orientation and/or initial training.

(When working with graduates from a nursing assistant training program at a convalescent hospital, I attended the nursing assistant training and orientation program. The training cost two days of my time, but proved to be a worthwhile experience. I drew on it for many years, when working with the convalescent hospital and other institutions. I felt better prepared to counsel and advise people who were interested in or considering entering the profession.)

☆ Send the employer a list of the assessment questions you will ask when screening applicants for the business. Ask for his or her comments and recommendations.

☆ Offer to use any assessment methods or tests the company uses to prescreen potential employees for their workplace.

☆ Make available to the employer a copy of all evaluation and assessment instruments used by your program to present the criteria you use to assess and evaluate your applicants.

☆ If the job description for a position you are requested to fill is vague (or nonexistent), offer to perform a task analysis of the job and assist in creating a job description.

☆ Invite employers to speak about opportunities at their businesses to relevant classes, graduations, or program functions so applicants can make informed choices about where they wish to apply.

☆ Meet with applicants before you send them to employers to ensure they are dressed appropriately and have all of the proper documentation (e.g., resume, master application, training certificate).

☆ When describing the person you are referring for an interview, take the opportunity to advise the employer about any special needs (or peculiarities) of the individual.

For example, if you have an applicant who speaks limited English, prepare the employer by suggesting interview questions to which the person will be able to respond comfortably. Or if you have an applicant who is passive in interview situations and will most likely not extend a hand or maintain eye contact with the employer, a comment like the following can go a long way to prevent the employer from forming negative judgements: *"I want to tell you that while Maria may appear less than assertive and confident in the interview, I have great confidence that once she's on the job, she will absolutely shine."*

Obviously, this does not mean sharing confidential information about the applicant, such as the nature or extent of a disability. Informing the employer about an accommodation for the interview situation is a separate issue. Telling an employer that an applicant who has a visual impairment will be accompanied by a reader in order to facilitate the application process only serves to better prepare the employer.

☆ If the person is applying in person, filling out an application or dropping off a resume or employment proposal, attach a personal note summarizing the applicant's strengths. This will let the employer know you are serving as both a personal and professional reference and set the application apart from the rest.

☆ If the employer requests resumes, applications or any other documentation, offer to hand-deliver them — promptly and personally.

☆ If you do not have an appropriate applicant to refer to the business, offer to call other programs that might. Specify when you will be back in touch to report your progress. Call the employer at the time agreed upon, whether or not you have identified someone to refer for the opening. If you don't have an applicant or referral, tell the employer you are not sending anyone at this time because you do not want to waste their time by sending someone who does not meet their specifications. Employers will respect the integrity of your screening process. (It proves that there is, in fact, a screen!)

☆ If you don't already use one, develop an Exceptional Candidate Listing which offers the names and summaries of experience of applicants who are ready to go to work and have skills and abilities of interest to employers. Update the listing regularly (i.e., monthly or quarterly) and mail, fax or personally deliver it to employers. An applicant listing is:

✎ A convenient way for employers to compare existing and potential jobs with the people you have available;

✎ A tool for keeping regular contact with employers;

✎ An incentive and opportunity for applicants to see their profiles included in the listing. (Where I worked, getting your name on the Exceptional Candidate Listing was a privilege.)

PRE AND POST JOB INTERVIEW PRACTICES

◆ Offer to accompany applicants to an interview so you are available to answer questions or offer any needed assistance.

For example, I worked with many employers who requested my presence when they interviewed people who spoke limited English. It was interesting to me that while I didn't speak any more of the applicant's language than the employer, just having me there put both the employer and the applicant more at ease.

◆ Meet with applicants before the interview to boost their energy and confidence. Pre-interview meetings with you not only help to minimize applicants' anxieties but they will also assure that they will arrive promptly at the interview with the employer.

◆ Offer applicants any and all information about the employer so they are prepared for the interview and can make informed decisions if offered the job.

◆ If you are not accompanying the applicant to the interview, ensure that he or she has directions and knows who to ask for at the company.

◆ Inform the employer about any special needs the applicant may have in relation to the interview.

◆ Carry out a reference check of your applicant's past employer(s). Jot down some quotes from past employers, and fax or mail them to the employer or have the applicant hand-deliver the highlights of the reference check to the employer.

◆ If you know some of the employer's concerns about an applicant, raise and resolve them before the interview. You also may recommend questions the employer can ask which will give the applicant an opportunity to resolve the concern.

◆ Meet with the applicant *after* the interview to elicit his or her thoughts, feelings and perceptions about the company, the employer and the interview. If the applicant's experience was positive, call the employer to report it.

Job development trainer Richard Pimentel emphasizes the importance of making a follow-up call after the interview. He claims that a call like the following one could be the deciding factor when an employer is on the fence about whether to hire the person:

"Mary came to see me right from your office. I don't know how you felt about her, but Mary was so excited about her interview with you! She's pretty pumped up by the possibility of working at your company. I want to thank you for meeting with her. Whether or not she gets the job, it was a good experience for her. By the way, when do you expect to be making a decision?"

When an employer is undecided about an applicant, it certainly can't hurt the situation to hear how positive the applicant feels about them! Bear in mind, a neutral response to an applicant following an interview is far more common than a decidedly positive or negative one.

◆ If the interview did not go well, call the employer to get his or her feedback. Ask if there are additional screening criteria you should use when referring other applicants to the business.

Use this opportunity to get employer recommendations or advice about other possibilities to pursue for the applicant. The perspective of an employer who has just finished interviewing an applicant is invaluable!

◆ Regardless of whether the person is hired, send a thank you note or make a call to express your appreciation for the employer's time and consideration. If appropriate, ask for additional comments about the applicant.

◆ Offer to hold an interviewing day for selected employers at your program or agency office.

◆ Offer to send applicants for practice with supervisors who are being trained as interviewers. Your applicants have an opportunity to practice interview skills and gain exposure to real supervisors and the new interviewers get practice and exposure to real applicants.

I found this idea can be rewarding in more ways than one. When I worked with Refugee Programs and had a caseload in the hundreds, I proposed that Marriott's Great America hold a "warm-up day" before their big push to hire staff for the spring-summer season. Knowing they hired a "fresh" staff of interviewers each year, I suggested they offer their staff one solid day of interviewing practice before the flood of applicants began. I suggested that the warm-up day would be a great opportunity for applicants to practice interviewing and if they were qualified, could "lighten the hiring burden." They liked and agreed to the idea. More than half the applicants interviewed on that warm-up day were hired! It's only fair to tell you that they were a bit surprised (overwhelmed?) to see us arriving in busloads!

EDUCATION, TRAINING AND SPECIAL EVENTS

•◆ Make available to employers any course outlines or curricula for relevant training or workshops you offer to applicants whom you will be referring to their company.

•◆ Invite employers to observe and participate in training and educational events.

•◆ Show how the performance objectives of the training program relate to performance standards of the employer's workplace.

•◆ If you don't already have one, develop an Employer Advisory Committee on Education and Training to invite employer feedback on present and planned courses and obtain ideas about additional funding and employer involvement in the training process. There's nothing like ownership of a program or an idea to inspire employers to invest in its success!

➡ Invite employers to contribute to your program's training efforts. They can offer materials and equipment as well as time and ideas. This invitation communicates confidence that your program is designed to benefit the private sector. In view of the potential "pay-off" for employers, it is not unreasonable to request them to invest in and contribute to the programs.

➡ Invite employers to attend and/or speak to classes, workshops, orientations, or graduations.

➡ Incorporate worksite tours as a regular part of training and workshop programs. This not only communicates to employers that your programs are reality-based, but also reinforces that the employers' workplaces are relevant to your applicants.

➡ Use job shadowing or work experience as components of your training efforts. These activities simultaneously offer employers the chance to see the abilities of applicants in action without having to make a hiring commitment and provide valuable work experience for trainees.

➡ Share training and supervising ideas from your curricula or course(s) which might be of interest to employers providing in-service or initial training for supervisors.

JOB COACHING AND SUPPORTED EMPLOYMENT

◆ Interview the new employee's supervisor(s) to learn their expectations, standards, and perspectives of the job at hand. Remember, the supervisor(s) may not have been the one(s) who made the decision to work with you, so be as informative as possible. Invite them to ask questions and express their concerns. Reassure them of your desire to keep as low a profile as possible and of your purpose — to facilitate the new employee's independence and success.

◆ Be aware of a supervisor's concern that he or she will have less influence or authority with the employee because you are present at the worksite. By asking for the supervisor's direction and approval of your job coaching efforts, you will lessen this concern and increase his or her willingness to work with you.

◆ Continuously work to build "natural supports" into the work environment. Any activity you perform that could be performed by an existing employee or person in the work environment should be encouraged. Naturally, you should not request or suggest performance of an additional task or activity if it compromises the worker's ability to carry out his or her present job responsibilities.

◆ Offer to orient co-workers to the special needs of the supported employee. Use this opportunity to model the use of valuing language and appropriate attitudes toward the individual. Respond to co-workers' questions and concerns. Encourage support of and good will toward the training endeavor by emphasizing that co-workers' and supervisors' comments and ideas are welcome and valued.

◆ Look for shortcuts and the way other employees approach the job. Requesting co-workers' ideas and insight strengthens their support of the new employee, and they are often able to provide fresh insight into the job coaching process.

◆ Always credit supportive co-workers by reporting favorable attitudes and actions to the supervisor(s). Similarly credit supportive supervisors by describing their efforts to managers or when appropriate, to the owner of the company. You can recognize them informally during meetings, or formally with a letter of recognition.

◆ If during job coaching efforts you have done a task analysis of a job that differs from the way the company has done it previously, offer your insight in the form of a detailed description of the job as you understand it. Your perspective may prove helpful to the company in terms of hiring, training and supervision.

◆ Keep copies of every job analysis and related job accommodations. Share this information with employers who have similar or comparable positions.

◆ As a job coach, in addition to ensuring that the supported employee can adequately perform all designated job responsibilities, look for additional ways to capitalize on the employee's abilities. Consider presenting an alternative employment proposal when you see the potential to increase the effectiveness or profitability of the supported employee.

We often view a job differently once we begin to work and gain a measure of experience. Don't automatically assume that your first impressions or instincts were either most accurate or best. To be an effective advocate for the employee and the business, you also must be a consultant and a resource, continuously offering ideas about how to improve employee productivity, satisfaction and profitability.

◆ Whenever possible, offer assistance to other employees as well as the supported individual. Make your time spent at the worksite as profitable for the business as it is for the individual.

◆ Help the new employee to apply the same principle of "going the extra mile" in his or her own work!

POST PLACEMENT AND FOLLOW -UP

➠ Write a letter or note commending each employee who took part in the hiring, interviewing or training of the new employee.

➠ Agree to the times and dates for follow-up contact.

For example, make a statement like the following to prepare the employer for follow-up:

"It is going to be important for me to know that everything is going well and to offer further assistance should you need it. I plan to call you (weekly, every two weeks) for a progress report. In fact, I am going to be in contact with you until I hear you say, 'Denise, we don't need to hear from you any more.' What would be the best day and time of the week for me to call you?"

Describing your planned follow-up at the onset of placement will prevent you from feeling awkward when you place your first follow-up call — the one that begins, "I'm just calling to see how things are going." Formalizing the follow-up process is not meant to complicate your contacts with employers, but rather to simplify and organize the content and outcomes of them. Efficient, consistent follow-up is more likely to result in favorable responses from employers and employees than random, haphazard or "crisis intervention" contact.

➠ Maintain regular contact with the new employee during the first 4 to 12 weeks of employment.

The initial 4 to 12 weeks on a job is the most difficult adjustment time for new employees. It is also the period of time when people are most likely to quit their jobs. The adjustment period is not over and new employees who are not sufficiently committed to or invested in the job will need your assistance to stick it out. Be prepared to offer support and encouragement to new employees during this critical adjustment period.

➠ During a follow-up call, ask open-ended questions.

For example, when you follow-up with the employer, rather than ask, "Is Joel's work meeting your standards?" which begs for (and usually yields) a "yes" or "no" answer, ask:

- *"How would you characterize Joel's first week of work?"*
- *"In what areas would you like to see improvement?"*
- *"What seem to be Joel's strengths?"*
- *"How close has Joel's actual performance been to our initial predictions?"*
- *"How well do you feel Joel's training prepared him for doing the job in your shop?"*

When you follow up with the new employee, ask open-ended questions such as:

- *"How is the job different from what you expected?"*
- *"What has surprised you most about the job?"*
- *"What is the most difficult part of the job?"*
- *"What do you like most about it so far?"*
- *"When are you going to send me a cut from your first paycheck?"* *(Just kidding.)*

➠ Keep notes on each follow-up call so subsequent conversations relate to previous ones.

   For example, *"You mentioned a couple of weeks ago that Joel wasn't integrating well with the rest of the folks in his department. What's happening now?"*

Approach your follow-up calls as authentic, personal interviews about the specific employment situation rather than memorized, mechanical procedures. Follow up as a consultant, not a technician!

➠ When an employee has a particularly positive or successful experience in a new work environment, offer to write an article about it. Make your article available for publication in the company newsletter, related trade/association newsletters and the business section of the local newspaper as well as newsletters or updates published by your agency.

➠ When an employee has a negative experience with an employer, do not burn your bridge with the employer by avoiding a frank discussion of the situation. Instead, strengthen the bridge by phoning the employer to open discussions about the situation.

➠ Recognize employer efforts, participation and support by hosting an employer awards function or presenting special plaques, certificates or letters of recognition. Reward employers for all levels of participation, not just placement. Take steps (a personal phone call or handwritten invitation) to ensure attendance of superiors — managers, direct supervisor, corporate president or designee — of the person you will honor at the recognition event. When superiors cannot be present at the event, be certain they are aware of the person's accomplishment and that they are recognized at the event. A brief note summarizing the person's efforts (accompanied by photos from the event) not only effectively updates the employer, but also reinforces the accomplishments of your partnership with the business.

➠ Whenever possible, become a customer or patron of the businesses that work with your program. You will accomplish two things simultaneously — maintain contact with employers and employees (especially persons hired from your program) and enjoy the product or service provided by the business.

➠ When you receive negative feedback from a new employee about the workplace, a specific co-worker or the company, provide counseling so he or she feels able to approach the supervisor. In many instances, it is not feasible or realistic for the new employee to approach the supervisor alone. In these situations it is best to contact the employer with suggestions about how to improve the new employee's present situation rather than with a laundry list of complaints or problems.

MAINTAINING CONTACT WITH EMPLOYERS

✭ Get to know your partners in business as individuals, not just as employers, but as people. Find out what they care about and like to do in their free time. (This happens naturally, as your relationship develops.)

✭ Identify each person's interests, strengths and values. When you know what someone does well and takes prides in, then you can look for opportunities to enhance his or her skills and capabilities.

For example, if the person teaches interviewing skills in the company, send relevant interviewing articles or materials that cross your desk. If the person serves on a committee for diversity, keep him or her informed about events related to diversity and arrange introductions to other local business people involved in diversity initiatives.

✭ Send your contacts newspaper or magazine clippings they might enjoy and articles related to topics you have discussed. When you spot an article about an important industry-specific issue or trend, mail or fax it to everyone who might be interested.

✭ When you run across an innovative idea or interesting resource used by an employer, ask for permission to share the idea with other businesses, ensuring the innovator that you will credit him or her for the idea.

✭ Keep employers informed about things you see other companies doing that could benefit their businesses.

✭ Send holiday, birthday or special event cards and an occasional note to let people know you're thinking about them and to encourage them to call you with any questions.

✭ Keep employers informed about functions and events you think might be of interest to them.

✭ When you hold functions employers attend, make them feel welcome by:

   - Following a written invitation with a personal call encouraging them to attend and conveying why you think it would be beneficial to attend.

- Faxing directions (and any other relevant information) to make travel and/or attendance easier.

- Greeting and orienting them to what will be happening, e.g., where they will be seated, how the event will conclude. Introduce them to other staff members with whom they have had or will have contact.

- Arranging seating according to expertise or interests (e.g., by industry or company function, chamber of commerce membership, enthusiasm for rock and roll).

- Inviting a mix of employers with varied levels of involvement with your program so newly recruited employers may receive support and encouragement from those with long-standing relationships.

- Following up with a thank you call or note expressing your appreciation of the employer's attendance at the event. When relevant, ask for employer comments about the event and guidance for planning future functions.

✱ Once you have established working relationships with employers, make sure they have ongoing opportunities to give you feedback about services received or desired but not received. (For strategies to solicit employer comments and opinions, refer to the next section, Inviting Employer Feedback.)

✱ Respond quickly and responsibly to employer complaints and problems. Use these situations as opportunities to go the extra mile to correct or improve situations. (The section entitled *Dealing with Employer Dissatisfaction* on page 244 describes how to approach dissatisfied employers.)

INVITING AND RESPONDING TO EMPLOYER FEEDBACK

Earlier in the chapter we distinguished between classic "customer service" and "customer satisfaction" and decided that "quality" is defined by the customer, not the service provider. To ensure that we are providing quality service which will result in high levels of customer satisfaction, we need ongoing, regular feedback from employers about services received and additional services they would like. The process of obtaining this valuable information from employers also lets them know we care about them and their businesses.

"The time to repair the roof is when the sun is shining."

John F. Kennedy, 35th President of the U.S.

FIVE WAYS TO RECEIVE AND RESPOND TO EMPLOYER FEEDBACK:

(1) Go out and talk to employers in person.

(2) Get employer feedback by telephone.

(3) Invite employers to respond to a survey.

(4) Organize focus groups and/or employer advisory committees. Invite selected employers to discuss their concerns, likes and dislikes in an open forum.

(5) Develop an employer newsletter or other communication vehicle to broadcast your desire for and responses to employer input.

FEEDBACK BY TELEPHONE

Keep in touch with employers to let them know you are interested in their success and well-being. Set up a tickler file with notes about each business and any personal information about the employer. Review the file before each call. Regularly (quarterly or semi-annually) contact employers who have participated in your program to determine how their relationships with your agency are going. Follow these simple guidelines to elicit employer feedback:

- Review the employer's original purpose for working with you. Reestablish the problem, concern, need or interest that attracted the employer to you in the first place.

- Explore employers' impressions about their first experiences using your services. Were the initial experiences helpful? Were there any problems? Ask for ideas or suggestions about ways to improve your services.

- Determine employer satisfaction with your service after a working relationship ranging from 6 to 18 months.

- Reassess employer needs. (To compare past and present needs, it is helpful to have notes from your original assessment.) Determine if the business has taken or is about to embark on a new direction.

- Determine how you can continue to meet their future needs.

- Ask employers if they would like to expand the relationship to include additional services or assistance? Present possible options.

For example,

"I see you participated in our summer youth program as well as the mentorship project. Are you aware of the component of our program which offers applicants for direct hire?"

–or–

"Thank you for taking part in the Employer Day we held last spring. You were terrific with the students, and your comments to them were very encouraging. In fact, I want you to seriously consider participating in our Mentor Program. It's a unique way to make a difference with these kids, especially for professionals who don't have many opportunities to spend time with kids from the inner city."

–or–

"I don't want you to respond to this request until you have more information on the program. May I send you some information about it?"

USING A SURVEY

While you are more apt to receive information in conversation, you may prefer to have employers respond to a survey. Surveys may be conducted by mail, fax or in-person. When you mail surveys, I urge you to follow up by telephone so you have some personal contact with employers. Use their comments on the completed survey as a springboard for your conversation. On the next page is a sample survey for obtaining employer feedback. Tailor this sample to meet your program's needs.

EMPLOYER FEEDBACK SURVEY

We appreciate your business and want to continue to provide quality services to meet your expectations. To assist us in our ongoing efforts to meet quality standards, please rate our services in the following areas using the scale below:

RATING SCALE: 1 = LOWEST SCORE, 5 = HIGHEST SCORE

(1)   Responsiveness to your needs: 1 2 3 4 5

(2)   Ability to follow-through on   1 2 3 4 5
        agreements:

(3)   Quality of applicants referred   1 2 3 4 5
        to you by our program:

(4)   Quality of training and employment   1 2 3 4 5
        preparation for applicants:

(5)   Program ability to respond to your   1 2 3 4 5
        changing needs:

(6)   Attitude of staff member(s):   1 2 3 4 5

(7)   Telephone communications with all   1 2 3 4 5
        program staff:

(8)   Quality of follow-up on the services   1 2 3 4 5
        provided:

(9)   Overall efficiency of services   1 2 3 4 5
        provided:

(10)   Overall quality of our communication: 1 2 3 4 5

(11)   Ability to keep you informed of the   1 2 3 4 5
        status of work we are doing for you:

(12)   Ability to meet agreed-upon   1 2 3 4 5
        deadlines:

(13)   Delivery of support services for   1 2 3 4 5
        the new employee:

(14)   Overall value of our services to   1 2 3 4 5
        your business:

GENERAL COMMENTS:

FALLING COCONUTS AND OTHER UNEXPECTED FEEDBACK

"It's always somethin'!"

Roseanne Rosannadanna
Saturday Night Live

Rosannadanna must have been a job developer!

Over the years, many job developers have asked me what to do when the employer's feedback is negative. I answer with the little story of the coconut:

The Coconut

A monkey on a tree
hurled a coconut
at the head of a Sufi.

The man picked it up,
drank the milk,
ate the flesh,
and made a bowl from the shell.

Anthony deMello, The Song of a Bird

Let's face it — we are only human and problems with employers are inevitable. Sometimes problems occur more than once, or even repeatedly with the same employer. Not infrequently, the experience is more like being hit in the head by a bowling ball than a coconut. Here are some true-to-life examples from my job developing experience:

The time an applicant showed up with all his friends and smoked dope in the parking lot before making his grand entrance;

The call from a business who complained that "my people" were squatting on top of the toilets, instead of sitting on them like "regular people";

The newly trained bank teller who left with a customer and had an extra fifty dollars in her pocket;

The employee who didn't show up for work in the middle of the week because, as she stated matter-of-factly, "Wednesday has been my laundry day for over twenty years!"; and,

The employee who signed up forty people on the company's insurance policy because in his culture "immediate family" includes everyone our society considers "extended family."

Less dramatic than these examples (I know you have all had your own), is the multitude of times when people just don't show up for their interviews at all. Or people who ask for twice the amount of money they had agreed to with you. There are people who just don't work out as had been hoped. Is there any way to prevent these things from happening? Can we really promise employers that these things won't happen?

My answer to both the questions above is "No." We cannot promise employers that unexpected things won't happen and we do not have the power to prevent these situations. In this context, here are some ideas to bear in mind as you face the day-to-day trials and mishaps that come with the job.

WHY ANGELS FLY AND OTHER THOUGHTS FOR A BUMPY ROAD

"Angels fly because they take themselves lightly!"

Anonymous and Airborne

"What on earth would a man do with himself if something didn't stand in his way?"

H. G. Wells, English novelist and historian

◆ We're working with people. Name a power, force or commodity, more unpredictable — chancy, erratic, mutable — than people. Okay, there's the weather. Yet even meteorologists have some warning about impending changes!

◆ Nobody's perfect. Not you. Not the applicant. Not the employer. It's not a perfect world and there are no perfect jobs. If we can agree on these points then we can probably also agree that in this imperfect world of imperfect people, we should expect the unexpected.

◆ Think of yourself as a problem-solver. I once read that if there were a tranquilizer to render us oblivious to all of our problems, few of us would take it because we know trouble often brings out the best in us. When trouble comes a knockin', let it be your teacher. Let it be the light that shines on your ability to handle it.

◆ We are a lot tougher on ourselves than employers are on us. It's easy to forget that employers are in positions similar to ours when they hire people for their business. What we experience as a "negative termination" or a minor catastrophe, employers experience as "turnover," an expected, planned variable typically affecting 10-20% of people they hire.

◆ When a person hired through your program does not work out, remember that it was a shared decision between you, the applicant and the employer. None of you are completely responsible for the situation, but all of you are partially responsible. Make a statement that reflects this shared responsibility. For example,

"I am so sorry it did not turn out as we expected. What did we miss?

Is there an additional question we should ask or another factor we should consider as we look to filling the position again?"

◆ In the event that you over-sold your services and committed to something you cannot deliver, call the employer and tell them just that. Being honest about your misjudgment of a situation or your inability to do what you promised is far more considerate than hiding behind your pride. I'm glad I don't have to give a nickel for every call I've made to say:

"I am really sorry. I was so enthused about the possibilities we discussed in the meeting the other day that I got a little carried away and promised too much too soon. The research for the employment proposal we talked about is going to take me at least another couple of days. I apologize if I have inconvenienced you. I truly value your time and appreciate your interest in this proposal, I hope I haven't discouraged you from being part of this. How does this revised timeline sound...?"

Or for a more recent example of eating humble pie,

"Gee Milt, I realize that I predicted this book would be just a couple of months in the writing, and now we are going into the twentieth month, but I am sure you are going to find the end product well worth the wait...Milt, are you there?"

◆ Don't expect to please everyone. No matter how patient, helpful and understanding you are, there will always be a percentage of people you simply will not be able to satisfy.

◆ Use problems and challenging situations with employers to your benefit. Many job developers take to the highway at the first sign of trouble with an employer. Problems with employers should draw us to them, not distance us from them. Willingness to resolve a situation at your own expense is an important investment in your relationship with the employer.

The following section provides guidelines to help you do more than survive negative situations with employers. These approaches will actually strengthen your relationships with them.

DISSECTING THE COCONUT

Tom Peters proclaims the importance of handling customer complaints in his book, *Passion for Excellence,* by distinguishing between two kinds of companies. One type, the most typical, views complaints as a disease to be gotten over, with memory of the pain rapidly suppressed. The other perceives a complaint as *"a luscious golden opportunity."*

Facing employers directly and actively soliciting feedback about dissatisfaction serves three important purposes:

"Experience is the name everyone gives to their mistakes."

Oscar Wilde,
poet, playwright
and novelist

"Robin, it's time we unravel this capricious caper!"

Batman,
Caped Crusader

*"*T*hose who enter to buy, support me. Those who enter to flatter, please me. Those who complain, teach me how I may please others so that more will come. Only those hurt me who are displeased but do not complain. They refuse me permission to correct my errors and thus improve my service."*

Marshall Field,
American
merchant

(1) It identifies areas in need of improvement.

(2) It may give you a chance to provide additional services to improve or resolve the situation.

(3) It is a wonderful opportunity to strengthen employer loyalty.

An important element of an employer partnership is the chance for them to teach us how to do business. We learn through dialogues, and the most useful dialogues are with people who value and trust us, but are dissatisfied with how we are serving them. The trusting, dissatisfied employer gives us clues about the marketplace we don't ordinarily have access to and can point to aspects of the program which need to be expanded, changed or eliminated. In our personal melodramas, many of the people we view as opponents or as "difficult" are not opponents, except when we perceive them to be. We need these employers to help us improve. We should be actively soliciting employer assistance to continuously improve our program, but:

It is difficult to receive criticism when we are ambivalent about whether we want to hear it.

Do you remember the old saying, "Don't ask questions that you can't hear the answers to?" A mature program, deeply committed to quality, invites criticism and constructive feedback about how to improve what it is already doing. This kind of program sets its sails on the winds of reality and charts a course toward success. Here are some general guidelines for using employer complaints as the "luscious opportunities" they are, and from which you can get the meat and the milk from the coconut.

DEALING WITH EMPLOYER DISSATISFACTION

(1) Welcome complaints. Without them we can't improve.

(2) Make it as easy as possible for employers to express dissatisfaction.

Think back to the words of Stephen Covey, and *"Seek first to understand, then to be understood."* In other words, listen and hear what people are saying, thinking and feeling. Listen for what employers don't say, and encourage them to express what they would like to say but have difficulty putting into words.

(3) Let employers know you value their thoughts and perceptions by responding promptly to complaints.

This doesn't mean that you will hold the same perspective as the employer about the situation. It just means you permit and encourage the employer to express his or her frustration, disappointment or anger. You respond with genuine interest in and concern about the employer's point of view.

(4) Make the employer's goal in the situation your goal.

The terms for satisfying their expectations in the situation should, to a great degree, define your own. When you share goals, it is natural to ask for the employer's advice and suggestions about improving the situation or dealing with the issue at hand. Follow these three steps:

(a) Ask questions to identify employer expectations.

For example,

- *"What is the situation right now?"*
- *"What would you like it to be?"*
- *"Will you please tell me exactly what you would like to see happen from here?"*
- *"Let's decide if there's something I can do to help."*

(b) Repeat the specifics.

"My student pierced her what?"

(c) Outline possible solutions or alternatives and agree on a course of action.

"As I see it, here are our choices... This is what I'm going to do... What do you think?"

"Here's my understanding of the situation and where we can go from here. Is there anything I'm missing in this assessment of the situation?"

"Where do you suggest we go from here?"

(5) Follow through on the agreement(s) made and monitor satisfaction by staying in contact with the employer.

(6) Treat the employer respectfully, even when you disagree with his or her point of view.

You may change the terms of your working relationship as a result of a disagreement. But at least agree to disagree! In the event employer complaints seem unreasonable, be kind. Remember, everyone you meet is fighting some kind of tough battle. You may not be the real target of this person's anger or frustration, but you may be in range when it is expressed.

"You'll never have all the information you need to make a decision. If you did it would be a foregone conclusion, not a decision."

David Mahoney, Jr., corporate executive

"A problem well stated is a problem half solved."

Charles Kettering, inventor

(7) For serious complaints or situations that are not easy to resolve, consider the following approaches:

✦ Direct communication of the employer's concern to the highest possible level in the organization. (A call or letter from the agency director may have greater impact than a call from the job developer.)

✦ Even in the event the employer does not want your participation to resolve the situation, follow up with a call to see how things work out.

✦ Once the fires are out and things have cooled down, contact the employer to ask for advice about how to prevent the problem or situation in the future. For example, how would you feel if after making a complaint about services provided for you, the provider says, "I would really like our agency to learn from this situation so it does not happen again. What recommendations would you have me share with our staff?"

A job developer in one of my workshops related a great story about dealing with an irate employer by asking him to come and speak to the staff of the program because, as he told the employer, "It's from people like you that we have the most to learn!" The employer became putty in the job developer's hands, because he felt valued, validated and understood.

A Tale of Two Gas Stations

As a freshman in college I pumped gas on the weekends. I will never forget this story which was passed on to me by my supervisor on the first day of my job. I later learned that this story was passed on by every supervisor to every employee on the first day at this particular "service station":

A man pumping gas at a filling station was asked why his station was always so busy while the one across the street selling comparable gas at an identical price was almost always empty. This sage businessman replied, "They're in a different business than us. They're a fillin' station - we're a service station!"

SUMMARY OF THINGS TO REMEMBER ABOUT PROVIDING QUALITY SERVICE TO EMPLOYERS

★ Employers will listen to what you say, but they will believe what you do. How you deliver the services you promise is where the rubber meets the road.

★ Research shows that the average business spends six times more to attract new customers than to keep existing customers. In relation to our business, this means employer loyalty is worth ten times more than a single placement made with an employer who will never hire again. Perhaps more of our resources — financial and otherwise — should be dedicated to confirming the loyalty of established employers rather than to developing new relationships.

★ Many job developers are pleased to deliver services that qualify as "good enough to meet employer expectations." But "good enough" only puts you in the game alongside the rest of the pack. It doesn't give you the service edge you need to compete with programs that offer the same services. You need to be the difference between what employers can get from your program and what they can get from other programs. This means "going the extra mile" in every way you can, in every aspect of service delivery.

★ Quality is in the eye of the beholder. For job developers, employers are the beholders...their perceptions of quality are the ones we must meet or surpass to create effective working relationships.

★ An employer partnership involves allowing employers to teach us how to do business. To encourage employers to educate us, we must not be ambivalent about our desire to obtain feedback and hear criticism.

★ The way you deal with employer complaints and problems is crucial. There are long-term consequences not only for future employer participation and loyalty, but also for the success of your program.

★ To develop long-term relationships with employers, you must reward employers for being in partnership with you!

★ Everyone is trying to accomplish something big, not realizing that life consists of little things. Michael LeBoeuf in his book, *How to Win Customers,* writes, *"Excellent service isn't the result of doing any one thing 1,000 percent better. It's the result of doing thousands of things one percent better."* In the book *Servicing America*, this process is described as handling the hundreds of "moments of truth" each day which, taken together, constitute customer service.

★ We need to expect the unexpected, rather than lose our footing in response to it. When we deal effectively with unanticipated problems and situations, we can actually gain ground and strengthen relationships with employers.

★ Set up a system to handle employer complaints. Seek, acquire and follow-up on information including:

- The nature of the complaint
- A mutually agreed upon solution to the problem
- A determination of whether the problem was resolved on the spot
- When a solution was promised to the employer
- The steps to be taken to resolve the problem, complaint or concern
- How the problem could have been prevented
- Actions or service improvements to prevent the problem from recurring
- Whether to compensate the employer for his or her inconvenience and the nature and extent of this compensation.

★ While it is important to take our work seriously, we need to take ourselves lightly. Employers do not expect us to approach perfection any more than they expect it from themselves. Similarly, we should not expect perfection from our applicants. We should accept mistakes as part of the woodwork. As a wise person once said, *Pain is inevitable, but misery is optional.*

★ Finally, take to heart the Chinese saying: *You can't prevent birds of sorrow from flying over your head, but you can prevent them from building nests in your hair!*

DISTINGUISHING FEATURES OF QUALITY SERVICE

Satisfactory service	Quality service
Views job placement as an end	Views job placement as a beginning
Quality defined by service provider	Quality defined by employer
Focus on placement	Focus on job retention
Aspires to be "good enough" in the eyes of employers	Aspires to go the extra mile to provide services
Deals with problems when they arise	Anticipates and plans for problem areas
Is open to customer feedback	Invites ongoing customer feedback
Views employer complaints and problems as things to get over with employers	Values complaints as opportunities to quickly strengthen relationships

*"If a man is called to be a street sweeper, (or job developer)
he should sweep streets even as Michelangelo painted,
or Beethoven composed music, or Shakespeare wrote poetry.
He should sweep streets so well that all the host of
Heaven and earth will pause to say,
'Here lived a street sweeper who did his job well'."*

*Rev. Martin Luther King, Jr.
Civil Rights leader*

APPLICATION: GOING THE EXTRA MILE
TO SERVICE EMPLOYERS

(1) Which is the most frequently occurring problem you have the capacity to change or control when providing services?

(2) If you were in complete control of your program and could make a single change to improve the quality of service provided by your agency, what would it be?

(3) Which of the ideas presented in the section devoted to going the extra mile would you like to apply to your work? List additional ideas about how to improve each of the following aspects of your services:

Communication Practices

Assessment and Referral Practices

Pre and Post Job Interview Practices

Education Training and Special Events

Job Coaching and Supported Employment

Post Placement and Follow-up Practices

Ongoing Contact With Employers

A Tribute To The Unsung Heroes Of Job Placement

Amazing things are accomplished every day by job developers throughout North America. Young men and women are breaking the cycle of dependency on social assistance. Individuals with disabilities are gaining recognition for their unique contributions to the workplace. People are leaving the sterile walls of prison cells and getting a second chance to participate in their communities. People who have been living in shelters are gaining access to a place to call home and to a workplace. Still others have been lifted from the shock and betrayal of company layoffs to heights of renewed self-awareness and second careers. Businesses once closed to the idea of working with people perceived to be in any way "different," are now actively recruiting such individuals as valued team members!

Many of these accomplishments are due in large part to the hard work, belief, inspiration, encouragement and talents of job developers. I am assuming that you, dear readers, are many of these unsung heroes.

Your accomplishments have been hard-earned; your knuckles callused from knocking on doors that didn't open, your spirits dampened by people who aren't ready to change or who refuse to cooperate. But in the face of adversity and difficult economic times, you have not given up. You have persisted and succeeded in being agents for change in the lives of the people you serve and your communities.

And given all of this, I just bet that many of you have not been thanked. Well, in acknowledgment of your efforts, thank you! I feel proud and blessed to be a colleague of dedicated people who, one step at a time, are changing the world.

Our work has just begun.

AN INVITATION

Dear Reader,

In many ways, this book is my correspondence to thousands of job developers I have had the privilege of meeting in my seminars throughout the past ten years. In fact, as each chapter neared completion, I was tempted to sign, "Fondly, Denise", drop it in the mail and await your reply.

As such, I would like to hear back from you. I invite your responses and reactions to the material presented as well as your ideas and philosophy of job development. I expect that this will be the first in a series of books relating to non-traditional job development. I envision future publications, however, to be more of a joint venture between us. This is an invitation to take part in those future writings.

So, if you have a winning strategy, valuable insight or an experience to share with your peers, this is your chance to see your name (and/or your agency's) in print. You'll also earn my gratitude and that of your colleagues.

To inspire you to put your thoughts on paper, here are examples of the types of things I'm looking for:

- Successful employment proposals
- Examples of how you and your co-workers go the extra mile to deliver quality employment services
- Fresh ideas about how to target and initiate contracts with new employers
- Novel marketing and communications approaches
- Strategies to help manage job pressures and maintain motivation
- Amusing, significant or otherwise extraordinary aspects of life as a job developer
- Stories of unique partnerships with employers
- Questions or issues you would like addressed in future publications

To ensure credit for your contribution, please be certain to include your full name and your agency name, address and telephone number with your submission.

Thank you for reading this book!

Sincerely,

Denise Bissonnette

BIBLIOGRAPHY

Rafael Aguayo, <u>Dr. Deming, The American Who Taught the Japanese about Quality</u>, (New York: A Fireside Book, Simon and Schuster Publishers, 1990).

Nancy Anderson, <u>Work with Passion</u>, (New York: Carroll & Graff Publishers, 1984).

Dr. Robert Anthony, <u>Doing What You Love, Loving What You Do</u>, (New York: Berkley Books, 1991).

Henry Beard and Christopher Cerf, <u>The Official Politically Correct Dictionary and Handbook</u>, (New York: Villard Books, 1992).

Geoffrey Bellman, <u>The Consultant's Calling</u>, (San Francisco: Jossey-Bass, 1990).

Warren Bennis and Burt Nanus, <u>Leaders</u>, (New York: Harper & Row, 1985).

Warren Bennis, <u>On Becoming a Leader</u>, (Reading, MA: Addison-Wesly, 1989).

Peter Block, <u>The Empowered Manager</u>, (San Francisco: Jossey-Bass, 1987).

Robert Bly, <u>Selling Your Services</u>, (New York: Henry Holt and Company, 1991).

Richard Bolles, <u>How to Find Your Mission in Life</u>, (Berkeley, CA: Ten Speed Press, 1991).

Lawrence Bradford and Claire Raines, <u>Twenty-Something: Managing and Motivating Today's New Work Force</u>, (New York: MasterMedia, 1992).

Lorna Catford and Michael Ray, <u>The Path of the Everyday Hero</u>, (New York: St. Martin's Press, 1991).

Jim Cathcart, <u>Relationship Selling</u>, (New York: Perigree Books, Putnam Publishing Group, 1990).

Gerald Celente, <u>Trend Tracking</u>, (New York: Warner Books, 1990, 1991).

Stephen Covey, <u>The Seven Habits of Highly Effective People</u>, (New York: Fireside, 1989).

Vernon Crawford, <u>From Confucius to Oz</u>, (New York: Berkley Publishing Group, 1988).

Anthony deMello, <u>Awareness: The Perils and Opportunities of Reality</u>, (New York: Bantam Books, 1990).

Anthony deMello, <u>The Song of the Bird</u>, (New York: Image Books, Doubleday, 1982).

Max DePree, <u>Leadership Is an Art,</u> (New York: Doubleday, 1989).

Peter Drucker, <u>Innovation and Entrepreneurship</u>, (New York: Harper & Row, 1985).

Rick Fields, <u>Chop Wood Carry Water</u>, (New York: St. Martin's Press, 1984).

Daryl Allen Hall, <u>1001 Businesses You Can Start From Home</u>, (New York: John Wiley & Sons, 1992).

Tim Hansel, <u>You Gotta Keep Dancin'</u>, (Elgin, IL: DC Cook, 1985).

Paul Hawkin, <u>Growing A Business</u>, (New York: Simon and Schuster, Inc., 1988).

Craig Hickman and Michael Silva, <u>Creating Excellence</u>, (New York: New American Library, 1984).

Tom Jackson, <u>Guerrilla Tactics in the Job Market</u>, (New York: Bantam Books, 1978, 1991).

Dennis Jaffe and Cynthia Scott, <u>Take this Job and Love It</u>, (New York: Simon and Schuster, Inc., 1988).

Susan Jeffers, <u>Feel the Fear and Do It Anyway</u>, (New York: Fawcett Columbine, 1987).

Michael LeBoeuf, <u>How to Win Customers</u>, (New York: Berkley Books, 1987).

Michael LeBoeuf, Imagineering, (New York: Berkley Books, 1980).

Lewis Losoney, The Motivating Leader, (New Jersey: Prentice Hall, Inc. 1985).

Charles C. Manz and Henry Sims, Jr., Superleaderships, (New York: Berkley Books, 1989).

William Marsteller, Creative Management, (Illinois: NTC Business Books, 1966, 1992).

William B. Martin, Managing Quality Customer Service, (Los Altos, CA: Crisp Publications, 1989).

William B. Martin, Quality Customer Service, (Los Altos, CA: Crisp Publications, 1987).

Alan Loy McGinnis, The Power of Optimism, (New York: Harper & Row, 1987).

John Naisbitt, Megatrends, (New York: Warner Books, 1982, 1984).

Roger van Oech, A Whack on the Side of the Head, (New York: Warner Books, 1985).

Roger van Oech, A Kick in the Seat of the Pants, (New York: Harper & Row, 1986).

Thomas Peters and Robert Waterman, Jr., In Search of Excellence, (New York: Harper & Row, 1982).

Faith Popcorn, The Popcorn Report, (New York: Doubleday, 1991).

Michael Ray and Alan Rinzler (editors), The New Paradigm in Business, (Los Angeles: Perigree Books, Putnam Publishing Group, 1993).

Robert Reich, The Work of Nations, (New York: Vintage Books, 1991).

Dru Scott, Customer Satisfaction, (Los Altos, CA: Crisp Publications, 1988).

Barbara Sher, Wishcraft, (New York: Ballantine Books, 1979).

Marsha Sinetar, Do What You Love, The Money Will Follow, (New York: Dell Publishing, 1987).

Studs Terkel, Working, (New York: Avon Paperback, 1975).

William Ury, Getting Past No, (New York: Bantam Books, 1991).

William Ury, Getting to Yes, (New York: Penguin Books, 1981, 1991).

Peter Vaill, Managing as a Performance Art, (San Francisco: Jossey-Bass, Inc. Publishers, 1989).

Steven Vanderstaay, Street Lives - An Oral History of Homeless Americans, (Philadelphia: New Society Publishers, 1992).

Dennis Waitley, Seeds of Greatness, (New York: Pocket Books, 1983).

Robert Wegmann, Robert Chapman and Miriam Johnson, Work in the New Economy, (Indiana: JIST Works, Inc., 1985, 1989).

Melanie Astaire Witt, Job Strategies for People with Disabilities, (New Jersey: Peterson's Guides, 1992).

Ernie J. Zelinski, The Art of Seeing Double or Better, (Edmonton, Alberta, Canada: Visions International Publishing, 1990).

Ron Zemke, David Osborne and Ted Gaebler, Reinventing Government, (New York: Penguin Books, 1993).

ORDER ADDITIONAL COPIES TODAY!

Must reading for everyone in employment training, this recent release describes revolutionary approaches to develop new employment opportunities and assist applicants to attain fulfillment from meaningful work.

Price: $29.95 Code: 250BC

Discounts are available for quantity orders.
Call (800) 626-3939 for volume discount prices.

Milt Wright & Associates, Inc.
Organizational Design, Training & Development

www.miltwright.com
(800) 626-3939 • (818) 349-0858 • FAX (818) 349-0987